Sentenced to Blindness – Now What?

SENTENCED TO
BLINDNESS
NOW WHAT?

A Journey from Hopelessness
Street to Possibility Road

By Morten Bonde

Translated from the Danish by

Sinéad Quirke Køngerskov

Sentenced to Blindness – Now What?
A Journey from Hopelessness Street to Possibility Road
by Morten Bonde
Copyright Danish original
Dømt Blind – Hva' så? Morten Bonde ©2019
English translation Sinéad Quirke Køngerskov ©2020
Forlaget Vision 2020
Cover design: Morten Bonde
Cover photograph: Brian Poulsen – Foto & Co.
Editor: Anne Gillion
Layout: Morten Bonde
First Edition
ISBN 978-87-971498-6-7

All content in this book is the story of the author's own experiences. This book is intended for inspiration and motivation and is not intended as a substitute for qualified medical or psychological advice. The reader should consult a physician or therapist in matters relating to their health, and particularly with respect to any symptoms that may require diagnosis or medical attention. Although the author and publisher have made every effort to ensure that the information in this book was correct at the time of press, the author and publisher do not assume and hereby disclaim any liability to any party for any loss, damage or disruption incurred in whole or in part as a direct or indirect result of the use of the ideas, experiences, tools and suggestions, and/or any and all errors or omissions presented in this book.

www.mortenbonde.dk

A huge thank-you to

My parents,
who have always been there when I needed them. Thank you for all the love and care you have always given me. That love enabled me to show and give the same love and care to my boys. And a special thank you to you, Dad, for driving me all over the country for all kinds of lectures.

My beautiful wife Mette,
who has been my counselor and discernment during a period when everything was chaotic. You've been by my side every step of the way. You have been able to both give me space and be present and attentive when I needed to discuss ideas and philosophies before I could concretize them in the book. I love you. You are—and always will be—my soul mate.

My two wonderful boys,
who have been interested, curious and kept an open mind to a dad who suddenly brought brand new ideas and principles into our little home. You have been absolutely amazing and I am so proud of you.

All my beta readers: You know who you are.

Various foundations for financially supporting the publication of this book.

Contents

PART 3 – ARRIVAL ON POSSIBILITY ROAD

FOREWORD

Let me just state for the record: writing this book has not been easy! Talk about an emotional roller coaster. There've been times when I was close to giving up, and times when I was sure the book was just right. When I first shared the manuscript with various publishers, their responses weren't exactly uplifting: *the book has too small an audience—you should delete this section—the book is too long—you write too much about yourself—you write too little about yourself—maybe we'll publish next year after a rewrite and* so on. It really put me in two minds and made me doubt both the project and my own abilities.

Should I do as they say—is the book not relevant?—will it make sense to others? I've thought about giving up so often!

After several rejections, I made a decision: I had to write this book the way I thought it should be written. It's my story, my experience, and it deserves to be presented to you as honestly and authentically as possible. One of the reasons for writing the book has been to demonstrate how the seemingly impossible is possible when you decide to make it possible. What you're about to read, therefore, is the book as it wanted to be written. It's MY story. Not a publisher's version of my story.

My role in the book is to be a living example of the exciting and life-affirming topics that I think we know far too little about and learn far too little about in our everyday lives. My ambition has been to illustrate how we can grow greater than all the imaginable and unthinkable problems and misfortunes life can throw at us.

The book contains knowledge that I've used to transform my view of the world we live in and to find my place in it. That I write about myself and share my experiences and my life, "my story," is a natural consequence of being the person I know best in the world, and that I happen to have a personal "misfortune" to tell you about. So, I volunteered to make my life story available to the author, who just also happens to be me. Are you confused? Don't be. I'm just playing with words and warming up to what we'll soon be doing together: discovering and playing. For what better playground is there than where words, ideas and thoughts come together in jest?

I'd come to a dead end, which forced me to find a way out of the situation I was stuck in. A life situation provoked by an eye condition that is slowly making me blind.

This means that the purpose of the stories you read in the book is to make you see the bigger picture. See a pattern. Maybe you'll discover it, maybe you won't. If you do identify the pattern, it'll be because you understand the deeper messages I want to give you, and if you don't see the patterns, it may be because you're not ready to see them—yet. And maybe what I'm saying is just a modern version of *The Emperor's New Clothes*, but I challenge you to explore it for yourself and find your own answer. I'm convinced that if you see the patterns, you'll change how you see yourself and change your life—I'm going to push and motivate you to see your life and your world from a different perspective.

Perhaps you're right in the middle of a life crisis or you feel stuck. Maybe your gut is telling you that you could do more with your life, but that something is impeding you? I've been there! And I found a way to move on. First, from a deep sense of hopelessness and powerlessness and later to a place of solid knowledge that I create my own life according to what I think about and think of myself. This simple sentence may not make much sense to you right now, but it can. Its importance is earth-shattering and can change your life, as it did for me when I first understood its enormous significance.

I'm going to tell you how I overcame an insurmountable challenge in my life and how I turned it into something that made me stronger, happier and hungrier for life than I'd ever been before. I'm going to share with you how we can cope with whatever comes our way in life, even if we don't—and can't—believe it when we're at the bottom of the black hole. Here, I'll tell you how I found the way forward in my life, despite blindness being my future prospect; how I became aware of the primary cause of my depression and my being stuck in my life; what was hindering me from living my life to the fullest.

And you know about that primary cause only too well. But it can be difficult to identify because it's well and thoroughly entangled in every aspect of our lives. It has engulfed us and has, in a way, become the modern definition of life. So, what is it? It's the eternal stream of thought, which is constant background noise in the mind and which is frequently predominantly negative. It's most often focused on worries about the future or memories of the past.

As Eckhart Tolle writes in his book *Gateways to Now*, the French philosopher René Descartes in 1637 formulated his famous quote, *"Cognito, ergo sum"* [I think, therefore I am]. It became the foundation for how Western culture perceives itself; our thoughts became synonymous with our being.

We may have learned to live with the endless stream of thought, but we've lost control of it, and now these thoughts have too much control over our lives. When I realized that it's up to ME to decide the direction of my thoughts, my life changed miraculously. I discovered I was, to a great extent, enslaved by my negative thoughts and feelings and the experiences I'd had throughout my life, and that all my decisions, thoughts and choices had been made from the perspective of my old limiting behavior. Behavior and a personal hell I'd created for myself, but which I had the possibility of changing to a new and improved version that agreed better with my wishes and dreams for my life. Everyone has inside them the capacity to change their thoughts and behaviors—if we want and believe we can. With this book, I show you how I did it.

I will still lose my eyesight and I am still legally blind, but that doesn't change anything in the life I am to live and the gift that it is. I know that we create our own reality, and I left Hopelessness Street forever to live on Possibility Road when I finally recognized that Descartes' definition on being was wrong. We are not our thoughts, but rather the consciousness, which is deeper than the flow of thought, and with our focused awareness, we can direct our thoughts and, thereby, create our lives according to our dreams and visions. Whether it is joy, happiness, grief or sorrow, the choice is ours.

Morten Bonde, May 2020.

A little on the book's structure

PART 1

When you get started with the book, you'll discover that Part 1 is about some of the challenges I've had to deal with in relation to my eye condition, but also about who I was as a person throughout my life until 2016. Part 1 is about how I slowly moved further down Hopelessness Street and ended up living a life of stress, depression and limitations. The purpose of Part 1 is to help you better follow my footsteps to the realization that I had to change the way I handled these limitations. And remember that the challenges I talk about in Part 1 could have been completely different challenges. They could easily have been the challenges you are experiencing in your own life. I hope it'll make you curious and interested in the tools I found to move forward and that you'll explore further how I was able to change the way I viewed my world and my life. The anecdotes and comments you're going to read reveal some of the topics that we're going to work on in Part 2. These little hints might just kick-start ideas in your subconscious—and that's what we're going to talk more about in Part 2.

PART 2

I hope that you'll stay with me throughout Part 1, but if for some reason you don't want to read my personal story in Part 1, then I'd recommend at least starting with the chapter "Meeting at the municipality: An experience that changed everything" and then delving into Part 2 where I share a lot of knowledge and the tools I used to change course from Hopelessness Street to Possibility Road. I'm still dumbfounded about the fact that I knew nothing about how to change habits and behaviors—something that so many people are now struggling with. I can't understand why we don't learn about this in school. If you find Part 2 too theoretical and distant from what you already know, or if you just can't relate to meditation, mindfulness or brain research for beginners, try moving on to Part 3, but remember that in order to understand the deeper meaning of the examples I share in Part 3, it may be helpful for you to go back to Part 2 afterward.

PART 3

In Part 3, I arrive at Possibility Road, and I share the story of how I used the knowledge that I tell you about in Part 2 to change many of my limiting beliefs. I'm going to show you how action, knowledge and determination gave me new, strong core beliefs and that these were now predominantly positive. You could say that Part 3 is a recipe and inspiration for how you, too, can work with your own limiting beliefs. The examples given could have been accomplished in various other ways. The most important thing to understand in Part 3 is that if you want to change your limiting beliefs, you have to DO instead of just THINKING, worrying and ruminating.

If, along the way, you find yourself wondering at strange encounters and conversations with the mysterious Letter Men, don't despair or get confused. Just read on. It'll all make sense in the end.

Happy reading.

PART 1
HOPELESSNESS STREET

A telephone call from a stranger

Friday, July 28, 2017:

I'd come to a standstill. I'd shut down. Didn't know how to move on. I was suffering from stress and depression; everything looked bleak. An inner voice ran on repeat in my head: *"You're going to be blind, and there's nothing that can change that. You're useless—just give up now."*

I have a disease that is slowly making me go blind. For years, I put on an Oscar-worthy performance, acting as if it wasn't a problem that I needed to deal with. But then the realities of the disease hit me: *"I'm going blind!"*

It was as I sat, feeling most saddened by this dark fact, that I got a mysterious call from an unknown number. Now normally I don't bother to take such calls—they're usually pushy salespeople trying to sell you something. But this was different. For some reason, I picked up my iPhone and swiped ANSWER.

"It's Morten," I said. There was silence on the other end. I repeated: "It's Morten—hello?"

Then I heard a faint voice: "Is that Morten?"

"Yes, it's me," I answered a little irritated, and the voice began to speak a little clearer, and what it said—completely out of the blue—had me sitting on the edge of my seat. "Morten, you're in a very dark place in your life, and right now you're wondering how to get back into the light. Am I right?"

There was silence for at least ten seconds. I was struck dumb. My summer vacation had started two days earlier and I'd been thinking a lot about how to move on with my life after spending six months ruminating and worrying about how to change my life from being sad and depressed all the time over losing my sight someday. I lost count of the times I'd asked myself, "What is my future going to look like as a blind person? Will I be able to do anything?" That someone should contact me without warning and put into words what I'd been brooding over, came as something of a shock. To put it mildly!

I was quiet for a moment. Thoughts rushed through my head. Who was this man? How did he know something so private about me; something I hadn't ever told anyone else?

I considered pressing the red telephone icon, but something kept me from ending the conversation. Something told me to listen to this man, despite another instinct saying, *"Hang up—now!"*

"Who am I speaking to?" I asked carefully, getting up from the sofa and walking out onto the patio. I had to be alone for this conversation.

"Morten, this is the call you've been waiting for, and if you listen to what I have to say, I'll help you with what you're going through right now, and, I promise you, you will become the person you dream of becoming."

I gawped. This was scary. I'd just started reading books on self-development, and I was inspired by reading stories about people who did the unthinkable, despite them having severe limitations or disabilities to deal with. Only the night before, I'd watched a video on YouTube about a man—Nick Vujicic—who was born without arms and legs, and yet had created an amazing life for himself, found the love of his life, had children, learned to walk without legs, learned to swim without arms, and who was now traveling around the world giving inspirational lectures to thousands of people. I'd asked myself, "How can he look so brightly on life when I look so darkly on mine? How can I change my life and see opportunities and possibilities instead of constantly seeing limitations?" I'd told myself I wanted to be that kind of person. But how? And how did this stranger know what I was thinking?

I gathered myself and said as resolutely as I could: "How do you know what I'm thinking and what exactly do you want with me?"

The answer came without hesitation, and I noticed that there was an unusually friendly and nice vibration in the way he responded: "If you dare to believe that you can change how you see your world, and if you believe I can help you, then it will happen. But you have to believe it 100 percent. Do you believe, Morten?" he asked.

Without faltering or thinking, the answer came out of my mouth and it surprised me. I stated loudly and clearly: "I believe you!"

We continued chatting over the phone and, after 15 minutes, I was convinced that this man could help me and that it was now or never. He made me truly believe that I could change my way of thinking and I could feel my mood lifting.

"I do have one condition for helping you, Morten," he said. "I'm going to give you some tasks, and you have to promise me that you will do your very best to accomplish these tasks. Do you promise?"

Energized by a rare, positive force, I answered again without hesitation: "I promise!"

"The first task I'm going to give you, Morten, is this: You are to write a book about the journey you are now embarking on, and you have to believe that you are absolutely capable of doing it. I'll help you. I'll make sure you make progress and I'll give you advice and guidance. You just have to accept these terms. What do you say, Morten?"

Now I hesitated.

"Write a book," I said uncertainly. "I've no idea how to write a book and I don't see why I should write a book.

Who'd want to read it? I don't believe I can."

"Don't think of it as having to write a book, Morten. You're going to do a number of tasks that, eventually, will make you think like a new person. A person who can see opportunities and who can get the best out of life. That's the most beautiful gift we've ever received. Trust me. You need to write the book to remind yourself of what you've accomplished and about what you've been able to do with your mind. You don't know what that is yet. Therefore, the book is going to act as a kind of diary for you. Something you can refer to later and that other people can be inspired by. Do it now. You can do it."

I let the words circulate in my head for a moment. It all made sense in a way, even if it was totally absurd and unreal. "Okay, I'll do it," I replied, feeling better than I ever remembered before.

"That was the first difficult decision, Morten. You're on your way now. Your life is never going to be the same again."

This was so incredible. I was still standing on the patio, talking on the phone with a stranger who was telling me he could change my life, and I believed every word he said—completely. I must have gone mad!

"You have to start your book now. Start by looking back over the life you have lived. I want you to tell me where you come from and share some of the highlights of your life. As you write, try to think about what beliefs and thoughts have dominated your mind during all these years. It may not make sense to you now, but it will. You have to trust me."

"Okay," was all I could say. "I'd better get started."

"Good, Morten," the man replied. "I'll contact you again and ask you to share with me how the manuscript is developing. I will then read it through and give you new assignments. My name is Mr. P and I am going to change your life. That is my promise to you. But there's something I have to warn you about."

I stiffened.

Ahhh, I thought. *Here's the catch.*

Mr. P continued: "I haven't told you everything yet. Two other people are going to contact you during this process. It's a condition you have to accept. A price you have to pay. These two people are my colleagues. They work for the same organization that I do. One is Mr. N, and the other is Mr. F. Our names are a tad enigmatic, but once this process is over, I promise that I will reveal our full names and what they mean. I will tell you more about who we are. For now, you need to know that Mr. N and Mr. F will try to confuse you and lay traps for you. They will try to talk you out of it and instill fear in you. It's your job to try to find a way through these challenges without letting them get to you. I'm sure you can, and I will help you.

"Uh, okay," I managed to stammer. "I'm starting to doubt that this is a good idea."

"This is the only way if you want to get on with your life, Morten. All you have to do is believe. Believe in that voice inside you that's saying yes to this project."

With those words, Mr. P hung up and the phone went silent.

How do you write a book? I thought. I had no idea, but I was determined to find out. So, two days after my conversation with Mr. P, I found myself sitting down in front of my computer, staring at a blank Word document. I decided to just start, and see what would come of it, and so I started to type . . .

The beginning

In 2002, I received a diagnosis that changed my life. I was 29 years old and just about to embark on life with a family and as an adult. My wife, Mette, and I had driven the long way from Kolding to the Danish State Eye Clinic (today the Kennedy Center) in Hellerup, near Copenhagen, and after a plethora of tests and investigations, we were now sitting in the consultant's office about to get the final verdict: "Morten, you have a genetic eye disease called Retinitis Pigmentosa, and it's going to make you blind."

Talk about a shock! I couldn't believe my own ears. It was as if everything had stopped—as if someone had pressed the pause button and was taking control of my life. It was as if the sounds coming out of the consultant's mouth were being spoken in a foreign language that I hadn't learned yet. And when he, patiently and compassionately, explained to me that the visual cells in the retina would die one by one, with no way to stop this process and that it would eventually lead to blindness, it was somehow the first day of my new life. My life as Visually Impaired. There I was, 29 years of age, facing the tragic news that I would slowly lose my sight and someday go blind. I was *sentenced to blindness*. And Now what? What was going to happen to me now? What would my life be like? How was I supposed to move on?

Today, I am the proud father of two wonderful sons, Mikkel and Rasmus, and I am happily married to the most beautiful and cleverest woman on earth, Mette. For the past 20 years, I've been working in communications at various advertising agencies, including as a senior art director in the LEGO Group for the past ten years, where I've written countless stories about the heroes of LEGO City. I've made heaps of TV spots that have been shown around the world. I've developed campaigns and concepts and presented countless of them to LEGO departments from around the world.

I grew up in a nuclear family in the 1970/80s, where I was raised by caring and loving parents who did everything they could so my two brothers and I got the best possible start in life. In many ways, I was an ordinary kid. I played soccer, was a skilled gymnast, was good at badminton and spent most of my childhood in a sports hall. I played with LEGO bricks with my brother, Henrik, his friend, Michael, and my friend, Kent. We built caves in the woods and cycled the trails around town. On the whole, a happy and ordinary childhood. My brother, Anders, younger by ten years, hadn't made his debut to the world yet, so the family consisted of us four.

But despite the loving environment, I'd had one primary, dominant feeling and thought about myself and my future ever since I was a little boy. I didn't think I'd be able to do anything special with my life, and I dreaded the day I'd be grown up and have to stand on my own two feet. I didn't believe I'd ever be able to have my own family, a home and a job I would love. And I carried this core belief with me into my adult life. It was a core belief I had, and I have been fighting against it all my life.

As a boy, I was often anxious, and insecure and unhappy with who I was. In kindergarten, I felt insecure and yearned for my home and the security there. I hated being in kindergarten, and I have a strong memory of the mornings when my mother drove me there. I would sit in the back seat, imagining I had my own steering wheel for the car, and every time we got to a turn, I would steer the car in a different direction, away from kindergarten. I could only have been four years old. I'm sure I had good times too in kindergarten, but I can only remember the bad ones. I clearly remember one day when I was asked to take the trash out to the refuse container. Two days before, some kids had thrown trash all over the playground, and they had gotten a good telling-off when the teachers had found out who they were. So I was terrified of dropping the garbage on my way out to the container. When I went to empty the trash can into the container, I couldn't lift the heavy lid, and as I struggled with the lid while trying to lift up the heavy can to the high edge, disaster struck: I dropped the trash can. Garbage splattered everywhere, spreading out over a few square feet.

It was the food waste from lunch. It was filthy. I felt indescribable terror because now I imagined that I would get a right scolding, too. I hurried back to my classroom and didn't tell anyone what had happened. For the next few days, I was terrified that someone would find out I was the one who had dropped the garbage, but no one ever did find out. For days, I'd been dreading a disaster that never happened.

Another episode I remember distinctly was a morning when my mom and dad had slept in. My class was going on a tour that day, and when I got to the kindergarten, everyone from my class had already left, and I had to spend the entire day in another class. Having to be in a strange place with teachers I didn't know was terrible. I felt lost and lonely.

Something else I remember was an exercise the teachers had developed to create peace and calm at lunchtime. The child who could be most quiet would receive a reward and I took this exercise very seriously. I always sat absolutely still, because I really wanted the reward, which was a small packet of raisins. But it was always some other kid who won the raisins. Not me. It was so unfair because I always thought I was the quietest child of all. One day, when my mother picked me up from kindergarten, I just sat completely still and said, "I didn't get it," and when she asked what it was I didn't get, the only thing I could say was, "I didn't get it."

I remember these three episodes so vividly and clearly that in some situations, in my adult life, I can still feel like the little four-year-old who didn't like being in kindergarten. How is that? How can I, as an adult, still feel these feelings so strongly?

Later, when I started school, I was a happier boy. Elementary school was definitely better for me than kindergarten, and before the invention of the internet, smartphones, computers and the PlayStation, entertainment consisted of exploring the area around our city and building with LEGO bricks. My father, an engineer, was able to construct the most amazing vehicles with turning mechanisms and other clever inventions, and my friends and I could spend days building spaceships and airplanes.

But, at school, I was always afraid of not living up to the demands the teachers placed on me. I was scared of making mistakes, and I spent a lot of time trying to anticipate everything that could go wrong. I did everything I could *not* to make mistakes. I *had* to live up to other people's expectations of me.

I discovered that being good at badminton and other sports was a great way to gain recognition and praise, but despite me having an obvious talent for both gymnastics and badminton, I never really made it to the podium at tournaments and came in, most often, in third or fourth place. In badminton—my favorite sport—there were always three or four others able to beat me. I accepted this, reluctantly, and really felt deep inside that I should be glad that I even managed to come in third or fourth at all.

I loved training for sports, but most of all, I loved the recognition and praise it gave me when I did well. And when I didn't do well, I had to make sure to improve so I could be even better next time. Living up to the expectations of others, not making mistakes and not standing out from the norm were important to me.

As I said, I had good and loving parents who ensured I had a safe home. I have no reason to blame my parents for the lack of faith in myself that I so often felt throughout my childhood. They did everything they could do and gave everything they could give with what baggage they were carrying from their own childhoods and with the knowledge they had at the time. But if you were to look at that little boy named Morten today, you'd probably make an extra effort to help him out of the obvious anxiety and inferiority challenges he was facing. That's exactly what we did with our own son when he showed the same traits and which he now has useful, practical tools to overcome.

My parents gave me a safe upbringing. I had a good childhood. I love my parents and am forever grateful for their love, and I have no doubt that they always wanted the very best for me and my two brothers. But there was always something inside me that didn't really believe that I was good enough. You could say I've always been subject to mental limitations, and I've always been plagued by deep questions like: Why don't I dare to take chances? Why don't I think I'm good enough, despite others telling me that I am? Why don't I just do what I set out to do? Why don't I dare? And when the questions rang hollow in my head, my heart and mind were filled with self-reproach and dissatisfaction with my mediocre achievements.

I left high school to try my luck with being a business graduate. At that point in time, I'd no idea what I wanted to do with my life, and my lack of vision for the future affected my time at business school because I had no motivation or purpose for studying. I did poorly, and in the three years I went to business school, my already poor self-worth and esteem took a right hammering. I hadn't the slightest understanding of business economics and math—two fairly central subjects in business college. I was good at writing, languages and marketing, but I didn't know what I could or would do with that. Several of my classmates knew they wanted to do further study and were, therefore, motivated by their goals, but I had no plans at all. I never did homework and didn't understand much of what was going on in the number-based subjects. I always got bad grades and was one of the worst students in the class. No one tried to help me, to help me catch up or do anything else about it, and my parents had no idea about the hopelessness I found myself in, because I didn't tell anyone. I had fun with my friends, but I was always the "stupid" one in class, and I kept believing I was the stupid one for years and years after business school. I managed to barely drag myself through college with passing grades. It's definitely not a period of my life I remember with fondness.

Fire, smoke and lost digits

I've always enjoyed listening to music, and I was interested in sound systems. That interest earned me an apprenticeship in an electronics store, where I became a pretty capable sales rep. I learned so much from that job—about appearance and making a good impression—that I still use today. I discovered that I had the ability to convince people and create trust in them. It's a very useful skill to have in all aspects of life, and an ability I try to instill in my boys, too.

After completing my education in sales, I served my conscription at the Danish Emergency Management Agency. I wasn't particularly interested in serving my military conscription, but I knew I would have to do something, so I volunteered. I'd been advised to sign up for the service with the shortest term of service. Some of my friends had been sent to the Danish island of Bornholm because they hadn't decided where to do their military service, so I volunteered straight away to join the Danish Emergency Management Agency in Haderslev, which was only six months of military service. I hated having to waste six months on this and, as a matter of fact, I had the same pit in my stomach as on the mornings when I was forced to go to kindergarten. It was an involuntary reaction, associated with some unpleasant experience in my life, an experience that had set itself firm.

But my time at the Danish Emergency Management Agency was actually well spent. It was exciting and I gained valuable experience. The Agency was central to the emergency services, so we had shifts to help the nearby fire department if they requested assistance with accidents and incidents, natural disasters or fires. I remember being called out to a fire a few times. It was a crazy experience that really got your adrenaline going. Imagine sleeping soundly in your bed, then getting rudely awoken by a siren at 3:22 in the morning and having to be in the emergency vehicle, fully equipped, five minutes later—you definitely have a pulse of at least 170. Such an adrenaline rush!

One Friday afternoon, we were called out to a farm where there was a fire in a workshop. The air was tense with excitement and anxiety as we arrived at the farm. Pitch-black smoke was rising in the distance, and I was the first self-contained breathing apparatus (SCBA) responder on the search and rescue team.

When serving conscription at the Danish Emergency Management Agency, you had to pass an exam in using SCBA, an extended first aid exam and firefighter training before being able to join the emergency duty team. Our training involved using the air tanks in a burning building in the exercise area. It was the job of the firefighter wearing the SCBA to search the burning rooms for injured people. In one of the exercises, I walked into the training building, wearing full breathing and fire equipment. The person who went in first was designated First SCBA, and right behind them came the Second SCBA, whose job was to help drag in the heavy hose. Black smoke poured out of the doorway, and the impulse was always to turn round, but it was something you just had to get over. It was pitch black inside the building during the exercise. I stood in the middle of the room, wondering why I couldn't see any fire anywhere when I noticed my boots getting hotter and hotter. I realized I was standing in flames up to my waist, so I immediately busied myself with spraying water everywhere. Now, when water is sprayed on fire, a powerful reaction occurs: a quarter of a gallon of water turns into about 396 gallons of water vapor. So the moment I sprayed the water on the flames, steam erupted violently and visibility was reduced to zero. In training, we had to find human-like sand puppets in the building and evacuate them, and that training was about to be put to the test in the burning building we were heading out to now.

As I said, I was the First SCBA responder on the search and rescue team, so I had to operate the fire hose and go in first. My heart was almost beating out of my chest, but I was also excited about what was going to happen. I was ordered to get ready for action, so I equipped myself. The fire captain, who was heading the mission, doubted anybody was inside the burning building, but we needed to make sure. I was particularly concerned about ensuring my oxygen mask was sealed tight to my face so that no toxic fumes would enter my airway. I moved toward the building along with my Second SCBA responder, who was my backup. When we reached the door and opened it, black smoke surged over our heads. We could feel the intense radiating heat, and I automatically thought: *What are you doing, Morten?* I was walking into a burning building—My first time to be in a real operation. I got another urge to tighten my oxygen mask and I told my Second to stop for a moment. I pulled hard on the rubber strap to tighten the mask again, and the worst happened: it snapped! Now I could taste, smell and feel the poisonous smoke, so, naturally, I started to retreat. We reached a safe distance from the building and I had to go back and change my mask. When I got back to the fire truck, there was a deafening crash behind me, and as I turned around, the building collapsed in a huge cloud of dust. There was silence all around me, and I remember the surprised facial expression of the fire captain who had ordered us into the building and who obviously hadn't imagined that happening.

Imagine what would have happened if I hadn't broken the rubber strap on the oxygen mask? It would probably have been the end of my life! I've always been an atheist, but I have to admit to thinking that some higher power was watching out for my partner and me that day, saving our lives. Or maybe my inner intuition caused me to thwart the possibility of facing my own downfall.

Just before my time at the Danish Emergency Management Agency came to an end, we were due to do a huge exercise in southern Jutland. We packed up all our gear and loaded our bags onto trucks. I'd snuck a large bottle of Coca Cola and two Snickers into my bag. Craving something sweet, I crawled up after a Snickers. It turned out to be the most expensive Snickers I NEVER got to eat! I climbed up into the back of the truck, found my bag, fished out the Snickers and got ready to scrabble back down. I took a step and, with my left hand grasping an edge on the inside of the back of the truck, I prepared to jump about two feet down from the final step.

And then something happened that I wasn't prepared for. My ring finger had obviously gotten stuck on a little nick in the metal, and as I made the hop to the ground, my left hand jerked violently. I landed awkwardly on my legs and looked at my hand. There, where my left ring finger used to be, was now a white and red, bloody bone with sinews sticking out everywhere. It was almost like watching Arnold Schwarzenegger in Terminator 2 peel the skin off his arm. But it was just my finger. Talk about a first-hand(!) demonstration of how to react in an extreme situation—that knowledge is actually nice to have, and as there's no going back to change it anyway, I'm grateful for this traumatic experience, which, of course, it was.

I looked down at the ground to see where my finger had landed, because, in the extended first aid course, we had learned that a severed finger could be re-attached if you made sure to bring it to the emergency room properly packed. So, I resolutely picked my finger up from the ground and started running into the barracks for help. The finger looked completely intact but was quite hollow. The ring had simply pared off the finger, leaving the bone on my hand. It dawned on me that my wedding ring had to be on the ground somewhere, so I stopped and turned around to shout at the others who had been standing next to me during the accident: "Find my ring and give it back to me later!"

When I share this story with people, they are generally speechless at how I was able to keep a cool head and had the energy to issue commands to my colleague about finding my ring. But, as I said before, this accident taught me something about myself: I can stay focused and keep calm in emergencies. It's something you never know until you've been in such a situation. I didn't know before this incident whether or not I would faint, howl and scream, panic, or react in some other way entirely, but I responded by keeping an overview and focusing on "surviving."

I entered the barracks with my finger in my hand and my left hand up in the air. I approached two Agency officers talking with their backs to me. I walked toward them calmly, and asked politely and quietly, "Can one of you help me?" I distinctly remember the expression on their faces when they turned and looked at me. Total amazement and shock! They rushed to get me to lie down, and

... I can't remember anything else. My body had done its job: getting me to safety as quickly as possible, so my mind shut down.

The next thing I remember is sitting on the stairs to the entrance of the barracks, waiting for the ambulance. What happened from when I was laid to the floor to that point has simply disappeared. I could hear the ambulance approaching in the distance, and my colleagues were doing everything they could to keep my mood up. I was able to joke a little bit about what had happened, and I jested about it probably being the most thorough and persistent attempt to avoid having to participate in an exercise— ever. Everyone did what they could to keep me thinking about something other than the hand now bandaged in white gauze that was soaked with blood. My superior officer held regular eye contact with me as he kept a close eye on my condition. I'm sure he was watching me for signs of shock.

My superior officer and a colleague accompanied me in the ambulance. Funnily enough, it wasn't a colleague I'd had much to do with, but as is often the case in these situations, you discover what people are made of. And this person was someone who cared about others and wanted to make sure I was doing okay. This was, in a way, another important lesson for me to experience, and it's what I always think to myself in situations when I can see that people need help. My instinct says, *Help those who need your help!*

The ambulance staff talked to me and kept an eye on my condition during the drive. Suddenly, the paramedic at my side shouted to the driver that it was time for Code 1, and the siren was turned on. I was bleeding profusely. I needed to get to the emergency room now. At the ER, I was rushed into an operating room and made ready for surgery. As I lay on the operating table, it dawned on me that the colleague who had driven with me in the ambulance, and whom I thought was someone I didn't know, was actually my big brother's childhood friend, Michael. Michael had been one of the childhood friends who'd spent hours and hours building with LEGO bricks with us, and when I was graciously allowed, I joined the gaggle of boys when we played in the woods around my home. I knew now he was an officer at the barracks of the Danish Emergency Management Agency, but I hadn't had anything to do with him since I was about ten years old and the only contact we had was saying hello to each other. Now, here he was, in the operating room, watching over me. That was clearly what he was doing, because he didn't move from my side.

The surgery was about to start, and I was still sure they were just going to re-attach my finger, as I'd heard on the first aid course, but that's not exactly what happened. The doctor told me that the finger couldn't be saved because it'd been so severely torn off. Had it been cut off, they might have been able to sew it on again, but that was almost hopeless in my situation. He told me that they could try, but it was almost 100 percent certain (if it didn't die from infection) that the finger would just stick out motionless.

But there was also another reason why he was reluctant to try re-attaching it. When you lose a body part, it's vital to bring it into the emergency room as clean and cold as possible. So don't go putting anything in your mouth— that's just an enduring myth. The best thing to do is put the body part in a bag of water, tie a knot, and put the bag inside a clean bag of ice. Which is not exactly how the first aid experts at the barracks had chosen to transport my finger to the emergency room. No. They had placed my finger directly on a block of ice and put another block of ice on top of it. You can probably imagine what happened to my poor finger. It was frozen stiff and, so, completely dead. I've always laughed at how the officers, who taught us first aid, could make such a blunder.

What was done was done. The finger couldn't be re-attached, so when the surgeon asked me to decide whether to cut off the bone or to try to sew the finger back on again, the decision was easy—the huge shot of morphine undoubtedly helped to make the decision easy, too. Off with it. And once the situation became clear to him, Michael took his leave. Somewhere in the room, a nurse said, "You'd better sit down." Michael had turned so pale that the nurse had noticed and anticipated he would keel over. He got through it though; obviously affected by the prospect of me losing my finger.

Having a finger amputated, under local anesthetic only, is a strange experience. Despite my finger and hand being locally anesthetized, I could feel it all the way up my shoulder as the doctor cut off the bone. The thoughts of it—and the sound! I'll save you that experience.

The surgery was over. I was stitched and bandaged. I'd received a hefty dose of morphine, so I was feeling fine and my mood was light. So I left the operating theater on my own two feet, but feeling pretty dazed. I was standing there in my uniform, with both hands down by my sides, when a nurse told me to hold my hand over my head; otherwise, it was going to hurt later.

To my surprise, I was sent home. I'd imagined they would keep me in for a night or two for observation, but they didn't. I was sent home with anti-inflammatories and paracetamol for the pain.

Michael borrowed a car from the barracks and drove me to Kolding.

That night was one of the most painful I have ever experienced. Only slightly sedated from the medication—which wasn't at all enough to numb the pain in my hand—I struggled through the night with help from

Mette. The pain was, of course, excruciating, but the traumatic experience had now caught up with me, too—and it hit me full force.

Now, most people would probably think that I drew back for a while, but I didn't have time to lick my wounds, because I'd applied for a position as a service consultant in the Danish KIM's group, and I had a job interview two days after the accident. Maybe it was madness, or maybe it was my upbringing—living up to others' expectations of me—that made me take the airport bus to the Propellen hotel in Billund, where the interview was to take place.

I have no idea today why someone couldn't drive me to the interview, given the circumstances. Anyway, I headed off on Bus 166—on which I would later become a regular passenger—and arrived at the interview feeling pretty groggy after the events of recent days. The interviewers seemed shocked by my appearance when I came stumbling in with a white bandage, stained with a little blood, on my finger. I didn't get the job, but I'm sure they didn't forget Morten Bonde in a hurry!

This episode taught me some important lessons. I knew I had the strength to cope with extreme situations. I was able to use that knowledge later in life when I had to seriously deal with my visual impairment. There was something else, too: I had gained a friend for life. Michael and I shared a special connection, and we developed a close friendship in the years that followed. A friendship that ended tragically, but an end that motivated me to find the strength and willingness to leave Hopelessness Street.

I wasn't yet aware of my eye condition at this point in my life, but there were a few incidents that have reminded me subsequently that I was probably already showing symptoms of Retinitis Pigmentosa back then.

There were a few times, when we were doing night exercises and I was a driver, that I didn't see traffic obstacles in the dark. Once, we were driving in a so-called "Signal & Special Service Vehicle," a mobile command center for emergency situations, where the two- or three-person crew sat in the back of the vehicle. Well, I drove this truck over a bump at nearly 40 miles an hour. I never saw the bump—you can imagine what that must have been like for my poor colleagues sitting in the back, trying to keep track of road maps and loads of other exercise-related tasks while talking on the radio and being full-focused on the job at hand. They flew around the truck and I was called names I don't want to repeat here.

This could have happened to anyone, but I can now see that it was probably the first signs of night blindness, which is the first symptom of Retinitis Pigmentosa. The cells in the eye that we use for night vision are the first cells to switch off. So, today I am almost totally night-blind and spend most of the winter months with a flashlight in my pocket and often wear a headlamp on my head at home, too. It's a weird experience for neighbors who drop by unexpectedly—I often resemble a miner taking a coffee break when I open the door to them. And if I forget to turn off the flashlight, they're welcomed by a cyclops-like creature with a 1,500-lumens-bright eye.

The first change of course

Unsurprisingly, I didn't get the job at the KIM's group, but I did get a job as a sales consultant in a cell phone shop, serving both commercial and private customers. But, after selling phones for a couple of years, I realized that wasn't the industry I wanted to develop and grow in. Being a seller was not for me. I was good at building trust and giving advice, but I wasn't that good at "fobbing something off on people." I certainly wasn't comfortable having to change my personality depending on whom I was selling to. I was having enough difficulty figuring out who I was, and being a sales rep wasn't making it any easier. One moment I had to play one type of person to persuade a customer to buy, and the next I had to play another when I was facing a new customer. I felt dishonest and fake.

I'd had a talent for drawing since childhood, and I'd always dreamed of becoming an advertising designer and working at an ad agency. I would spend hours and hours in my room, music blaring, with a pencil in my hand. I started out drawing Donald Duck characters and later moved on to superheroes like Batman and Superman. And then came heavy metal covers.

Sitting for hours under the hypnosis of the creative process was amazing. Being able to create something out of nothing—to start with a blank piece of paper and slowly see something come to life before your eyes.

But when I left business school and had to choose between further education and work, I didn't believe that working in the field I dreamed of would ever be feasible. The guidance counselors at school, who were supposed to help us find our future dream job, made it clear that there was little chance of me getting an internship at an advertising agency as it was much-sought-after, and getting into the advertising industry at all was a million-in-one shot. I believed the counselor. That I'd be lucky enough to do it never crossed my mind, so I didn't dare hold onto my dream or go for it. I just thought that if I were to actually land a job one day, then I should be happy with that and just count myself lucky. I hadn't yet learned to dream or imagine that I could become anything I wanted to, if only I believed in both it and myself.

One of my missions in life now is to encourage my boys and other young people to pursue their dreams. When I found my way off Hopelessness Street later, I found this quote, often attributed to Henry Ford, founder of Ford Motor Company: "Whether you think you can or you think you can't, you are probably right."

One day when I was sitting in the cell phone shop staring into space, a thought came to me: *Morten, what are you doing here? You have to do something. You're not happy!* The voice was rather powerful and it echoed and clanged in my head. The kind of experience we get when we go into a trance and get lost in our thoughts. Doing this can be compared to the state achievable through meditation. When we meditate, we come into contact with ourselves in a way that causes us to lose our sense of time and place, and if we are fortunate enough that our conscious awareness abates sufficiently, we may experience what can be called clear-sightedness. For a moment, everything makes sense and it's all so simple. I'm sure you know what I'm talking about and that you recognize this feeling. Most people have had such an experience at some point in their lives—waking up at night after a dream and immediately knowing what to do with your life, but the next morning you can't remember the epiphany. The feeling is gone and you can't understand what made you think that you had all the answers to life's important questions in your grasp.

Later, I decided to seek answers to what was behind this phenomenon, and the answer made a major difference to my life. Actually, it changed it completely. When you're in a state of inner focus, at the level where you're just about to fall asleep, you can circumvent the filters and limitations that our conscious minds are trained to believe. And when you can sidestep the filters, ideas and wishes that are usually sorted from the consciousness's filters can resonate in our minds.

That's what happened to me that day in the cell phone store. And I was able to take the vision out of my drowsy state and let it manifest. I dozed off and realized that I wasn't happy, and my filters were absent just long enough for an idea to manifest itself in my mind.

It's fascinating and I believe it's deeply regrettable that we don't have a subject in school that teaches us more about this while we are children. If more people were equipped with the knowledge that I have today, then disorders like anxiety, stress and depression could be substantially minimized. I'm aware, at least, of the mental mechanisms we humans have. I would like to teach my two boys about them as I'm sure it will benefit them later in life—I'll return to this, but we're not ready for it just yet. You need to know a little more about my backstory before I can tell you about the insidious eye condition that was going to rule most of my life; about how it completely pulled the rug out from under me at first, and about how I later discovered the secret of overcoming the challenges and limitations we face in life.

So hang on in there.

For me, that day in the cell phone store, a door in my

mind opened and I saw a whole different life for me than the one I was living at the age of 24. I realized that if I wanted something more than selling cell phones (not that there's anything wrong with that), then I had to start now. And opportunities began to emerge entirely by themselves over the next few days. It was as though all that I needed to attract opportunities that would help me to fulfill my desire to "do something else with my life" was a great and heartfelt wish.

I was reading the newspaper one day, when I spotted a little ad at the bottom of the page: "Would you like to work in the advertising industry?"—my childhood dream. So, I was definitely interested in finding out more. It was a course in graphic design and communication—a Danish academy degree program of two-and-a-half years, consisting of lectures and an internship at an advertising agency. A few weeks later, I took the entrance exam, and six months after that, I started college.

For the first time in my life, I experienced everything coming easy to me. Driven by a wish and a deep desire to do something I loved, I did really well in college. I graduated top of my class and got a job at the advertising agency, I'd done my internship in. It was huge, and when I think back, it was actually a major achievement. Completely without external motivation or help, I'd made a major change of course for myself. Back then, I didn't think any more about it, but I had done something

I should have noticed. I had gotten a vision for my life. I believed in it. More than anything, I had wanted to be accepted onto that college course. And I had wanted an internship with all my heart. I had made a decision that changed my life. I had set a goal and I had achieved it.

But I neither celebrated it nor give myself credit for it. That wasn't me and it wasn't how I'd been brought up. And after reflecting on this now, in my forties, I can see that this was the first time I had worked on a goal for my life. Setting goals for your life is a prerequisite for personal and professional success. If you don't yet have a goal in your life that's greater than yourself, then start thinking about what it could be. Setting goals opens you up to the possibility of going to new and amazing places.

I now had my dream job in the advertising industry, and I worked hard over the next few years to find my feet in a profession that's always in the fast lane. When you work at an advertising agency, you quickly have to get used to there being a campaign at least once a week—you get briefed on a job and then, typically, have a few days or a week to come up with a creative concept consisting of ads, brochures, logos, visual identities, TV spots and so on. All you have to start with is a white, blank piece of paper.

At the beginning of my career, having to constantly re-invent the wheel was exhausting. It was fun, but it was incredibly hard. I did quite well, but I still had huge self-worth and esteem issues—despite the success. I often said to Mette that there was no way I was going to last my entire life in this industry. The job was way too demanding. My gut feeling told me I wasn't going to be able to keep up with the pressure I was exposed to every day, and I often caught myself thinking that if I could just retire early, or something like that, then I'd be saved. Given these thoughts and the desire for early retirement to get out of my predicament, you might be almost tempted to think that I got what I asked for later. When I started in the advertising industry, I imagined I wouldn't survive in this business, and four years later, I was diagnosed with a rare, genetic, hereditary eye condition that no one else in my family has and that would cause me to retire early. Be careful what you wish for—you just might get it!

The first meeting with the Letter Men

Thursday, August 10, 2017:
It had been two weeks since I'd had the mysterious conversation with Mr. P, which had somehow set in motion a fierce round of self-examination and scrutinizing of my life up to the time I started in the advertising industry. Thinking back over your life and describing its events is a difficult task. I could now see details of myself that I hadn't been aware of before. I really had spent an unbe-

lievable amount of time worrying and feeling anxious, and I'd been terrible at celebrating my own victories!

As I sat thinking about this one night in my home office, my cell lit up on the table, followed by the familiar buzz of a phone set on silent. PRIVATE NUMBER said the display. I hesitated for a few seconds, well aware of who this call was probably from. Mr. P had announced that he or one of the other "Letter Men" would contact me, asking for the status of the writing process. Maybe that was now? My heart began palpitating and my hands started sweating at the thought of it. What if it was one of the other two men, Mr. N or Mr. F! I was dreading talking to them, thanks to Mr. P's not-exactly-positive cautions. I stared at the cell that refused to stop its humming, and finally, I pulled myself together.

"Hello?" I practically whispered.

"Is that Morten Bonde?" said a sharp commanding voice down the phone.

This was definitely not the friendly voice I'd spoken to that night, two weeks ago. Of that much, I was certain.

Softly I answered, "Yes, it's me. Who am I talking to?"

"This is Mr. N, and I would like to emphasize that I am the one asking the questions here."

"Uh, okay," I replied, astounded at his unfriendliness. But, for whatever reason, I didn't have the courage to protest. There was something terrifying about Mr. N's voice, and I knew instinctively not to cross this man. I can't say why I felt like that. Something deep inside me just told me to obey him—as if my life depended on it. "It is time for you to present the progress of your work on the book. We, therefore, ask that you come to the address I will send you in an encrypted message after this conversation. You will need to bring three copies of your manuscript. We will then review it, though I highly doubt you have written anything useful, and I have voiced this skepticism repeatedly to my team. I certainly have strong misgivings about getting anywhere with you, Morten Bonde. I am rarely wrong in my evaluation of people, and my assessment of you is that you do not possess the strength, the will or the skills to complete this project. It will be a waste of everyone's time, and I will be proven right, yet again."

I had no idea what to say. His words seemed to make complete sense—I had a strong feeling that his assessment of me was absolutely correct.

I can't do this, said a voice in my head. *He's right.*

Mr. N continued in the same cold tone: "This conversation is now over. You will receive information on where and when to meet, subsequently." The line went dead.

I stared at the phone and when a message beeped in, I jumped with fright in the chair. I hardly dared to pick up the cell and look at the message, but there was no way around it. I had to listen to Mr. N's orders and as I looked at the phone, I stiffened with distrust.

"You are to come to 1 Castle Alley, in Kolding, on Friday, at 10 p.m. Please bring three copies of your manuscript for the presentation. Under no circumstances are you to discuss this meeting with anyone. Messrs. P and F and the undersigned will be in attendance."

The next few days were awful. The first chapters of the book, that I was now due to present in less than two days, still weren't finished. I hadn't told anyone about my telephone call with Mr. P because it was all too crazy to share with anyone. I had, of course, told Mette that I wanted to write a book—it'd come as a surprise to her, but she thought it was a good idea.

The writing was actually going well. It'd been easier than I thought. After all, I'd written numerous stories and manuscripts during my time at the LEGO Group. But would I be ready? Would what I had written be good enough? Would I be made a laughing stock; thereby fulfilling Mr. N's predictions of my uselessness?

I spent the next two evenings finishing the first chapters of the manuscript. I thought it was surprisingly good considering that I'd neither written a book before nor learned how to.

On Friday, at 10 p.m., I found myself in front of the entrance to 1 Castle Alley, hesitating to use the ancient doorknocker that would announce my arrival. The doorknocker was shaped like a dark demon writhing in agony, and it reminded me a little of the situation I now found myself in. It didn't bode well for the meeting I was about to attend.

I clenched the manuscript under my arm close to my body, as if I was afraid that someone would snatch it from me or that I would lose it and so come empty-handed to the meeting. I felt terrible. My mouth was dry, my hands were clammy and my heart was pounding in my chest. My body was ready to do battle, and I was constantly on the alert for the slightest sign of danger. I raised a hand and grabbed the dark demon, lifted it up, and dropped it against the heavy oak door. Three times. A hollow knock, knock, knock resounded from the antique door. There was complete silence. No reaction. I let the demon fall three more times, and could hear slow steps approaching from behind the door. With a protracted creak, the ancient door opened, and an older man appeared in the doorway. He was dressed in an elegant tuxedo and, on reflection, was probably a butler. *What am I doing?* I thought. *RUN, RUUUNN,* while you can, Morten, pleaded an inner, desperate voice.

"Welcome, Mr. Bonde," rattled the butler in a hoarse voice. "They are awaiting you in the library. May I take your coat?"

I fumbled with my manuscript, managed to get my jacket off and handed it to the butler, who walked laboriously toward another heavy oak door at the end of a long hall. A dim light shone from the door opening that had to be from candles.

The butler pointed to the door and said, "This way, Mr. Bonde. They are awaiting your arrival."

I swallowed a lump and moved slowly and hesitantly toward the door. It was as though something inside me knew that if I stepped inside, something terrible would happen to me, but I conquered the fear, put my hand on the old door and pushed it open.

"Come in, Morten," said a friendly voice. It was Mr. P. Relief and thankfulness flooded through me. "Thank you," I stammered, immediately wishing I could have said it with more confidence.

The room was an ancient library of thousands of antiquarian books. Brown wainscoting and old paintings of people I'd never seen before lined the walls. I guessed they had to be members of some kind of secret society. Professor Dumbledore's office at Hogwarts flashed into my mind.

Two other people were present besides Mr. P. I looked at them nervously, barely able to see them in the glow of the candlelight, as the eye condition made my vision almost useless in dark surroundings. I stepped closer to the large round table located in the center of the room, and now I could better see the three men. I guessed who Mr. P was from the direction of his voice. He was a slightly gray-haired man in his mid-forties. He had a friendly face that looked at me with glowing empathetic eyes. It was weird—I had a strong feeling that I'd met him before, but I couldn't figure out where or when. He winked encouragingly at me without the others seeing it, and it felt nice to have an ally. He seemed sincere; like he was wishing me all the best. Next to him sat a man of the same age, who looked anything but friendly. He had dark penetrating eyes and not a black hair out of place on his head. He remained quiet as he looked at me intently with his probing eyes. And, as with Mr. P, I had the sensation that I knew this man, but I still couldn't figure out when I'd met him. He opened his mouth and introduced himself.

"Good evening, Morten Bonde," he said with a sharp, shrill voice. "My name is Mr. N and next to me is Mr. P." He gestured with his arm toward the man I'd guessed at once was Mr. P.

"And this is Mr. F," continued Mr. N, looking at the other gentleman who was also observing me intensively. "You are here today to present the first part of your manuscript. We will read it through and give you feedback so you can move forward in the process."

He pointed to a fourth high-backed chair at the round table and asked me to take a seat.

There was a moment's silence and I watched them while they watched me. I looked at the third man, who hadn't said anything yet. Mr. F was also in his mid-forties, and incredible as it was, he seemed familiar too. His hair was cut short, almost clean-shaven, and he looked at me nervously. It seemed as though he wanted to say something, but then decided not to.

Mr. P broke the silence: "Morten, we are excited about what you have brought us today. Would you please submit your manuscript so we can review it?"

"Yes, of course," I answered quickly, pushing my stack of printed pages toward him. They were quite damp where I'd been holding them. I hoped no one would notice. Mr. P passed a copy of the manuscript to the other two and they began to read.

I sat watching them as they read, all the while keeping an eye on their reactions. Mr. P seemed happy and grinned once in a while, occasionally looking over at me and smiling warmly. Mr. F seemed concerned as he read. He sat uneasily in his chair and closed his eyes every so often, as if what he was reading pained him. Unsurprisingly, Mr. N seemed to dismiss what he was reading; shaking his head and sometimes making small mocking noises, as if the manuscript was completely useless.

It was nerve-wracking to witness. I wanted to flee and forget that I'd ever been in contact with these three; pretend it had never happened, and just be myself again. Live with the limitations I had and return to living the old life I knew, despite everything. It was crazy to think I could change and make any kind of difference.

Finally, Mr. P broke the silence: "Morten, I have to say I'm impressed. I'm pleased with what you have written—I can see how much thought you've put into this. What do you think, Mr. N?"

Mr. N sat with his arms crossed, his expression far from one of satisfaction.

"As it is, this book is unpublishable. It is uninteresting; there is no substance. Readers will get bored. It has not gripped me at all. The language is too simple; it is laughably amateurish. It is simply not good enough."

Mr. P thought for a moment and then looked over at Mr. F.

"What do you say, Mr. F?"

Mr. F shifted uneasily in his chair, as if having to say something made him uncomfortable.

"Eh, I have my doubts," he stammered. "I'm afraid it's too personal. There's a risk it will change Morten's life completely—in a bad way—if he shares so generously from his private life. I would not be so open and honest."

He looked directly at me.

"Morten, you have to be absolutely sure that what you write won't have any consequences for you. This could trigger events in your life that you can't foresee. Your position at the LEGO Group may be at stake if you go ahead and publish this. Who can use a visually impaired senior art director? You risk being fired and that people you care about will turn their back on you."

He looked back at Mr. P, the apparent leader of the group. He seemed to have the final say in decisions. He smiled and said, "I hear your concerns, but I'm sure Morten is doing the right thing. I'm convinced he can only benefit from telling his story. It needs to come out, Morten, because not only is it going to help you—" He looked me straight in the eye. "It's also going to help others. And if you can help others, you'll help yourself, too. What do you think?"

Thoughts swirled in my head. I was appalled at how hard Mr. N had criticized my writing, and I was angry and upset at his comments. And I worried about what Mr. F had said. Imagine if what I wrote did have a negative impact on my life—what if I was fired when they discovered that my vision was so limited? It was a revelation that could cost me dearly, both in my career and my life. Should I listen to his warning? It made sense. Who would want to hire a half-blind art director? It was ridiculous to think I would keep my job at the LEGO Group if I revealed these things about myself. But when I searched within, I could feel that Mr. P's words had left the deepest impression. Imagine if there was another life for me. One not full of limitations. A life where I could just be honest and be myself! And could my story really help others? That was reason enough to continue working on the book.

I looked at them all one after the other.

"You all have a point in what you say, and I am inclined to agree with your arguments, Mr. N and Mr. F, but Mr. P makes the most sense. I feel I've done a good job with this first section of the book and I want to continue."

Mr. N snorted and threw out his arms. Mr. F shook his head reluctantly. But Mr. P jumped up out of his chair, exclaiming, "THAT'S IT, MORTEN! That's what I needed to hear from you. You can do this. You have my full support."

I was delighted at his outburst. I felt more confident and up to going against Mr. N and Mr. F's warnings.

"It's time for you to go home and continue writing, Morten, but you also need to start learning how you can move forward. Only YOU can do that. You have to be persistent in finding all the literature you can get your hands on that can inspire you and make you progress."

I knew exactly what he was talking about. I'd already begun this work, and now I was more inspired than ever to continue.

"In the next part of the book, we want you to describe what it was like to work in the advertising industry, and I'd like to hear about how you discovered you had an eye condition that is making you go blind. What happened and what did it mean for your life? It's a vital story for you to tell, and for others to hear."

Everyone around the table got up and the meeting was adjourned. The old butler escorted me out to the door. My first meeting with the Letter Men had come to an end. I had passed the initial test and was now highly motivated to continue my writing and my work to get away from Hopelessness Street and onto Possibility Road.

I was in my office again the very next evening, writing.

Sentenced to blindness

One day, in 2002, after four years in the advertising industry, the chief accountant at the agency I was working for at the time came to me and asked if I could be the fourth player in a badminton double later. I was delighted to have been asked. It'd been almost ten years since I'd last swung a badminton racket, and my fingers were tingling to do it again. That evening, we met in the badminton hall and the match started. Apart from cramps in my buttocks and a sharp pain in my shoulders, I hadn't forgotten the tricks from my time as a young badminton player. I was probably the best player on the court, but something strange happened that evening. I lost sight of the shuttlecock in multiple duels. It was comical—I could dazzle with backhanders, drop shots, jump smashes and other fancy footwork, but then, in the midst of an intense match, I stopped and stared into the air after the birdie.

Where the hell was it? It was gone, but a few seconds later it landed squarely right next to my foot to the great delight of my opponents and the despair of my partner. "What the hell are you doing?" my partner shouted at me, and all I could say was, "The birdie disappeared." It was bizarre and we laughed. I put it down to the poor lighting in the hall, which was probably quite normal when I think about it. The badminton matches continued for the next few weeks, and each time, I experienced similar weird episodes on the court.

These incidents gradually aroused the attention of my colleagues, who urged me to get it checked out. So I made an appointment with the ophthalmologist and, after measuring my eyesight and examining my eyes, the doctor determined that nothing was wrong. He couldn't explain why I'd lost sight of the shuttlecock, and sent me home again with the explanation that "our eyes play tricks on us sometimes."

The months passed, and it felt like the badminton matches were getting harder and harder to play. I went to a new ophthalmologist and got pretty much the same answer as I got from the first one, but this time, however, the eye doctor referred me to the ophthalmology department at Vejle Hospital. There, I was subjected to a lot of complicated tests and examinations, but all with the same result. The consultant couldn't give me an explanation and he began talking about tumors of the optic nerve or in the visual center of the brain. That the ophthalmologist wanted to do tests for this type of disease came as quite a shock, and I was referred for an MRI scan of my brain a few days before the Christmas vacation. However, there was a unique opportunity in all the sadness. For years, Mette and I had had a lively discussion: Mette was sure that if my brain was scanned, it'd reveal nothing but a little nut in a large cavity.

It was the longest Christmas of my life, and not in a good way. Mette and I bit our nails almost down to their beds over the holidays; both pretty worried about what the results of the scan would show. After the Christmas vacation, I got the result. There was no tumor on the optic nerve or in the brain. I was right and Mette was wrong. There was no small nut but a perfectly ordinary-looking brain.

However, the specialist at Vejle Hospital couldn't explain my vision problems either, so I was referred to the Kennedy Center, a national counseling and research center for genetics and visual impairments in Denmark.

At this point in our lives, Mette and I were in the process of making plans for our future together. We were close to entering into an agreement with a construction company to build our dream home where we would live and raise our future children together.

We drove to Zealand, and I was put through even

more tests, and after half a day in the clinic, Mette and I found ourselves sitting in the consultant's office, finally about to get a clear message. The doctor looked at both of us thoughtfully and then began to explain: "Morten, I'm sorry to have to tell you that you have a genetic eye disorder called Retinitis Pigmentosa, which will slowly make you blind."

The room was completely still. I stopped breathing for a moment that seemed to last forever. It was a shock. I didn't believe my own ears. I had come to the clinic with the conviction that I had a vision problem that could be fixed with surgery or medication. Now the doctor was telling me I had an eye condition that would make me blind! A myriad of thoughts flew through my head as we sat there in the consultant's office. What about my job? My future plans? Building our future home? Should we have children? What about Mette? What about my life? I remember thinking: My life is ruined. I couldn't see the sense in having to care about houses, children and jobs when there would come a day when I wouldn't be able to see them anyway. I looked at Mette and she looked at me. Nobody said anything, because neither of us could understand what we had just heard.

The specialist explained to me that the visual cells in the retina would turn off one by one. First, I would become night-blind, then my field of vision would narrow; eventually, leading to blindness. He also told me that, regrettably, there was no cure for the disease—yet. But he guessed there would be a cure within ten years—an overly optimistic guess, as there is no sign of a cure for the disease in the near future. If a cure for the disease is to be found, it needs to be able to replace the defective gene and restore lost vision cells. Unfortunately, science isn't there yet.

There I was, 29 years old, facing the tragic news that I would slowly lose my sight and, one day, be blind. The consultant asked about my professional background, and when I replied that I was an art director, he looked satisfied and said that was a fine profession given the future that awaited me. He said that had I been a bus driver or roofer, I'd have had to retrain for a new industry and a new way of life.

It was so surreal. You don't realize how quickly your life can change sometimes. There, in that office, my life changed with the snap of a finger. I imagined how many people had received the sad news that they had an incurable disease that was going to change their lives before me. I know my condition can by no means compare to life-threatening illnesses, but being blind was one of the worst fates I could imagine. Not being able to see my future children, see Mette or see the great world that was just out there still waiting for me. This was a disaster. Even if the symptoms were only going to initially present themselves in the distant future.

The doctor explained to me that I had probably inherited the disease from my mother or father, or that I could have been born with an uninherited mutant gene. At this point, in 2002, there wasn't the same possibility of determining this as there is today. Only recently, I discovered that my eye condition is due to mutations of the USH2A gene, which is associated with isolated Retinitis Pigmentosa (RP) and the so-called Usher syndrome, which causes both blindness and hearing loss. Personally, I don't think I suffer from hearing loss, but my dear wife has stubbornly disagreed with that self-diagnosis—but that's a different story entirely.

Retinitis Pigmentosa (RP)

Retinitis Pigmentosa is a hereditary eye disorder that slowly degenerates the retina. The condition, which is most often abbreviated to "RP," can be a difficult disease for outsiders to understand, meaning life with the disease can be quite lonely. People who don't themselves have RP, can't understand what it means to gradually lose your eyesight. RP is not actually a disease; it's a term for a group of hereditary eye disorders that have in common the progressive degradation of the photoreceptor cells in the retina of the eye. This often leads to severe visual impairment, which can develop into blindness over a number of years. It is estimated there are more than one million people with RP worldwide. The condition is typically detected in childhood or adolescence and is one of the most frequent causes of poor eyesight and blindness among young people aged 20–64.

The disease can develop in many different ways, but usually with a slow, persistent shrinkage of the retina's cells that starts with night blindness and an increasing degree of visual field impairment, color vision problems, contrast problems, reduced sharpness of vision and, in some cases, blindness. I have all these symptoms except reduced sharpness of vision.

For some people, myself included, the vision loss happens slowly and there will be only a small amount of loss over about ten years. Others have periods of rapid sight loss, interspersed with years without any particular deterioration. Some people realized that they saw poorly in childhood, and may have had difficulties in school when training or playing a particular sport or traveling at dusk. Others may never have noticed that they had poor vision, and were diagnosed with RP at a later age—like me.

Some people develop a severely narrowed field of vision, but retain near-perfect central vision, as is the case for me, while others retain their peripheral vision but have limited or foggy central vision. The latter type finds it difficult to read, but are able to get around fairly well using their peripheral vision.

With so many various presentations of symptoms and variations, it isn't surprising that outsiders find RP a difficult disability to understand.

People in the early stages of RP may have near-perfect vision during the day, but at night, in bright sunshine or under rapidly changing lighting, they may experience themselves as almost completely blind.

The loss of sections of the field of vision is just as difficult to understand. When people with normal vision look straight ahead, they can see objects on both sides and above and below the point on which they are focusing. It brings about an awareness of what is right in front of the person. This awareness helps to warn them, so they avoid tripping over things or bumping into people or other obstacles. But it also means that losing your peripheral vision reduces your mobility or ability to move about in your surroundings. One moment, a person with RP can read or see something at a distance, observe something specific or respond to a passer-by's smile, and the next moment, they're wading into a row of bikes on the sidewalk, creating embarrassing situations for themselves. It can be difficult for others to understand that one moment you seem to see just fine, and the next you're behaving like someone with a severe visual impairment. People with RP who cause these minor mishaps are often perceived as being intoxicated or severely confused.

The retina, which is located at the back of the eye and lines its inside, works by perceiving the light we see and transmitting the signals to the optic nerve and the brain. The retina is a fine layer of visual cells that capture the light and translate it into electrical signals, which are then transmitted through a network of nerve cells to the visual center of the brain. In humans, there are two types of photoreceptor cells called rods and cones. Rods are to ensure that we can see in twilight or in poorly lit rooms. There are about 120 million rods in a healthy eye, concentrated particularly in the outermost regions of the retina, and these cells perceive only black and white, which is why our vision in the dark is always perceived as monochrome.

The cones—we have about 7 million of them—perceive colors and give our vision the sharpness that enables us to read and see things clearly and distinctly. There are fewer cones than rods, and they are especially concentrated in the central part of the retina called the "macula lutea" or the yellow spot (*lutea* is Latin for yellow). With RP, the photoreceptors gradually decay and cease to function normally. Typically, the rods (ability to see in the dark) are the first to break down and then the cones, which is also why people with RP develop night blindness first.

The necrosis or degeneration of the retina that occurs with RP is hereditary and is, therefore, due to changes (mutations) in the body's heredity factors (genes) concerning the functioning of the retina. Years of research have—to date—led to the identification of over 160 genes in which mutations can cause hereditary retinal diseases. RP can be inherited in several different ways; for example, via the inheritance pathways called recessive, dominant and x-linked.

RP may present as an isolated eye condition, but in up to 30 percent of patients, other parts of the body are also affected, in the form of "syndromes." RP is a factor in thirty different types of syndromes, which makes this grouping even more complicated and diverse.

And just to make it extra complicated: mutations in the same gene can cause different variants of the same retinal disease. For example, mutations in the USH2A gene, which is what I have, can cause Usher syndrome with both hearing and vision loss, and RP without loss of hearing. I don't experience any loss of hearing, but I've never had it tested. And, somewhat similarly, two people with the same type of retinal disorder can have mutations in two completely different genes.

Going home from the eye clinic

On the way home from Copenhagen, thought after thought whirled through my head, but inside the car remained silent. We didn't talk about the disease or the future that awaited me, as we both had to digest the facts at hand. As I watched the landscape whizz past at eighty miles an hour, I sat in my own world—and then an idea formed in my head. I made a decision. I said to myself, "Morten—this disease mustn't get to decide your life or throw a spanner in your plans."

I would continue to live as before. We had our dream house to build, children to make and raise; life had to go on as if nothing had happened. I listened to the inner voice, because life as an art director went on. I threw the eye disorder into a closet, locked the door and threw away the key. I couldn't think about an eye condition that was going to make me go blind. I would deal with it once it actually became a problem.

We built a house and had two lovely boys, Mikkel and Rasmus, and I told only my family, my closest friends and the people I worked with directly about my condition. It was as though my family couldn't quite understand the news, and so we talked very little about how the disease might impact my and their future. It was so intangible for them because I could still see, and it was mostly in my own little world that the condition developed.

Later, when my vision started to weaken and I started to experience limitations regarding my sight—such as in situations where my challenges couldn't avoid being noticed—those around me could see for themselves the consequences of the condition; for example, when I was sitting in company in a dark restaurant or when I tried to make my way in places I didn't know.

If I drop something on the floor, it takes me ages to find it again, even though everyone else can see that it's right in front of me. These situations are often stressful and embarrassing, as I can easily be perceived as flustered, nervous, stupid and confused for no apparent reason.

My coping mechanism was to have as little as possible to do with the condition. I didn't get into it; I avoided meeting other people who had it, and I kept as far away from considering myself "SICK" as I could. Picturing myself with a cane and being helpless was unbearable, so I avoided the thought. Retinitis Pigmentosa was packed tightly into a box at the very back of my mind, and I wasn't going to open it again until it became absolutely necessary.

The advertising industry

The advertising industry is a tough one to be in—you work under constant pressure. There's always a tight deadline to meet and every campaign starts with a blank piece of paper. And despite creating and inventing, developing and executing ideas nonstop being absolutely fantastic, it's exhausting and it can wear you out. Given my progressive loss of vision, my life was often tough, and I was probably under constant stress for years in the industry.

I've always been a thinker. Ever since I was a little boy, I've been able to come up with the wildest scenarios imaginable—I often ended up frightened out of my wits. I pictured how everything could go wrong and I always devised strategies for how to save myself from these THOUGHT scenarios. I've spent tremendous resources on preparing for disasters that often never happened. But this ability to visualize and fantasize made me a really good creative ideas person and thinker in my job as an art director.

Have you thought about whether you are a thinker? Do you have conversations with yourself in your thoughts? I've always done it. Long internal discussions with my-self have always been a part of my life, but I discovered that using this ability properly can become a source of self-development. But you really have to think about and control what the inner dialog is about, because if you talk to yourself in your mind, your negative and self-re-proaching self-talk can have a huge negative impact on your self-worth and esteem and your ability to achieve your goals and desires. The interaction between your conscious mind and your subconscious mind is crucial to your personality and behavior, and it's based on the core beliefs we have and the way we choose to see the world. And believe me: it is a choice! *It is always your own choice* and I am the living proof. Our core beliefs and our way of seeing the world determine how we live our lives.

I did quite well in the advertising industry despite my disability, but one feeling that still dominated my adult life was, "I'm not good enough!" Can you remember how I had it from childhood? It was still part of my life. Even though I delivered great creative campaign ideas and did well, I couldn't let go of the thought that I should be grateful for even having this job and that I'd probably never find a similar one anywhere else. I wasn't good enough for that. I was stuck and I didn't make any significant advancements or developments. I knew what I had and not what I might get, so I was always seeking for what was safe and well-known and moving away from the new and unknown.

Do you see? Having an invisible condition that you try to downplay—keep secret, if you will—makes for a lonely life. Nobody could step into my shoes to see the challenges I faced, because I only shared my experiences relating to visual impairment with others when the situation was embarrassing—when I knocked over cups of coffee, glasses of water, couldn't see the cursor on the screen or couldn't find things that were right in front of me. The guiding rule of my behavior was to try to look like someone who didn't have a disability. Thus, my visual disability became a controlling factor in my life. And I was completely unaware of it.

When you choose such a strategy, your life can slowly and stealthily be governed by the feeling and experience of being limited, because the ideal—being able to see like others—is impossible to achieve. I feared standing out, feared feeling embarrassed, feared making mistakes; feared not being good enough, feared being a failure, feared losing my sight entirely, feared losing my home, feared being fired—fear, fear, FEAR. And, for me, that became a slippery slope to depression and a life filled with stress.

My life slowly became one long obstacle course, where the obstacles were challenges and the consequence was lost opportunities. More and more, it became a question of not being revealed as "the blind man," and I spent years missing out on rejoicing in what I actually had—my two boys and my beautiful wife, Mette. I'm not sure if anyone consciously noticed my behavior, but I had built my identity around having a visual impairment that had to be masked in every way, and so my limitations became a controlling factor. These limitations came to have far too much power in my life. I was living my life without accepting that I was who I was, and that created an inner conflict. A gap between who I thought I should be and who I really was.

For the first ten years of my career, I worked at what are

called full-service advertising agencies—agencies that cover any communication tasks the customer could have, such as launching a new product, an in-store campaign, online communication, e-commerce, a new visual identity, TV and radio spots, events, trade shows, and so on.

I learned a lot in my first decade as an art director, but I felt like I never really got deep into the projects I was working on. I often felt that the campaigns were developed over such a short period of time that not enough thought had been invested in them, and that what I presented could have been better if I'd had more time. This gave me a feeling of being inadequate and insufficient, but in hindsight, I could have chosen another way to see this. I could have chosen to say to myself: "Morten—what you have managed to achieve in such a short space of time is amazing! You're the coolest art director in the world!" I could have said, "You're doing this with a visual impairment!" But instead, I chose to tell myself: "This isn't good enough, Morten! My colleagues could have done better. You're not good enough! Get yourself together, Morten!"

Do you see that I actually had two different possibilities for how to judge the same situation here? One perspective was to see it as weakness and the other was to see it as strength. Same situation, two different judgment calls, and who gave the verdict? Me! Is one of these perspectives more correct than the other? The answer is simple: The perspective you CHOOSE to believe in automatically becomes the perspective expressed in your reality.

But what about my boss and colleagues who also judged my accomplishments? I never experienced anyone complaining about my work, so almost all the negativity I'd built up was a product of my own thoughts. Spiritual teacher Eckhart Tolle describes it like this: "The primary cause of your unhappiness is never the situation, but your thoughts about it."

There were rarely major problems associated with my visual impairment. I got to work, turned on my computer, got a cup of coffee, and then I was up and running. I developed a system for looking at the whole computer screen with my tunnel vision. A technique I still use today. Finding a little arrow on a 21" screen with Retinitis Pigmentosa was quite an arduous task. As I could only see through a tiny hole, the cursor disappeared on the screen all the time. One way to get around this was to make the cursor huge, via the computer's settings, and then to constantly move the cursor up to the top left corner every time it disappeared on me on screen. Then I followed it back with my eyes to the area I was working on. It became quite natural, but it was yet another obstacle on a list of many on an already long workday. Something else that was particularly challenging was giving a presentation to a customer. Presentations were often made on a big screen or via a projector, and finding the cursor could be a real nightmare. These situations were extremely stressful for me. I had to present with great conviction and confidence while not being able to see what was happening on the screen properly—I lost sight of the cursor on the big screen all the time. And even with all that going on, I didn't want to reveal to anyone at all that my eyes were causing me major problems.

The Finnish world champion

One day in 2005, my boss gave me a very special assignment. I was to travel to Finland and do a photo shoot for VARTA Batteries, a major supplier of—you guessed it—batteries. They sponsored the world-renowned rally driver Marcus Grönholm, who was to front an advertising campaign throughout Scandinavia and the Nordic countries. My project manager told me I was to go on the trip myself, which really triggered my anxiety as it was extremely difficult to navigate and orient myself in foreign environments with my Retinitis Pigmentosa.

I remember almost panicking at the thought of getting lost in the airport, having to find my way to check-in and then finding the right terminal. My entire body went into alert-mode. But I didn't want to show my fears or concerns to my colleagues, so I pulled myself together and headed off.

It was only a short hop to Finland. I was to leave in

the evening, spend the night in Helsinki, show up for the photo shoot with Markus Grönholm the next morning, somewhere in Helsinki, rush back to the airport and be home again in the afternoon. This trip was really going to test my tolerance for stress and my eyesight. I was to take the train from Kolding to Copenhagen Airport and from there, a plane to Helsinki. I made sure to leave in really good time, and I'd planned everything as best as I could from home, which is a trait that often characterizes people with visual impairments. I had a great need to plan every detail, so as to minimize any mistakes or miscalculations that might occur due to my poor ability to orient myself. When you can't see very well, any deviation from the plan can cause stress and nervousness.

I quickly found my train (thankfully, there are only two tracks) at Kolding train station and everything else seemed to be in order. It was a direct connection to Copenhagen Airport, so what could go wrong? But two things I hadn't allowed for were the weather and a drunken Croatian first mate in the Great Belt.

First the weather. A snowstorm suddenly appeared on the way across the Danish island of Funen, which meant the train had to travel slowly. I started to worry about the time and kept a constant eye on the clock as the train snailed by. I began to doubt whether I'd make my flight at all. As I couldn't orient myself very well, a fear of traveling alone had gradually built up. Traveling by myself was—and is—enormously strenuous, as much of my visual reality is hidden behind a large, round, opaque, flickering ring. My blindness isn't darkness, as many people believe. Instead of darkness, my half-damaged vision cells still send signals to my optic nerve, but as the signal is poor, my brain perceives the signals as luminous, flashing flickers. A bit like the flicker you can experience if you get up from a chair too quickly. Both your entire eyes flicker for a moment, but then they slowly return to normal. My sight just doesn't return to normal, so around my center of vision are constant flickering lights, and it is exhausting to look at. Neither does it help to close my eyes, because the flickering is still there when my eyes are closed. Given my vision, it was obviously difficult to find info screens and other important information, and I wasn't good at asking people for help either.

There was now about an hour before my flight departed, and long past the time when I should have checked in. I began to wonder whether I should take a train back if I didn't arrive at Copenhagen Airport on time. It was an unpleasant thought, because I would have given anything to do the job I'd been sent to do. Making mistakes and the fear of failure was like a poison evoking a feeling of disability in me, and that this was only a taste of the future to come. Completing my mission meant everything for my life!

And then, as if that weren't enough, it also turned out to be the day of the greatest collision into the Great Belt Bridge—on precisely the day when I, with an already pounding heart and sweaty palms, was trying to plan my return trip back to Jutland. The Croatian first mate on the ship M/V Karen Danielsen sailed directly into the West Bridge just as the train arrived in Zealand. So, of course, the bridge had to close, which sabotaged my plan-B return trip. I felt sick to my stomach, and when I finally arrived at the airport, half an hour before the flight to Helsinki was due to take off, I had to figure out where to check in first. Trying to cope with the combination of a pulse of 120, my stress, and a face the color of an over-ripe tomato, was impossible for me. I needed to find someone who could help me, and, fortunately, I quickly found a staffed information desk that pointed me in the right direction.

What normal-sighted people don't think about is astounding, so here is a request to all of you who can see: When a person comes to you and says, "Excuse me, I'm visually impaired. Can you tell me where to go?", it's not always appropriate to say, "Can you see the little blue counter about 200 feet away, at the other end of the terminal? You need to go there." Which is exactly how the lady at the information desk choose to help me, after which she was on the phone again with another customer. I hurried in the direction she had indicated, and after some frantic searching, I found the check-in to my airline, but a huge queue extinguished my brief optimism. I had to wait until it was my turn, and when I finally made it to the counter, the airport employee looked at me with a discouraging expression.

"You're VERY late," he said. Then he picked up the phone and called the gate. He waited a long time, but no one answered, so he resolutely hung up, gave me my boarding pass and said: "RUN!"

I asked the way to security, and when it was finally my turn to go through the metal detector, it—of course—began to ring and beep. I'd forgotten to take off my watch, and so I naturally had to be patted down. I asked the security guard if he could tell me where my gate was. He looked at me teasingly and answered, "At the very far end of the airport," and added that I'd have to get my skates on.

My heart was in my mouth as I sped toward the gate with everything I had, weighed down by my bag and wearing too many clothes (it was winter and snowing, after all). When I finally reached the gate, they were closing it. I shouted "STOOOP" and, thankfully, they heard me and opened the door again. I hurried onto the plane and found my seat and, exhausted, threw myself into it. I was absolutely shattered and bathed in sweat. I hadn't had anything to eat and, unfortunately, there wasn't anything to eat onboard the short flight to Helsinki, so I spent the entire flight with a growling stomach, too. But I had made my flight and I'd lived through all the horrors I'd hardly been able to imagine before leaving my house. *Why did this SHIT always happen to me?* I thought, cursing to myself. *If only I didn't have this damn disease!*

I arrived in Helsinki at 11 p.m., grabbed a quick sandwich, took a taxi to my hotel, checked in and fell into bed. I had to get up at five o'clock and find my way to the studio where the photo session was going to take place, and I had no idea how to find the studio yet. It took me ages to fall asleep because my pulse was racing.

The next morning, I hopped into a taxi and arrived at the studio 45 minutes later. It was an old warehouse and there wasn't a soul in sight. The place was completely deserted and abandoned; the taxi had gone, so here I was standing somewhere outside of Helsinki all by myself. This was before smartphones and fast internet, so I'd no idea how to get hold of a taxi if no one actually showed up. I was beginning to wonder whether anyone would turn up, and I was also beginning to fear that the advertising agency had made a mistake and given me the wrong address or that I'd come on the wrong day. It caused me quite the stomachache.

But, fortunately, people soon arrived. I'd arrived at the studio before anyone else, so now that people were showing up, I relaxed a bit. Notice how my thoughts led me into all kinds of disaster scenarios. Our thoughts can cause the brain to release neurotransmitters, chemical messengers that enable it to communicate with parts of itself and the nervous system. These chemical messengers can make us feel panic, stress and ready for battle or they can create feelings of peace, calmness and happiness. We have the ability to control this process, but more often than not, we run on autopilot, letting our experiences of the past control how we anticipate the future. It's an unfortunate way to deal with your situation.

I'll return to this later in PART 2 of the book. These examples in PART 1 from my past give you a foundation to understand PART 2. I promise you will be rewarded if you stay with me and my stories for a little while yet.

Such a trip would have pushed many people past their limits, while others would have found it easy and natural. But considering that I could only see the equivalent of through the inside of a roll of aluminum foil, this was a major achievement for me and genuinely pushed my boundaries. But no one knew that was how I felt. I didn't share my concerns and challenges with others, which, of course, only made things even worse.

Soon the photographer arrived, and then Marcus Grön-holm. He turned out to be a completely ordinary guy with his feet planted firmly on Finnish ground. With his driving suit on, we were ready to start. I had created a layout, so we knew exactly what pictures to take. Marcus was to stand with one hand by his side and the other holding a battery out toward the camera. The idea was to shoot the image twice and create the effect of Marcus holding the battery very close to the camera; thereby, making the battery large in the foreground and Marcus smaller in the background. It was a way to create an exaggerated wide-angle effect that would bring the product into focus.

We took photo after photo, until Marcus started complaining that the muscles in his arm were starting to burn. The atmosphere was light and we laughed at the fact that a world champion couldn't hold a few grams of battery.

When the photo shoot was over, the photographer got me a taxi to the airport. Without any trouble this time and, fortunately, I quickly figured out where to check in. I'd also arrived four hours before departure, so as not to risk being late—I'd rather spend hours at the airport than go sightseeing. Everything went according to plan, and I returned safely to Copenhagen.

When I think back on the trip today, I can see that I often made life extra difficult for myself by keeping my problems a secret. I'm glad I was able to make the trip and overcome my worries, but I'd never subject myself to such experiences now.

Back then, I was driven by the fear of being revealed and that fear is devastating. Now that I've dropped the mask and laid all the cards on the table, I'd only go on such a trip alone if I wanted to challenge myself—for ME. But that insight was gained slowly over the years, and I wouldn't be who I am today if I hadn't lived through what I lived through then. I have learned so many lessons through the years as visually disabled, and the most important one is never to let myself feel pressured because of fear. Later, I realized how, through my thoughts and concerns, I created situations that made everything worse for myself. Just think: had I not worried myself sick on this trip and taken things as they'd come, I'd have done my job without tormenting myself. Because, in the end, everything went according to plan, and not because I was consciously doing something to make that happen. I could have been better at accepting what was, but I didn't have that ability. Which is one of the things we're going to look at in PART 2 of the book.

LEGO

In 2009—after 11 years in the advertising industry—it was time for me to find new challenges. The advertising industry was under maximum pressure due to the financial crisis of 2008. Many agencies were closing and customers (businesses) didn't want to bet on expensive advertising campaigns. This is when I had the idea to work for the LEGO Group. Again, the idea popped up quite randomly. I have no recollection of where it came from, but I'm pretty sure now that it was the same again as that day in the cell phone store. I'd grown tired of the advertising industry, where everything had gradually become a matter of delivering as much as possible for as little money as possible. The companies were putting pressure on the agencies, and keeping customers and surviving had become a bloody battle for the agencies. There was pressure on all fronts. Creatives, who once had weeks, were now harried into completing projects in only a few days. It was unsustainable and not at all fun, and neither did it harmonize with being a father and being present and attentive at home. So, the situation inspired me to seek out new challenges. But, to be honest, it was probably more about me getting away from what I was in. Again, it was probably more the dissatisfaction with my situation that motivated me rather than a desire to seek new adventures.

I decided to send an unsolicited application for a job as an art director to the LEGO Group, presenting my accomplishments throughout my now 11-year career and introducing myself, and I was subsequently invited to an interview. So now, here I was at the reception of the LEGO Group headquarters. Talk about a pretty nerve-wracking experience! I was standing in the foyer of the LEGO Group itself—the toy that had meant so much to me as a kid and that my friends and I had played with for hours and hours, day in and day out. I loved building and playing with LEGO bricks.

I was shaking with nerves. I'd heard that those who worked here were super talented, so my head was already full of stories about my not being good enough and why I should stay in my old job. That should have put a stop to any attempt to feel entitled to a job at the LEGO Group. But here I was. From working at small advertising agencies with 15-20 employees, I was now in a company with several thousand employees. I was shown into the meeting room, where I was welcomed by a creative director who was to lead the job interview, and his introductory comment was really promising: "I've been looking forward to meeting you all day."

Wow, that gave my confidence a boost and soon any nervousness was gone. I've always felt that I get terribly anxious just before having to present anything. My heart pounds, my breathing quickens, my hands get clammy and cold and, most of all, I want to run away from the situation. But once I start talking, any edginess quickly disappears. It has controlled me and restricted me and annoyed me my entire life.

I presented myself and my merits to the director, and

about ten minutes into the interview, he interrupted me and said they were looking for people for several different positions. In addition to an art director, they were looking for a creative manager for a team of art directors and graphic designers. A little confused and not quite knowing where this was going, I listened patiently. Finally, he got to the point. He believed I should go for the position of creative manager instead of art director. I was absolutely dumbfounded. That wasn't at all what I'd had in mind, but I went along with it, letting the director do the talking. From being a candidate for an art director position, he was now talking to me as if I were already employed by the company; as if it was just a matter of where and what to work as. It was a fantastic feeling and, as I was leaving the meeting, I was told to go home and think about whether I would like to be considered for the executive or the art director position, which gave me something to think about for the next few days.

I've never perceived myself as a leader of other people. So this thought was brand new to me. Today, I know exactly what was happening in my mind and body when I had to consider my options. My considerations were focused primarily on my shortcomings, my low self-worth and esteem, and—as I will tell you later—there was a true battle going on between my conscious and my subconscious mind. My conscious mind said, *Wow, this is a huge opportunity—go for it.* My subconscious responded by sending feelings of anxiety, inferiority, unease and all sorts of other clear signals to my body that this was dangerous and that I should watch out. You could say that there were no values in my subconscious mind that supported the ambitions my conscious mind was striving for. What happens between our conscious and subconscious minds is fascinating, and one of the purposes in me writing this book was precisely that: to tell you about the forces at play when the two layers fail to agree with one another.

But, to start with, I was onboard with the idea of being a creative manager, so I said so to the director. Now, an even greater recruiting process than I could have imagined was implemented: two more interview rounds, but before I could go to the first one, I had to undergo a comprehensive online personality analysis that looked deep into the kind of person I was. Completing the test was both fun and a little daunting. It was the first time I'd done anything like it, and I was surprised at how difficult it was to answer some of the questions. The test was compiled in such a way so that you actually had to answer the same question several times, just phrased in different ways, so there was no way to cheat the system by plugging attitudes and opinions that didn't actually reflect the person I was.

I arrived at interview number two and couldn't believe my own eyes when I entered the meeting room on Åstvej

1 in Billund, where two "LEGO men" sat waiting for me. We call them "Minifigures". But these were not miniature. No, they were flesh and blood. In the meeting room were two creative directors and one HR partner, and the two directors were both bald and wore thick, black spectacles. Guess who they also looked like—ME! And, as I stood in the doorway, I couldn't help but comment that the three of us were perfect for working at LEGO—all we needed was a little stud on the top of our heads and we'd look like LEGO Minifigures with glasses. It was absolutely comical and with that intro-line, the ice was broken. Humor is always a good way to start a relationship—it works every time. We laughed and it was the perfect start to the interview.

The two interviews went well, but I simply didn't have the heart when it came to being a people manager. I'd been ruminating on it for weeks and had asked all my close friends for advice, without being any the wiser in my decision. I just didn't believe in my own abilities, and the people at LEGO had definitely spotted it, because after the two interviews I got the message that they would like to hire me as an art director with the potential of revisiting the possibility of recruiting me as a manager later.

In actual fact, I was relieved that they had made the decision for me; it was quite symptomatic of the way I was thinking and had thought my entire life. Never setting goals for myself or believing that I could accomplish anything great. It's weird because when I asked my friends for advice when I was ruminating on the managerial job, the reaction from everyone was that they were sure I'd do a great job. They all said that I was sympathetic, empathetic and skilled and that anyone would be lucky to have me as a boss. But I didn't believe it myself and, interestingly, when you don't really believe in yourself or when your heart isn't in it, you're more likely to listen to the negative arguments presented to you than the positive ones. The mind will seek the solution that gives you the least risk of failure or of being hurt.

I wasn't my own best friend, so any negative consequences of a new opportunity in my life outweighed the potential positive outcomes. Which is a typical reaction when your life is in "fight or flight" mode, where the body is more used to living in a state of fear and stress than in one of joy and harmony; so it was a relief to be able to say no to the unique opportunity that had opened up in front of me — the managerial job.

But I did get the job as an art director and I got it because I was able to convince people that I'd be a brilliant art director. I exhibited sureness in the job because I knew how to be an art director. But I *didn't* know how to be a creative manager, so I didn't dare head in that direction. I could easily convince the people at LEGO that I'd be good for the company — as an art director — not as a creative manager.

Starting at LEGO was a culture shock. From working in a small cozy business of fifteen people, I was now surrounded by hundreds of colleagues. It took quite some time before anyone even noticed that a new employee had started in the large open office in Billund. So many people work at LEGO and the workforce counts loads of freelancers, too. Therefore, it was difficult for other employees to figure out whether you were a freelancer, working here for the short-term, or whether you were a new full-time employee. A few months passed before I was really noticed, and it was the project I'd been hired to do that got me noticed.

When I started at LEGO, I was told that I was going to work as an art director on the global LEGO Christmas campaign, which was to be bigger and more ambitious than ever before. I was to be the driving force in the creative process, responsible for its progress, but I wasn't to do all the work myself. I was supposed to work with colleagues on the project, but I was the lead on the assignment. So I was pretty excited about how it was going to go. Could I do it? Was I in way over my head? Anxiety-provoking thoughts for someone who saw mostly disasters ahead of them.

But those first few months at LEGO didn't go quite as I'd imagined. I was hired in August and, at first, did different assignments for different teams—LEGO NINJA-

GO, LEGO City and LEGO ATLANTIS. After a while, I knocked on the window of my creative director's office to find out if we shouldn't get started on the Christmas campaign anytime soon. I was beginning to get nervous about whether we'd have trouble finishing the campaign before Christmas, now that we were in October. That's when I got my first *eureka* moment into what it takes to prepare global campaigns for one of the world's largest toy factories. The LEGO motto, *Only the best is good enough*, which was coined by the company's founder, Ole Kirk Kristiansen, was—and is—taken very seriously in the group. The creative director was obviously amused by my question and replied with a smile on his lips: "It's the Christmas campaign for next year, Morten."

Just as he said it, I could hear how silly it was to think that a worldwide company like the LEGO Group could create a Christmas campaign to be rolled out across most of the globe in only a few months. The logistics behind such a huge campaign are enormous, and the machinery behind all the markets involved in approving such a large campaign is equally as huge.

But now I started working with one of the two creative directors who had hired me and a planner (an analyst who knows the trends, tendencies and needs of different consumer and customer groups), and a few months later, we presented the campaign to the international committee that was to implement it worldwide. I have to admit, going from working in the domestic Danish market to communicating in markets around the world was a giant leap. I now had to understand how a German child, an American child, and their parents, thought in their respective cultures. It was super exciting and very educational.

Another thing was the language. English is spoken at the LEGO Group, which is something I had to get used to, because despite having a fair grasp of the English language, initially it was a barrier. Conducting all workshops and presentations in English was a challenge, but I soon overcame it. Now, I actually prefer reading and listening to books in English, which has the added advantage of having a much greater selection of non-fiction to choose from than Danish does—something I took great advantage of when I started my research. I'll return to this in PART 2.

After proving my worth on the Christmas campaign project, I was quickly promoted to senior art director and was assigned more of a leadership role in projects. I was now responsible for making presentations, directing the creative process, leading and facilitating workshops and being a motivator and the "go-to" person for the other art directors who worked on my team. It wasn't difficult for me to fulfill this task—it turned out my ten years in the advertising industry had prepared me well for the position.

The LEGO Agency, where I now work, is LEGO's in-house advertising and communications agency, and to many people's surprise, it's Denmark's unrivaled and largest advertising agency. We develop the majority of the LEGO Group's global campaigns, and if you want to work creatively with animated films and TV production, there is nothing greater in Denmark than the LEGO Group. Over the years, I've made over forty TV spots and more than twenty small animated films in collaboration with various film production companies.

Did you notice that not a single word about my eye condition was mentioned in this quick review of my years at the LEGO Group? There's a good reason for that. Before my job interview, I decided that I wouldn't tell anyone about my condition, in case it minimized my chances of landing the job. I wasn't going to let my eye disorder give them an excuse to disregard me as a candidate, and that way of thinking was in line with the decision I'd made on my way home in the car from Copenhagen that day in 2002 after I'd been diagnosed. I'd managed all these years with a visual impairment without anyone complaining about my work, so why shouldn't I be able to do the job? I've never kept my condition secret per se, but I certainly didn't talk about it unless it was absolutely necessary for me. My plan at the LEGO Group was to show them that I worked with the same ability and with the same capacity as anyone else with full vision, and once I'd proved that, I would begin to talk to the people I collaborated with about my disorder.

And that's what happened, but as I've experienced countless times before, people have a hard time taking me seriously when I talk about the disorder, because it's almost impossible to tell by looking at me that I have a visual impairment. I don't use a white cane when I walk, and neither do I wear the badge that many blind people wear. I've developed so many coping strategies that people would have to observe me carefully before they could see that I handle everyday life differently than people with normal sight do.

Many people are surprised when I tell them that I am visually impaired and they are absolutely astounded when I add that I work with visual communication. And really—can you blame them?

Breakdown

Over the years, my vision gradually got worse and worse. I sometimes went to the ophthalmologist to follow its development, and it was clear that the field of vision was narrowing year after year. I still had enough sight to drive a car—that was what the old ophthalmologist I went to in Kolding had said, at least—so I was still driving.

This was probably one of the biggest reasons why I kept the development of my eye condition to myself. I wanted to keep driving for as long as possible. Being able to drive equaled freedom. It was my way of getting back and forth between LEGO and home, too. And it also kept me in my state of denial: I absolutely did not have a disability. At least, not one I was prepared to talk about aloud. I realized that if I talked too much about my vision problems, people would start wondering about my still driving a car.

I never drove the car whenever we went anywhere as a family. Mette always drove then. Neither did I ever drive in the dark. I agreed with my boss at LEGO that, in the winter months, I could arrive at work when it was bright and leave to drive home when it was still light. I would continue working when I got home, without having to risk my life and the lives of others in the dark traffic. Another reason I stuck to driving a car was that if I crossed that line, and accepted that I could no longer drive, I was also then officially disabled in a way. It was an invisible limit for me that was difficult to cross, so I held onto the car for as long as I could.

When I was with the eye specialist, sometime in 2007, I asked him if it was still okay for me to be driving a car, and he gave me this slightly vague answer: "Hmm, I don't know if the surgeon general would say you driving a car is a good thing." So that was the last time I went to the ophthalmologist. Staying away wasn't a conscious choice, but I didn't make another appointment when the time for the next annual check came around. They couldn't do anything anyway! I was slowly losing my sight and nobody could do anything about it.

The years passed and life became harder for me to bear. I was getting more and more stressed at LEGO. I remember a particular episode where I was developing twenty-two short two-minute animated films simultaneously. I wasn't producing the films myself, but I'd written the scripts and developed the initial storyboard to ensure the cool LEGO City models and the right balance of humor and action that characterizes LEGO City stories were included. Once I'd written the stories and gotten them approved through the system, a film production company was then called in to develop the films with me as an approver, which meant I was constantly receiving new versions and had to comment and give direction to the production people. It demanded that I tread carefully. Having to keep track of all the different versions, while also doing campaign development and being the go-to person for the other art directors and their projects, was very stressful. It all simply became too much. One morning in 2014, I was sitting on the edge of my bed, and the thought of going to work caused my whole body to shake. I just couldn't take it anymore. I went on sick leave for a while, and the next few years of my life at LEGO were characterized by stress and depression. It was something that had slowly crept into my life.

In August 2016, after struggling through years in the advertising industry as an art director, the last of which had been with stress and depression, too, I still wasn't aware that this state could be due to my loss of sight. In fact, I was still living in a world where my vision challenges weren't to be an impediment, but where self-reproaches and self-criticism had become like a heavy and warm overcoat embracing me completely. I constantly heard an inner voice say, "Why can't you handle this anymore? Why are you getting tired so quickly? Pull yourself together, man!"

Despite being well aware that I'd now lost much of my vision, I didn't make the connection at all between it being hard to live a perfectly normal and busy life on the same terms as a person with normal vision. Working full time as a senior art director at LEGO, without any visual aids, was wearing me down. Over the years, I had grown accustomed to my vision and found ways to survive getting through the days.

To better understand why having RP can be a bit of an ordeal, I've tried to describe an ordinary day on the job. When I think back on that time, I can't begin to fathom how I endured it for as long as I did. The little excerpt that follows is from the time when I was still driving a car and under serious pressure in my day-to-day life. I wrote it one day after coming home from work extremely frustrated, exhausted and completely burned out. For some reason, I needed to get it out of my system. This was before I realized that my poor eyesight was the cause of many of my everyday problems. That it didn't immediately make sense to me that there was a connection between my stress and my loss of vision is quite incomprehensible to me today, but again, that is what is remarkable about our minds. Our subconscious mind will try to hold on to its learned habits and ordinary everyday way of life for as long as possible. I tried to hold on to the "SELF" that I'd built up over many years. If I admitted to myself that I was now challenged by my disability, I'd have to take a good look at my life and make major changes to it. It was far more difficult to change ingrained habits and beliefs than to continue living with the challenges. The idea of becoming someone else, a "disabled" person, kept me from looking reality in the eye.

A Friday in spring 2016

I get up and want to have breakfast. I go out to the kitchen, open the drawer and find a packet of crispbread. I open the fridge and scan it with my eyes for the cold cuts of chicken. When I move a few packets of meat to better orient myself, five packets of sliced cheese tumble out of the fridge. They crash to the floor. "Damned eyes," I curse. I pick up the mess and put them back in the fridge, but the chicken isn't where it used to be. After scanning the fridge in vain for a few minutes, I call Rasmus and he comes to my rescue. Rasmus looks in the fridge, and after a few seconds, he reaches out an arm and takes the chicken from the front of the top shelf.

"It's right here, Dad. Right in front of you," he says, smiling.

"SO it is," I smile, cursing inside.

I didn't see it and that annoys me. *"Why can't I see a damned thing?"* complains a voice in my head.

I find everything else that I need and eat my breakfast. After eating, I take the plate and glass and carry it over to the sink. I forget to scan the kitchen counter, and as I reach out my arm, I don't see a glass that one of the boys has placed on the edge of the counter. I knock it over, sensing the glass falling in slow motion to its end. It shatters on the tiles, spraying glass shards all over the kitchen floor. Annoyed at myself again, I start picking up the fragments.

Typical! Idiot! Why didn't you look around properly?

Rasmus comes out to the kitchen again and says, "There goes another glass, huh, Dad!"

He smiles and asks if he can help. I politely decline, and continue picking up pieces of glass from the floor. He shouldn't have to pay the price for his father being a blind fool who can't see! I take out the vacuum cleaner and vacuum everything I can see, knowing that Mette will come home this afternoon and see all the glass shards

I've overlooked.

I'm finally ready to head to work. I walk out to the car, turn on the engine and roll out of the estate. At the end of the road, I stop and scan the road I'm turning onto. First left then right. I slowly let my eyes slide once again from left to right, making sure I haven't overlooked anything. Meanwhile, the driver of the car behind me has become impatient. He lets me know with an irritable beep, beeeeeeppppppppp! And startled, I respond by setting off.

I drive from my home to Billund. A 25-mile ride with little traffic, and I feel comfortable driving this route in daylight. I've long since stopped driving a car in the dark. I reach the first roundabout at Billund and scan the area thoroughly. My eyes moving back and forth; everything looks good, so I drive forward calmly. Out of nowhere, there's a van right next to me on the roundabout. I slam on the brakes and the van does the same. The man in the van looks at me angrily while he gives me the finger. I pretend it doesn't bother me as I drive into the LEGO parking garage with my heart in my mouth. I stop just before the entrance and switch from sunglasses to regular glasses and slowly drive into the dark. The darkness seems all-encompassing as I go from the sharp daylight into the parking garage. There are people and cars everywhere, so I drive quite slowly, so as not to hit anyone or anything. Slowly and with a tail of cars behind me, I come up onto the third floor and park the car. I get my bag from the trunk and head to the stairs. On the way over, my eyes continue to scan my surroundings. It's so embarrassing and annoying when I overlook colleagues politely greeting me. I don't see anyone—I'm all alone.

"Hi Morten," says a voice right beside me. I get a fright but overcome the impulse to let him know. It's so embarrassing!

It's a colleague I work with every day. I pretend that I knew he was there the whole time, and we head to the stairs together. He steps ahead and jogs down the stairs. My eyes still haven't quite adapted to the dark, and I stop at the stairs to orient myself thoroughly before taking a step down. As I can't see both my legs and the stairs due to my narrowed field of vision, I have to be brave and concentrate. Otherwise, I could fall down the stairs.

When my colleague notices my hesitation, he turns around and asks what I'm doing. I reply that I'm not in any hurry to get to work and we grin at each other. This is always how it is for me when I have to go down the stairs. I feel clumsy and count the steps down to the middle landing. There are eight steps. Phew! Made it!

We descend the stairs, as my colleague fills me in on his plans for the weekend. I'm only half-listening as my full concentration has been on getting down safely. I don't think he noticed anything and we exit the dark parking garage together. The light hits me like a laser beam. Suns, moons and stars flicker before my eyes. I quickly put on my sunglasses and can now glimpse my surroundings. Again, it takes a few minutes for my sight to adjust to the daylight.

In an attempt to keep up with my colleague in the bright light, I walk smack into a roughly twenty-inch high concrete pillar with flowers—OUCH! *Who the hell decided to put that there?* I think to myself. The pain in my shin makes my eyes water, but I bite it back, because— fortunately—my colleague didn't see my clumsiness. With a thumping tibia, we walk the last few steps into our shared workplace.

We go our separate ways after entering the building; me to my desk and him to his. As I walk through the large open office, I think about how many people are greeting me silently right now, and what they must think when I don't return their hellos and good morning nods. I scan my surroundings again as I make my way forward, trying to avoid all the obstacles en route. The entire office has just moved from one building to another, so there are moving boxes everywhere; plants aren't where they should be, and some desks have been placed a bit randomly. My full concentration is on finding my desk safely. I've no idea who I may have involuntarily ignored on my way.

I greet the colleagues in closest proximity to me, find my Macbook Pro and start work. It's been a typical and very ordinary morning for me. I don't think about it anymore. That's just how it is. This is my everyday life and I've learned to live with it as best I can. I don't know any other reality anymore. My Retinitis Pigmentosa has slowly worn away much of my vision, and as with people who gradually lose their hearing, I'm gradually losing my sight. It's happening in small sneaky stages, so I'm probably unaware of how bad it really is.

"I'll have to do something about it soon. I'll call the ophthalmologist tomorrow and make an appointment. Or the day after tomorrow—No, next week is better. I have a few important meetings tomorrow, and a birthday party next week. So maybe next month is better. Yeah, I'll definitely do it then. And my eyes probably aren't that bad. I won't have to stop driving. What happened this morning at the roundabout was certainly due to that idiot in the van driving erratically. Besides, nobody can tell that I have difficulty seeing. I'm good at hiding it and explaining the stupid daily mishaps. I'll call the doctor next month. Definitely!"

When lunchtime comes around, a colleague asks if I'd like to go to the canteen. I don't really want to. It's been like that for a while now. I prefer to prepare lunch at my own pace and eat alone. But I know going to lunch with the others is good for me. I've gradually become so isolated that it's starting to get a little lonely. But it's easier to be alone, as then I don't have to keep up the façade and pretend that I don't have any challenges. And I don't make a fool of myself when I'm by myself, because no one's around to see it!

We arrive at the canteen. It's thronged with people. Long queues at every counter. I hate eating at this time of day. There are far too many people—it's extremely stressful to be in the canteen during peak lunch hours.

We look at the day's specials on the menu board, and I comment to my colleague that the kitchen staff must have forgotten to write the menu on the large whiteboard.

My colleague gives me a strange look and says, "What do you mean?" Then she starts to read aloud, and I realize that the whiteboard I'd perceived as empty, actually had scrawlings in faint ink. Practically illegible to me, but obviously not to my colleague. I apologize, saying I must have overlooked the text because of the way the light is falling on the board.

SO EMBARRASSING I think, hoping my colleague will let the incident go. *Why can't you just be like everyone else? Blind idiot.*

We stand in our respective queues and I decide to take

the salad counter. I can't see the plates. They're not where they usually are. I look around the crowd and finally ask a stranger by my side if she has seen any plates anywhere. She laughs at my question as she points right in front of me. "They're right there," she smiles. And right in front of me are the plates. I can't understand how I missed them, and apparently, she can't either. Again, I pretend that it's nothing embarrassing.

I fill my plate with different salads and glance around, but I can't see any of the others I came to lunch with— they've disappeared. I ring a colleague and ask where they are and she tells that they're upstairs. I go upstairs and look out over the sea of tables. I can't see them.

Blind idiot.

Then I hear familiar voices calling my name, but I still can't see them, and I frantically scout the crowd. The voices continue to shout my name and, finally, I spot a table of waving arms and legs, like shipwrecks who've finally spied their rescue ship in the distance.

They must think you're so weird.

I prepare myself for the onslaught of questions now awaiting me: "What the hell were you doing? Couldn't you see us?" Sometimes I explain that I'm challenged by my vision; other times I just laugh with them and pretend that my bumbling and blundering is an expression of absentmindedness. Explaining my level of vision is too hard and no one understands it anyway.

Yet again, I'm the last one to sit down at the table to eat. Getting food often takes me longer than it takes other people, but I've learned to live with it. That's just how my life is.

After spending years wrestling with stress and depression, the project I'm working on is actually going really well, but I still don't quite feel that I'm able to keep up. Which is weird. Why am I having so much trouble getting over the sick leave I took over a year ago? It's as if something is keeping me stuck in my melancholy. Not even all the conversations I've had with psychologists and my family have helped me understand the cause of the stress and depression I'm dealing with. It is so frustrating. Am I just worn out? Am I burned out? I don't understand. On the one hand, I love my job but, on the other, sometimes I'm not able for it at all.

You're useless! You're not good enough!

This was an ordinary day at work for me, on a regular Friday. Ignoring these challenges in everyday life for so many years was, naturally again, my way of coping with life. Of dealing with the fact that I would slowly become blind. It was unbearable. I couldn't bear thinking about it, so I didn't entertain it. But what often happens when you try to push things aside is that, at some point, it becomes too hard to keep pushing them away. That's what happened to me. I'd been pushing things aside for so long, that it all became too much and my world collapsed. I broke down one morning before I was supposed to go to work. My body simply said no more. I shook all over. I couldn't think a single rational thought and couldn't cope with anything. I had to take sick leave and was then absent from work for almost six months. During that time, I had no energy for anything—not even being together with my family. After half an hour, I had to go back to bed and sleep for two hours. My will to live was broken. I was done for!

One day, my wife and I were sitting in the kitchen, chatting, and she asked me, "Morten, how exactly is it going with your sight?" It was during the summer of 2016.

She had been living with the Morten, who had been living with RP since 2002, without talking about it very much, and she had recently observed that I'd become more awkward and clumsy in my behavior than before, and that I could no longer see things as well as I use to. For example, on our recent vacation to Crete, I'd demonstrated my bad ball-eye coordination on several occasions in the hotel pool when playing with the boys. It was almost impossible for me to see the little yellow tennis ball we were throwing between us, and I often had trouble navigating the sudden little stairs and changes in levels in the hotel.

It had, after all, been years since I'd been to the ophthal-mologist, so neither of us knew what condition I was in, but there was no avoiding it anymore.

Mette and I had long asked each other why life was so hard for me and what the cause could be. I'd been through several rounds with stress management psychologists, and would soon have been through my childhood inside and out. But my gift of gab and my ability to hide my RP had deceived all the psychologists and, apparently, even Mette. My sight had only been mentioned briefly at the psychologists and none of them had seen the connection between my stress and my impaired vision. In fact, once or twice in my conversations with psychologists, I cau-tiously mentioned the theory that my stress might be due to my eyesight, but I don't think the psychologists truly realized that this was a problem for me. After all, my dis-ability is completely invisible, and I drove to my appoint-ments, so how could I be visually impaired?

At the psychologist's

Going to therapy is a bit weird. You meet a person for the first time, and then the timer is set, and you share private issues that you wouldn't normally tell a total stranger. As I said, I went to various psychologists with expertise in stress management, and I have to admit it didn't help a whole lot. The reason I ended up seeing several different psychologists was that I couldn't cope with going through the therapy process without a clear plan and a goal for what it was that we were going to achieve with the counseling. It was mostly chitchat, and when the hour was over, the psychologist would say: "Goodbye. Thank you, and see you next time." And the next time we'd start at a completely random place and just talk. It made no sense to me. Plus, I had an expectation about needing to be "fixed," and when I wasn't fixed, it had to be the psychologist's fault!

The fourth psychologist was nothing like the first three. At our first appointment, we talked for ten minutes in her office, and then she asked if I'd mind if our meetings were spent walking in the woods. There was a comfy bench, with a nice view of the fields, where we could sit and talk.

I wondered a little at the suggestion, but was also pleasantly surprised by such a different approach to what I had experienced before.

I had one goal: to be fixed so that I could get my life back on track and live the way I used to. My mentioning the little excursion with the psychologist makes much more sense later in the book. I didn't understand the true meaning of this nature walk until a year and a half later—and you'll have to wait a bit longer to hear that, so remember the story I'm telling now. Its significance will be revealed later.

We left her practice and strolled toward the forest that was right next to the building. She explained we had to walk for a while before we'd reach the bench. But there was a twist—we weren't going to walk like we normally did. Well, I wasn't to. I was only allowed to walk by putting one foot directly in front of the other, heel-to-toe. Small steps only. It was a strange task, but I joined in and I tried to walk as slowly as I could. In the meantime, she continued talking, and I tried to concentrate on walking heel-to-toe, heel-to-toe as I answered her questions. It was immensely difficult. I could barely keep my balance, and I kept increasing the tempo subconsciously. She had to gently remind me each time to take my time, to walk at a slow pace. I couldn't help but be amused by this comical walk, and neither could I help but shrink a little when passers-by glanced strangely at our performance.

We continued steadily, and then she asked me to notice what was going on around me. What could I detect? I commented, that I could hear the birds. That was curious—I hadn't noticed them at all just minutes before. A woodland bird was screeching somewhere, and a little while later another bird responded. She asked me to continue paying attention to the outside world, and now I detected the sound of the wind in the trees. A soft rustling sound, like when the sea rushes in to the shore. It was quite soothing. I began to feel the same wind touching my cheek, and my lips rose in a smile at the sensory experiences that were popping up for me now, but that had been there all along. We walked (well, I wobbled—I was still having a hard time keeping my balance), and finally, we made it through the woods and arrived at a little meadow. There, in front of a large grassy field with grazing cows, was the little forest bench. We sat down and just looked at the animals in the field. I hadn't had the mental energy to think of anything other than the way I was to walk. Putting one foot in front of the other without falling, answering questions and noticing nature had taken every bit of my concentration. But now that we were sitting still, I began to wonder what all this was about.

She was a quirky psychologist, and when would she start fixing my problems? I didn't understand and just as I was about to ask her, she interrupted me and asked me to close my eyes and feel how my buttocks were in contact with the bench underneath me. *What?* But I did as she said and felt the solid bench against my bum. It was a hard seat and not overly comfortable. I noticed that now.

Then she asked me to notice how my feet were in contact with the earth beneath me. I focused on my feet, and was reminded of something I'd tried once before. A few years ago, I went to a coach who introduced me to something called a "body scan." The idea is to take your awareness into your body to scan it. I'd done it a few times, but hadn't really understood what it was all about. "Feel your big toe," the coach had said, and I smiled again at the thought. "That's ridiculous. How is that supposed to help?" said a critical voice in my head.

This was reminiscent of a body scan, but the psychologist hadn't called it anything or prepared me for what I was to do, so I'd gone along with the experience without judging it too much. I certainly thought it was a little weird, but I was open to the idea.

So here I was, sitting on a bench with my eyes closed, feeling my feet on the ground, and then something absolutely crazy happened. Something I'd never ever experienced before. As I sat there with my eyes closed, I had the very real experience of my lower body remaining on the bench while my upper body hovered sideways beside me in the air—as though there was no contact between my upper and lower body. It took all my willpower not to open my eyes, and I informed the psychologist of the feeling of my upper body being separated from my lower body. The psychologist reassured me that my body was still in one piece and that I should try to just let it be.

After sitting and talking on the bench for 20 minutes, we returned to the practice at a regular pace and finished the session. They were peculiar meetings, and I left each time with a feeling that my problems weren't really being solved. We never got to the bottom of why I was so stressed all the time and why I had to take periods of sick leave from work. My bad eyesight never came up, but I discovered something else that I promise to share with you later in the book. Remember this story and it might just give you an *a-ha* moment like it did for me, too.

Back at the consultant's

But let's get back to Mette's question: "When were you last at the ophthalmologist, Morten?"

Naturally, Mette had some insight into my visual limitations, but only I knew what it was really like to be me and what it was truly like to see with my eyes.

Slowly losing a sense is an odd experience. You gradually get used to the loss, while other people often notice that something is wrong long before you yourself do. Think about elderly people steadily losing their hearing. They say "What?!" twenty times during a brief conversation, and they believe their hearing is just fine. "You keep mumbling," they point out when you mention that they might need to get their hearing checked. Losing your eyesight is somewhat similar.

Through the course of fifteen years, I developed coping strategies so almost no one discovered that I was losing my sight. I began slowly and subconsciously to avoid engaging in social activities where there were many people and I started to let old friends go. When you have RP, you first lose your ability to see at night, and then your general vision goes, so I declined parties where I knew there would be low lighting. I always came up with excuses to cover up my lack of desire to party and have fun with my colleagues. It was just my way of covering up my poor eyesight. Over time, I became more and more isolated, and eventually, colleagues and friends stopped inviting me. Having RP is a lonely journey!

In August 2016, Mette and I were sitting once again in the waiting room of an ophthalmologist in Kolding, like we had done many years earlier at the State Eye Clinic in Copenhagen. By now, the previous eye specialist I'd been to in Kolding—the one who thought the surgeon general might not let me drive—had retired. So we were there to see the new, younger ophthalmologist, for what would turn out to be yet another shocking meeting. Mette came to the appointment with me as she has quite a unique way of listening and remembering. Her job as an emergency room nurse has sharpened her ability to pay attention in the moment. I can't thank her enough for all the help she was, and still is, to me in my life.

A perimetry—or vision field—test was carried out to check how much vision I had left around my central vision, and the result was alarming.

In a perimetry test, you are placed in front of a simulator

and you have to look through a small hole at a large white screen with one eye at a time. When you have healthy vision, you see the entire white screen in your field of vision, except for the retina's little blind spot, where the optic nerve is attached to it. Everyone is blind there, but it's such a small area that it's impossible to notice in everyday life. Discovering your blind spot is like locating a certain star in the night sky. The purpose of the test is to discover how great a field of vision you have.

I was asked to look at a little cross in the middle of the white screen; I was to keep my vision focused on it. A small remote with a button was put into my hand. I was to press the button every time I saw a small bright spot on the white area. The problem with noticing my own RP was that I didn't know everything I couldn't see, which is why I myself often thought that my sight was fine. But this simulator meant registering all the areas I couldn't see.

I concentrated, looking intensely at the white screen. I looked and looked, and I looked and looked some more. I was just about to stop the test and ask why they hadn't turned on the light on the screen, when the technician came over to check if everything was okay. I asked if the machine was working and the technician said everything was fine. Finally, I spotted a bright light and pressed the button. Again, a long time passed, and then another spot of light. After about five minutes, the test was over and I didn't think I'd seen very many bright spots on the white screen. Mette and I returned to the waiting room for our turn to see the ophthalmologist. We were called in and I sat down in the patient chair. You know the one—covered in leather and a footrest at the bottom.

He looked at me and then said quietly, "Morten, do you know that you are legally blind?"

"Eh, what?" was the most intelligent thing I could say.

The test had shown that I now had only four degrees of vision left in my central vision. Roughly the equivalent to seeing through two thin cardboard rolls with a length of two-and-a-half inches (six centimeters) and a diameter of about an inch (two-and-a-half centimeters). If you take the inner tube from a roll of tinfoil and look through it, it corresponds approximately to a four-degree angle. Try looking through a tinfoil roll now. Welcome to my world. The ophthalmologist then asked: "What do you do for a living, Morten?"

When I replied that I was a visual senior art director at the LEGO Group and made a living developing visual communication, he was surprised, to put it mildly.

"Well, that must make everyday life very challenging for you." And finally, it dawned on me—could my stress and depression be due to my poor eyesight? Of course!

I gathered my thoughts for a moment, and then I asked, slightly embarrassed: "I suppose I should stop driving now?" "WHAT!" The ophthalmologist exclaimed.

"YOU'RE STILL DRIVING A CAR?!"

I was legally blind. Legally blind! It was the second time in my life that an ophthalmologist had managed to pull the rug out from under me. It was the second time I received a sentence from a person in a white coat. The first time I'd been "sentenced to blindness" in the future, and now I was "sentenced legally blind" in the present. The future I'd so persistently tried to push away for years and years had finally caught up with me. I was legally blind!

But what exactly does that mean? And how do you explain to others what it means to be able to see and not see at the same time? I was legally blind, but I could still see! It was confusing and I couldn't explain it properly to either my family or colleagues.

One night as I sat thinking about my new condition, an idea came to me. I was going to make a video that simulated how I saw my world with my RP vision. Making short videos was a regular part of my work, so this project was something I could do relatively easily. I'd spent the best part of twenty years of my professional life visualizing and communicating solutions to problems. That's what an art director does. So, I decided to visualize and communicate my own problem so it could be understood.

That I'd been able to go for so long with such poor eyesight, without myself or my immediate family noticing, surprised me. I didn't blame anyone, but if I was to get better at communicating my challenges clearly to those around me, I'd have to try and visualize my vision for myself and others. I didn't spend much energy thinking about how to make the film. It just came to me one night. I walked around the house taking pictures and video of furniture and situations—everyday things. My son Rasmus helped, too, by letting me use his face for one of the image experiments, and after a few evenings, the film was finished.

I hadn't shown the short to anyone during its development, so when it was finally done, I showed it to Mette without much introduction. She watched the entire thing—a little over four minutes—in silence. I was excited to hear her reaction to it. It was evident that the more of the film she saw, the more it was affecting her.

When it was over, her eyes were full of tears as she said quietly: "Why did you never say anything?"

"What do you mean?" I said.

"Why did you never tell me how bad it was?"

I didn't really know what to say. I found myself trying to explain what the video illustrated so many times.

Then it dawned on me: I myself was shocked at the footage. Seeing my vision from the outside was quite different. Now, I could actually see the flickering ring where I was blind. Usually, when I look at something, I don't see anything there, as I continuously move my eyes when

Simulation of my eyesight with Rasmus as a model.

I need to see what's in front of me. I suddenly realized what having only four degrees of vision really means. It's not a whole lot of eyesight.

The rest of the family reacted in much the same way as Mette. It was an eye-opener for everyone. Now my having had such a hard time made complete sense. This video was an immediate and effective tool for me to describe my eye condition to other people, and I used it when I had to explain to the LEGO management team, friends and authorities what it was like to be me.

I even decided to publish it on my YouTube channel and on my Facebook page, because if I could benefit from it, then other people with RP might find it useful, too. After all, I knew first-hand how lonely it'd been dealing with the "condition" by myself, so I imagined that others with RP probably experienced something similar.

I got a lot of inquiries from friends, but also from many people with RP who were grateful for the tool. And I was so happy to be helping other people with RP. A few months after I released the film, I was contacted by the Copenhagen Metropolitan Area Department of Education, who wanted to know if they could use my video for teaching. Of course they could! And, if you'd like to watch it, please visit mortenbonde.dk.

Eyesight is divided into two categories: central vision and peripheral vision. Central vision is our eyes' ability to focus straight ahead, allowing us to read and see details sharply. Central vision only extends about three degrees of our visual field, but it enables us to make vital judgments, such as estimating distance and discerning details in the path ahead. Peripheral vision is the field of vision outside of central vision.

I'm blind from four through to 50 degrees. In the blind ring-shaped area of my central vision, I have what is called acute central ring scintillating scotoma—a large donut-shaped ring around my central vision that flickers and flashes. If you've ever experienced standing up too quickly, then you've probably also experienced your eyesight flickering and disappearing for a moment, then slowly returning. That's what I experience all the time, just with a little peephole in the middle. In the flickering area, the cells in the retina are turned completely or nearly off. But our amazing brain is a trouble-shooter. So it still tries to decode the light picked up by the retina into signals for the brain. However, the signals are distorted and full of errors due to the defective gene causing the condition. Thus, the signal is transmitted incorrectly through the cell membrane, and on through the optic nerve to the brain.

Instead of receiving pictures, like you and everyone else, my brain translates the signals into a firework display of flickering light that's constantly visible, even when I close my eyes. I've gotten used to it, but when I think about it, it does wear me out. I just don't think about it anymore. After all, it's there all the time. But when I've been looking through the flickering for too long, whether it's at work, leisure or when doing something else during my waking hours, I need to turn the "noise" off—that is, shut out the outside world.

Another aspect of having a blind area in my field of vision is the brain's ability to fill those blind areas with what it expects to see. Our expectations of what we experience have a specific effect on what we see, and it can cheat our senses and our bodies completely—which is why I don't always realize that I haven't seen something. The brain and the subconscious immediately assess what I'm seeing and try to fill in the blind area with something that makes sense. Therefore, I'm often under the impression that I can easily see what's right in front of me—my brain tries to form the full picture, but I can get quite a fright when something then suddenly appears in my real field of vision.

Once, my dad, my sons and I went to Esbjerg Harbor, in western Denmark, to see the annual Tall Ship Races. The harbor was full of old, large and impressive ships. As we passed one of the ships, I looked up at it and noticed the white galion figure on the prow of the ship, and I nudged my boys and pointed up at it.

"Look at that galion figure," I said, and we stopped.

They looked up at what I'd been pointing to for a while, looking clearly confused.

"Where?" they said, looking around everywhere.

What I had decoded as a white galion figure was, in fact, a white folded-up sail. My brain had instantly decoded it as a galion because I'd had a previous experience and an expectation that there would be such a figure on the prow of the ship. When I couldn't see it properly, my brain simply decided that what my eyes were seeing had to be a ship's figurehead, and so that's what my brain saw.

Subsequently, I discovered that this is what our brain does constantly. It puts labels on what we experience based on our previous experiences. We don't think about it, but the incident at Esbjerg Harbor demonstrated clearly that the brain sees mostly what it wants to see. What

we expect to see is often what we do see. It's our perspective on the world that makes it what it is. In PART
2, we'll explore what this discovery really means for our
lives. Does it mean that if I constantly think and expect
that I am limited and worthless in any given situation,
then that's what I'm going to unconsciously experience?
In other words, is it my own limited worldview that decides what kind of life I get? PART 2 reveals the conclusion to these questions, but maybe you know it already?

RP seen through funny glasses

But not everything is bad, so I'd like to share a few fun
anecdotes with you. My visual impairment has also often
been the cause of a lot of laughter in different everyday
situations. Thankfully, I have a great sense of humor, so
I've always been able to laugh at my unfortunate episodes.

Like when Mette or the boys throw a ball at me, forgetting about my tunnel vision for a moment, and it hits me
square in the forehead or somewhere equally as comical.

Or being in the dark, steamy Turkish bath at the swim-
ming pool, where I've lost count of how many times I've
sat on other bathers when I was trying to find somewhere
to sit in the dark. It's an unpleasant experience, because
other people can't tell by looking at me that my vision is
impaired.

One day, after I'd shown my movie to Mette, I came home from work, burning to tell her something exciting that had happened that day. I rushed in through the hall door, threw down my bag, and started gesticulating wildly as I told her my news. I talked and talked, focusing only on Mette's beautiful face, when it dawned on me that she wasn't really listening to my exciting story. That annoyed me and as I slowly let my eyes wander down, her being so unresponsive made sense. There she was, in front of me, standing with her blouse pulled all the way up to her chin, exposing her breasts to me. I was completely lost for words but absolutely delighted at the same time when it dawned on me what that could mean for the evening! I'd been talking to her for almost a minute without noticing those two beautiful brown eyes staring at me, glowing and inviting. I hadn't seen anything. But promises of an amorous evening or not—Mette pulled her blouse down again just as quickly and gone were the beautiful brown eyes, and then she said dryly, "I just had to check whether or not you could actually see."

Another little anecdote I'd like to share with you demonstrates the benefit of being visually impaired, and we also have to remember to encourage the advantages. My little brother, Anders, and I were at a concert together in Copenhagen to see the American progressive metal band, Dream Theater. We were standing in the middle of Valby

Hall when the concert started. I was fine with where we were standing, but Anders, who is a bit of an adventurer and has always had the ability to get himself right in front of the stage at concerts, wasn't so pleased with where we were. You probably know that if you want to get up close to the stage, you either have to arrive very early or be cheeky enough to get yourself moved up there. We hadn't arrived early, so Anders, who wasn't satisfied standing where we were, decided to look for opportunities rather than limitations. He shouted to me to follow him and, of course, I did as he ordered, because he was my eyes in the dark, and if we got separated, it'd be difficult for me to find him again. We'd shared a bottle of rum, which probably wasn't going to help me get my bearings or navigate through the crowd either.

We made our way forward and, at one point, the crowd was so thick it was impossible to move. At least I didn't think it was, but we were so close! What separated us from a spot in the first row was a wall of two large hardcore metalheads with skulls on their denim vests, long ponytails, nose piercings, and goatees that were nearly a foot long. Anders had obviously decided we WERE going up to the stage, and nothing—not even these two—was going to stop his determination. He made an executive decision.

Looking at me resolutely, he shouted, "LOOK BLIND."

"What?" I shouted back, but Anders had already

turned around again, and now he was tapping the two "gentlemen" on the shoulder. They turned. Anders shouted something to them. It was impossible for me to hear what he was saying thanks to the noise of the drums, electric guitars and yelling crowd. The two tall metalheads seemed to be listening, and about ten seconds later, they looked back at me, giving me quite a fright. I hurried to "look blind" and turned my head slightly, putting Stevie Wonder himself to shame in the process. The two large men stared at me with a mixture of compassion and curiosity, and before I could think another thought, they both stepped aside and almost guided me past them. *What the hell*, I thought, hurrying after Anders. Like Moses at the Red Sea, Anders had parted the waters, and we had a free path to the Promised Land: the stage!

There was too much noise to understand what Anders had said that had transformed two tough metalheads with skulls on their backs into gentle and sensitive helpers. I'd have to ask him after the concert.

When the concert was over, we headed toward the exit, and I asked Anders what he had said to the two men. Anders grinned stupidly—still under the influence of the rum.

"I told them you were my legally-blind brother, who would soon lose his eyesight." He could hardly keep a straight face as he was telling me, but he continued: "Then I told them that your greatest wish was to experience Dream Theater up close before you go completely blind and that this was your last chance."

We had a good laugh and wandered off to the toilets to empty our bulging bladders. We each found our cubicle and I closed my eyes and breathed happily. Emptying a full bladder is true bliss. Once I'd emptied my bladder, the mandatory squirts came, reminding me that I'm now in my forties, I went to the sink and washed my hands. Metal concerts can be very civilized, you know. I checked myself in the mirror and feeling quite pleased with the reflection, I finally looked to the side. There, next to me, was a disaster waiting to happen. One of the metalheads from before was standing at a washbasin, staring at me. Good thing, I'd just peed or I'd have pissed in my pants at the shock. I didn't look very blind right now and he seemed to have noticed that, too.

"Aren't you supposed to be blind?"

I blinked a little, pretending it was hard to see him.

"Ehhh, yeah," I answered. "But not completely blind."

I'm in for a beating now, I thought.

He looked at me suspiciously, for what seemed to be an eternity, and finally seemed to accept my explanation. *Phew!* Anders and I exited the bathroom at speed and headed for the main train.

There is only one conclusion to make from this episode: it's an exemplary example of seeing POSSIBILITIES rather than LIMITATIONS. But I have to admit—it was mainly Anders who saw the possibilities here.

Bye, bye to the car and freedom

Obviously, the visit to the new ophthalmologist changed the course of my life. The consultant's judgment was clear: my sight was now so bad, I was in the "legally blind" category, so I had to stop driving immediately. When he reviewed the eyesight test that had been carried out several years earlier at the old ophthalmologist's, he was slightly appalled that he'd let me drive back then. He was absolutely sure that the surgeon general would have forbidden me from driving given my vision. So, Mette and I agreed on the spot that we wouldn't take the issue to the surgeon general. This was the end of my time as a driver. Imagine if I caused an accident and people were injured. I wouldn't be able to live with that, so the decision was simple—though getting used to life without a car was— and still is—a struggle.

Driving a car with my level of sight surely sounds completely insane, but I'd developed the technique of constantly scanning my surroundings and, therefore, I rarely missed anything. The technique simply involved me rapidly moving my eyes over everything in front of me, which enabled me to detect my blind spots. It worked quite well, but I'd never considered what employing this technique would do with my health over time. Using your eyes like that is similar to the way you use your eyes when you're in imminent danger or suspect a situation of becoming dangerous. Making your eyes rush around in this way puts your body under a constant strain. It was, undoubtedly, one of several reasons why I eventually succumbed to stress. My body simply quit. It could no longer withstand the pressure it was being exposed to.

I put my driver's license in a drawer and sold my two-year-old Skoda Octavia Elegance, with cruise control, Bluetooth system, 18-inch rims, and four cup holders. I wrote a long post on Facebook telling all my friends, family and colleagues about my condition and what it was doing to me. It was the first time I'd made it public. I was a little apprehensive about the reactions to being so open. I'd spent so many years doing everything I could to keep that door locked, and now I was sharing my secret with everyone on Facebook. But I received tremendously positive responses to my honesty and openness, and many people expressed compassion and sympathy. People wrote to me, calling me brave, but really, I had no choice. Life had somehow pushed me to where I was now, and telling it to the whole world seemed to be the only logical choice. Brave? Yes—maybe. But maybe more out of necessity. Writing the update was a relief. It was as though I finally felt honest about and was accepting my situation. For years, I'd lived with a feeling that my deception could be revealed at any moment. That might sound a tad harsh, but the one thing I'd been with myself for years, was harsh!

I was now about to experience just how limiting my disability was on my freedom. Losing the right to drive was life-changing. It might just be me, but being able to get into a car and drive wherever I wanted was a symbol of freedom. Owning a car and driving at leisure was an integral part of my manhood. It's a way of thinking we were brought up with. Men don't cry, don't talk about emotions, don't wear pink and ALWAYS control the car! That's how it is. You don't just change it. PERIOD! So, now I was no longer a man, because I could no longer drive a car. From now on, I would have to rely on other people for a ride, if I wanted to go anywhere that couldn't be reached with public transport. My independence was gone. My freedom was gone. From now on, I'd be locked in my home, dependent on the goodwill and grace of others. It was an awful thought and feeling. I think almost every man can relate to those feelings and the dark thoughts that having to stop driving a car evoked. Taking the bus and organizing my life according to timetables was my future. Never again could I go anywhere when I felt like it.

Would I lose my job now, too? How was I going to get to Billund from Almind, where I lived? Getting to Billund with public transport had to take at least a day. I'd lost my freedom. I was no longer ME. I was about to become someone else; an image of "visually impaired Morten," who was no longer worth anything, began to form in my head. I wondered if the boys and Mette wouldn't be better served by a father and husband who wouldn't become a shackle. I thought Mette would get tired of living with a worthless man who was slowly losing his sight. For a while, I thought many dark thoughts.

My employer, the LEGO Group, was, however, absolutely fantastic. They gave me the time I needed to find myself again. During the worst period of my life, I received only huge support and an assurance that my job was in no way at risk from the LEGO management. I just had to take whatever time it was going to take and come back when I was ready. That saved me so many concerns, and I would like to say a huge thank-you to the world's best workplace, for all their help and understanding. I won't ever forget that.

Through fall 2016, I was in talks with the LEGO management and the Municipality of Kolding about my situation. We were to figure out how I was to adjust to both my job and my visual disability—how could my working life be organized so I wouldn't keep hitting a wall of stress in the future? We realized that working long hours without breaks and taking on visually heavy tasks were not an option for me. Nor was I able to keep a general overview to the same extent, as all the years of stress had pushed me out of balance. Being in the middle of this inquiry was very uncomfortable. I felt stupid and superfluous, and I felt guilty about no longer being capable of doing the same level of work that I'd always been able to do. My boss kept telling me that I was doing an exceptional job, so I had to try to relax my need to perform and accomplish for a while. It was hard, because, after all, that was who I was. I was Morten, the senior art director who always did his job, and if I was no longer him, then who was I? Now I was Disabled Morten who needed special arrangements and who couldn't do the same things as his colleagues. I was a marked man. Disabled.

I'd been through an assessment process at IBOS (the Danish Institute for the Blind and Visually Impaired), too, and despite the process giving me plenty of knowledge about life as a visually impaired man, the meeting with the "system" slowly confirmed to me that I was limited and that my life was now subject to these limitations. I found myself where I'd struggled not to be for several years: in the "blind system." And I began to get used to the idea that I was limited, because I had a diagnosis that confirmed it. I was legally blind!

I began to feel more limited and experience more limitations than ever before. I suddenly thought my sight had become even worse. The counselors at IBOS also told me that having RP was exhausting and that being affected by stress and depression was normal when you were losing your eyesight. The dear people at IBOS were helpful, and they only wanted the best for me, but as I accepted that people with RP got tired faster, were placed on a job-placement scheme or retired, I experienced BEING more tired than ever before. I could no longer manage and deal with the same things as *before* I started talking to people who confirmed my limiting thoughts about myself and my situation. RP had made me legally blind. I finally had the reason for my stress and depression. It was the fault of my eye condition. Having RP was like being fatigued and tormented; I now had to settle for being put on a job-placement scheme—not that there's anything wrong with that. It's a great solution for many people. I shouldn't expect more of myself and it was okay now to sit back and hide behind my condition. RP was to blame for my life being ruined and there was nothing to be done about it. That became my core belief. I accepted both that I was limited and that that was how I was supposed to live. I was unhappy. I'd hit rock bottom. I had traveled so far down Hopelessness Street that I'd gone astray. I felt lost.

A call from Mr. F

Thursday, September 14, 2017:

It had been several weeks since I'd last heard from the Letter Men, and the writing was going well. Reliving the past like this was strange, but it was also a very useful way of summarizing all the events that had happened over the years. A kind of pattern of how I'd reacted to different situations throughout my life slowly started to form. I realized I probably hadn't handled my eye condition as well as I could have. I could think of many experiences, where it'd been difficult to deal with my disability, and I noticed that how I'd acted hadn't always served me or those I loved. But I couldn't really see what to do about it. After all, I was who I was, and that's something you just have to live with. Isn't it?

Just as I sat down, late one evening, with the last few pages of the part of the manuscript that I'd promised to write for the Letter Men, my phone rang. As always, it gave me a start, because it wasn't often that anyone called me so late.

"Hello, it's Morten," I said a little more confidently than the other two times my phone had rung at this time of day. I had a pretty good idea of who was calling—one of the Letter Men.

"Hi Morten, th-th-th-this is Mr. F. Is now a good time for

you to talk?" He asked nervously.

"Yes, I can talk now," I answered, reflecting for a moment on how different these three Letter Men were, and I wondered briefly how they'd ended up in the same group, given those dissimilarities.

"I'm calling to hear how things are going with the manuscript, because we would like a status report on your progress. And eh—if it suits you, we would like to meet you tomorrow. I mean, if you can and would like to."

The disparity between the way Mr. N had commanded me to meet them three weeks before, and the way Mr. F was asking for this meeting, was striking. I remembered shrinking in my chair upon hearing Mr. N's tone, and now I was actually having a hard time taking Mr. F seriously. He seemed nervous, almost anxious.

"Of course I can," I replied, looking at the screen where my manuscript was illuminating my darkened office.

"Where are we going to meet this time?" I asked, shivering at the horror of the old library in the Letter Men's headquarters.

"I'll send you a message, Morten. But, before I do, I must express my concerns regarding your involvement in this project."

I raised an eyebrow and sat up in my chair.

"Yeah?" I answered slowly. "What are your concerns?"

"I'm afraid you haven't thoroughly thought through what you're doing," he said almost angrily. "You're putting your life at risk by writing this book. You run the risk of annihilating yourself and everything you know in your life."

I frowned, growing quite worried.

"What do you mean?" I asked apprehensively. "Is my life in danger? How?"

Mr. F responded immediately, his voice almost manic: "The life you know is in danger, Morten. Doing what you're doing now—writing this book and communicating with the three of us—risks the life you once knew being wiped out. Everything will change. It might get much worse. I must urge you to reconsider your participation in this experiment. Eh, I meant project," he stammered, correcting himself quickly.

But it was too late. I had caught the word he'd accidentally uttered.

"Experiment?" I repeated quickly. "What kind of experiment are you talking about? Am I part of an experiment? You never said anything about that. If I'm in some experiment, I want to know what it is!"

I was very angry. I'd felt well and truly bossed around over the last few months. Now we were getting somewhere.

"What kind of experiment, Mr. F?"

"I can't say anymore, Morten. I can only say that you need to stop now, otherwise you will have to pay the price. That's not a threat—it's a fact." Then he hung up.

I sat in the dark for a few minutes, collecting my thoughts on the conversation. I speculated on how I could get out of this experiment that I'd apparently ended up in. What was the experiment, and who was conducting it? And why? The familiar buzz of a text message startled me, and the cell phone lit up as a message appeared on screen. "We would like you to meet us for a review of the next chapters in the book. Please bring three copies and meet us at 1 Castle Alley in Kolding at ten o'clock tomorrow evening."

I wasn't quite comfortable meeting up in that disconsolate place again. Something inside me was divided over it. I was somewhat appalled at Mr. F's gloomy warnings, and I was almost afraid of Mr. N's icy and hostile manner, but something inside me kept going over Mr. P's words that first night we talked on the phone.

"You need to know that Mr. N and Mr. F will try to confuse you and lay traps for you. They will try to talk you out of it and instill fear in you. It's your job to try to find a way through these challenges without letting them get to you. I'm sure you can, and I will help you."

Mr. P had warned and prepared me for this exact situation. It was as though Mr. N and Mr. F were trying to lure me away from the project. As if they didn't want me to succeed. Why? And, equally, Mr. P seemed determined to help me through the plan I had for myself: Moving on with my life and out of this stagnant situation I found myself in—hopelessness.

I closed my eyes, took a few deep breaths and heard a faint voice. I jumped in fright. Mr. P's voice was in my head. *You can do it, Morten, you can do it . . .* and then the voice faded slowly.

The next evening, I found myself standing once again in front of the gloomy door of the Letter Men's headquarters. I grabbed the demon knocker and knocked on the door three times. Moments passed, and then I could hear the door being unlocked on the other side. The elderly butler greeted me again, and politely invited me inside. He guided me toward the same room we held our last meeting in, but he didn't stop at the door. We continued down the hallway, reaching a staircase at the end that led down to a lower floor.

The butler pointed down into the darkness and said, "Down the stairs, Mr. Bonde. You will be received once you are down."

I stared nervously down into the darkness. I couldn't see anything. My night blindness made it impossible for me to see just a few feet down the stairs.

"Eh, can I ask you to turn on a light on the stairs—I can't see anything in the dark?" I managed to stammer. The butler looked at me blankly, turned around, and walked back toward the entrance.

I gawped. *What an idiot,* I thought, almost following him, wanting to forget everything about the Letter Men and just work on my book without them. The writing was going really well. Maybe I could easily continue without them? But something inside me made me walk toward the stairs anyway, and before I thought anymore about it, I began to grope my way into the darkness.

It was pitch black and I counted the steps to calm my nerves. The manuscript was clamped firmly under one arm and I held the railing tightly with the other. I sensed I was on a spiral staircase because I could feel myself walking around and around and down. Finally, I glimpsed light beneath me. Slowly, it grew brighter and brighter, and then I reached the bottom of the stairs. What I saw there shook me. I could never have imagined what was at the end of the spiral staircase.

I descended the stairs from the old building, with its antique wainscoting and paintings. Everything seemed hundreds of years old there, but here, one floor below, was a completely different environment. This was state of the art. I was standing at the top of a long corridor, almost reminiscent of a research environment or something futuristic that you might expect to see in a James Bond movie. It was clinical and cold; there were light panels in the ceiling and a polished black floor. There were flat-screen TVs on the wall. As in, covering the entire wall. It was one giant flat screen for as far as I could see.

On the screen, I read: "Welcome, Morten Bonde. You are expected in Q7. Please follow the LED lights on the floor."

A strip of blue light appeared, illuminating the shiny black floor. This was evidently the guide I was to follow, so I stepped forward. I walked and walked and walked, and when I thought about it, I must have long since left the building above behind me. On closer reflection, I had to be under Koldinghus, which was right next to the Letter Men's' headquarters. Koldinghus was an old Danish royal castle, and was one of Kolding's proud symbols. Talk about surreal. It felt like being in a science fiction movie or a dream. Maybe I was dreaming. This couldn't possibly be real.

I reached the end of the LED-guided corridor: a large metal door. On the door stood the sign Q7. As I approached it, it opened automatically and I saw a futuristic room with large screens everywhere. Carefully, I entered, speechless at what was playing on the screens. It was me! Video clips of me in all sorts of situations were playing on every single one of the screens. In *all* kinds of situations and at all possible times in my life, too. There were sequences from my childhood of me cycling through the woods around my home town. There were sequences of me and my brothers and friends, lying on the floor of my childhood home, building with LEGO bricks. There was a sequence from when I was only four years old, trying to steer the car away from kindergarten. There were sequences from my first day of school, from my first day at the LEGO Group, from when I lay on the operating table, and from when I first met Mette. It seemed like all of the most important situations and events of my life were playing on the screens. What was going on here? It was impossible for all those memories to have been filmed. I was sure of it. Not possible at all! But how was it all being played on the screens? I was getting dizzier and dizzier, and I could feel the panic starting to rise. I suddenly remembered Mr. F's warnings about this project being dangerous to me, and I remembered his slip of the tongue—that I was part of an experiment.

I walked into the middle of the room and looked around at the screens lining each of the walls. I was paralyzed. Panic-stricken. But, at the same time, fascinated. Part of me wanted to escape, but something else held me where I was. I had to know what was going on. Without warning, a voice from a hidden speaker said:

"Hi Morten." It was Mr. P's sympathetic voice. "I've been looking forward to showing you this room, and I'm looking forward to talking to you about your manuscript, too."

"What is all this?" I asked, so clearly articulated that I

surprised myself. "How do you have all these video clips of me? You can't possibly have filmed all that! That's impossible!"

"It's your life, Morten. Your entire life, and you've gotten a unique chance to look back on it. This is what you have been doing for the past few weeks as you've been writing on your book. You've relived many of your childhood memories and high points from your adult life. Reflected on them and thought about them."

"Yes, I can see that," I replied. "But how do you have video clips of these episodes? I don't understand."

Now another voice spoke: "I warned you, Morten." It was Mr. F's concerned voice. "I told you there would be consequences that could be dangerous and create fear, but you wouldn't listen. Now it's too late. You can't go back now. It's happened. Your life, as you knew it, is over and nothing is certain anymore. Anything can happen and it will probably end badly."

Mr. P interrupted Mr. F's excessive talking, which had become increasingly excited.

"It could, Mr. F, but it could also end well. That is a possibility I hope Morten will dare to seek."

Now another voice joined in with the conversation.

"Opening up to these thoughts was a mistake, Morten." It was Mr. N. His cold voice was unmistakable. "This will most definitely end badly and you will soon be left without your job or your family. Mark my words."

I couldn't take anymore. I shouted "STOOOOP!" as I started to turn around, but they were all talking over each other. They spoke louder and louder and everything began to spin. Faster and faster, and eventually it went black. Everything went black. I was gone.

The next morning, I woke up in my bed. It was Saturday, and I wasn't sure where I was. The last thing I remembered, from the night before, was being at the Letter Men's headquarters, but I couldn't remember what had happened. It was all foggy—as if I had amnesia from the moment I'd reached the end of the corridor by the dark staircase down to the lower floor. I exerted myself trying to think about what had happened, but nothing. I was blank. I couldn't even remember if I'd handed over my manuscript, but I couldn't see it anywhere near me.

I got up from the bed and had to steady myself on the wall so as not to fall over. I was completely beside myself. Thoughts rushed through my head, but not a single thought on the evening before surfaced. I went into my study. There was no trace of the manuscript there. I must have handed it to the Letter Men last night. What was I supposed to do now? I didn't remember getting any directives on what I should write about next or on whether what I had written was good enough.

I checked my phone. There was an unread message on the screen. I hurried to put my finger on the fingerprint reader and was immediately into the phone's texts.

It was a message from Mr. P:

You did well yesterday. You've written a great manuscript. Keep going. Continue writing the book. This time write about what made you understand that you had to do something to change your life. Figure out what you want to focus on in the future. Identify your goal. Write about that, Morten, and you will begin to understand what all this is about. We will contact you again when we want an update from you. I know you can do it. You've got this. Stay well, Morten.

Warm regards. Mr. P.

Meeting at the municipality:
An experience that changed everything

One cold December day, I found myself at the municipality's offices near Koldinghus, nervous about the approaching meeting. There was so much at stake for me. My future and my destiny were about to be negotiated and finalized, I had to be on the ball. I would by no means appear as a victim—which I was—or as a person who couldn't look after their own life. So I'd come to the municipality and called this meeting myself. I was going to manage this process myself! It's probably me over-dramatizing here again, but I felt that my destiny was to be decided that day, and it all depended on my ability to communicate.

Attending the meeting was a consultant from Dansk Blindesamfund (the Danish Association of the Blind), a retention advisor and a social worker, both from the local Job Center. We were to decide how I could get a job through a job-placement scheme. Yes, you read that right—that's where I was. Not that there's anything wrong with job-placement schemes. They help many people remain in the labor market. But, for me, it was a completely inconceivable situation that I hadn't seen coming just a few months before. A major part of my identity was bound to my work and my job. I was a senior art director and now I was going to be part of a job-placement scheme. If I wasn't a senior art director, what would I be? Just Morten, who struggled with his vision and his faded self-worth and esteem?

Something happened to me in the middle of that meeting. The social worker, who was helpful, understanding and accommodating, began to talk about the measures that would need to be taken to get me into a job-placement scheme. The Job Center advisor talked about assessment processes, job testing, interdisciplinary committees that would judge my case and action plans. The consultant from the Danish Association of the Blind talked about the limitations and challenges generally faced by blind people. I felt lost. Actually, right there in that moment, I felt that nothing mattered. They could take my job, my house, my damned car, my family, MY LIFE! I'd lost everything. I'd lost ME.

Municipal rules and clauses were mentioned and, from the emptiness, I heard a clear voice speak over the people sitting around me. *What do you want to do with your life, Morten?* But the voice didn't come from anywhere in the room. It was inside me. Just like back in the cell phone store, I experienced an unexpected ability to see clearly and, for a brief moment, it felt as if I had unlimited access to infinite knowledge. Knowledge that was telling me what to do. The epiphany lasted long enough for me to interrupt the social worker in the middle of his sentence. I distinctly remember his astonished expression as I burst out: "I don't want to be placed on a job-placement scheme so we might as well end this meeting." There was silence for a moment and everyone looked at me a little confused. "I'm not at a stage where I need to be placed on a job-placement scheme yet."

I experienced something that many people will nod to having experienced themselves. A moment of complete insight into your life and the world in which we find ourselves. An instant of such deep insight that you ask the absolutely right question at the absolutely right time. It was an overwhelming experience and something I was able to explore further over the next year. A year that changed my life and made me view my life and the world we live in, in a completely different way. That day in the municipality's office, I changed course from Hopelessness Street. Now I was headed for Possibility Road and, thus, started the first day of my new life! It was the day when old Morten died and a new one was born. Newborn Morten decided to choose life and embrace its possibilities. Without knowing it at this point, it started an inner journey that has given me knowledge that I had no idea existed. What happened in that office?

When I heard the voice and was filled with a new inner energy, I felt lighter than I'd felt in years. It was as if an elastic on the heavy baggage I'd been dragging around snapped. I felt free and relieved. One moment, I felt that my life was over. I'd lost everything. My position at the LEGO Group, my sense of being in control and being the master of my own life. I'd lost my identity. The one I'd desperately been clinging to all these years. The identity that made me *me*. Without my identity, what was I? Now that the elastic had snapped, where the old "me" was dead, I felt freer than ever before, because I still existed. I was still alive, I could breathe. I could feel life inside me. Despite my identity now being dead, I wasn't dead. I was finally free! It finally dawned on me that I was not my identities, my thoughts and my limitations. I was the consciousness that noticed all these illusions. I no longer needed to be anything specific. I just had to be. I AM!

For several days after the meeting at the municipal office, I walked around, strangely cut off from all my old problems. I could no longer see why they were so problematic and worrying. It was as though I'd been distanced from it all.

Everything that I later came to realize about my meeting at the municipal office, I hadn't realized at this point. I didn't understand what had happened. I could just feel that something was happening. It was only several months later that I gained the knowledge needed to understand it. Or, viewed in another way, I created a new story—the story we call our lives.

Question upon question began to emerge. New doors had opened in my mind. Unknown doors that might have been there all along, but which I just hadn't been ready to see. Doors to be opened and explored. I was slowly beginning to see a meaning in all of it—I knew I had to find a way out of the situation I was in. Now I had a mission. I had questions that I needed to find answers to:

1. How do I move from a life of limitations and hopelessness to a life of joy and freedom of mind?
2. How can I, with joy, openness and curiosity, find the will, power and desire to face my uncertain future?

I concentrated on these two visions. My job at the LEGO Group was, of course, important; my family was important, but if I didn't clarify these two matters, I'd find neither my way nor my future. I'd glimpsed Possibility Road. But only a peek. I was still on Hopelessness Street, but if I was going to find Possibility Road again, I would have to change how I dealt with my challenges. I was on my way; I'd formulated goals for my life in the form of questions. They became the objectives I was now going to pursue, and as they weren't material in nature, weren't superficial, but rather prerequisites for a happy and fulfilling life, they were goals that received my absolute focus. I couldn't think of anything else. A voice kept repeating in my head, *Morten, what do you want to do with your life?* Every cell of my body knew that I had to do this. I wrote down the new goal for my life on a piece of paper and held it up in front of me. I had written this:

Despite RP, I want to live a happy life
and see possibilities rather than limitations.

Both my conscious mind and my heart knew that this was my life goal, so it was already certain that I would find my way. I had decided I would!

And in the hunt for answers to those new questions, answers to some of my old questions, which I listed at the beginning of the book, surfaced. They would prove to be of great importance for my continuing journey, because the old questions (or blockades, if you will) turned out to be the cause of my hopeless state of mind and dark thinking—not my eye condition! These old questions were:

- Why don't I dare take chances?
- Why don't I think I'm good enough despite others telling me I am?
- Why don't I just do what I set out to do?
- Why don't I dare?

And so, with no idea of how the answers were going to come to me, I embarked on my new mission. I had my goal—a desire my heart burned for—though without any expectations of how to find the answers. I already knew they would come. I had formulated my goal for the Universe. Now, it was time to allow greater powers to do their work and to trust that my belief in myself would help me further.

"Open to everything and attached to nothing"

My surprising revelation in the municipal office kicked off a lot of thoughts. But how should I move on from here? My goal was clear in my mind, but how was I supposed to change my way of thinking about myself and my situation? I hadn't become happier or a new person as such. I was still experiencing all the same old sad thoughts, and when I faced a challenge in my everyday life, I reacted like I always did. I worried, and I said no to opportunities that could have nudged me out of my stagnant positiojust because they didn't feel right. I still reacted like the old Morten, despite burning to become a new version of myself. One that automatically saw the possibilities instead of the limitations.

I had to learn to think in new ways. I needed to find inspiration to become a new and more resilient and sustainable version of myself. I had to discover a way to overcome my feeling of being limited, and I had to figure out how to convince myself that I was good enough as I was. YouTube and audiobooks provided a lot of inspiration. One day I watched a video on YouTube about a guy named Nick Vujicic. Nick was born without arms and legs, but despite that, he enthused and motivated people all over the world with inspirational lectures. He had taught himself to see possibilities instead of limitations, and he seemed determined to become the master of his life. Discovering him made me reflect on my own situation.

An inner voice said: *Well, Morten—you have problems with your eyes. That's frustrating, but you have so much else to live for.* Which was so right. I hadn't thought about it before! I started to think differently. Could I also become the master of my life?

But then something happened that shook me to the core and even more out of my own state. It involved my childhood friend, Michael, the corps commander who had jumped into the barracks ambulance the day I'd torn off my finger. Michael, who'd never left my side during the operation. Michael, who'd subsequently become my closest and best friend.

The day before New Year's Eve 2016, there was a story in the Danish media about a cyclist who had disappeared on his bike ride in the area around Kolding. He'd apparently cycled out that morning, and when he hadn't returned by the scheduled time, the authorities were alerted. The Danish station TV2 broadcast special coverage throughout the day. Mette and I were following the story closely, like everyone else, but never thought it could be someone we knew. Late that evening, I was sitting on the couch by myself, surfing online and checking my Facebook profile. An update from among my friends caused my blood to freeze. There was a picture of a helicopter taking off from a wooded area and under the photograph was the text: "My beloved brother flying his last trip." Michael's sister had posted the update. It hit me like a bucket of cold water. Michael had tragically and senselessly perished on a bike ride in the forests around Kolding.

This news struck me like a bolt out of the blue. Michael was my best friend. We'd lost touch, unfortunately, over the past few years—we'd both been dealing with difficulties: He had gone through a divorce, started a new family and had a little girl, and I'd been busy keeping my head above water and had slowly lost touch with most people in my circle of friends. I'd had absolutely no energy for friends.

A few months earlier, I'd written to Michael on Messenger, and we'd agreed to meet again soon, drink a few cognacs and philosophize on the great issues of life—both of which we were good at. But time passed slowly and neither of us had done anything about finding a date and time to meet. I often thought about how this period of our lives was a time when we rarely saw each other, but that we'd both have the energy and time to see each other again one day. *There's plenty of time*, I thought. Now he was dead. Suddenly and senselessly. He left behind three children, his new girlfriend and loads of people who couldn't believe he was gone.

I contacted his sister and corresponded for the next few days. Everyone in his family was, naturally, devastated by the tragedy. The family asked me to be one of the pallbearers when the coffin was to be carried out of the church. That was both an honor and a privilege. Being by Michael's side on his last journey, like he had been there for me on the operating table, helped the wound of losing him a little. A wound of regret and remorse that I would never again spend time with my good friend. Mette and I attended the family's private memorial service; grateful that the family wanted us there during this sad time.

Although Michael's tragic death happened six months before I started writing this book and began the process of creating a new ME, it played a huge part in helping me realize that my life is a precious gift and that it is my own responsibility to get the very best out of it. As Mette and I stood looking at Michael's grave one cold January day, unable to fathom that he was lying down there in the earth, I felt how much I loved life, loved Mette and my boys. But I also felt how I didn't love myself. I'd struggled with low self-worth and esteem for most of my life, often scolding myself for not being good enough, reproaching myself and getting annoyed at myself whenever I had little mishaps that were associated with my poor eyesight. A voice in my head was always blaming me for not living up to my own expectations of myself. Blaming me for making mistakes and being clumsy. Criticizing me when I couldn't find something and for being limited by my poor vision. Maybe I even blamed myself for having an eye condition that was now limiting my life and for being guilty of feeling inadequate. But it wasn't fair of me to treat myself like that. The insight came clearly: if I was going to start changing myself, I'd have to start with how

I viewed myself. I needed to start listening more to what my inner voice was really saying to me.

How could I become my own best friend? How could I create balance in myself? How could I change my inner voice from being reproachful and harsh to being caring and supportive? Only when I could accept both myself and my situation could I move on. Only when I could do that, would I be able to challenge my fears, my low self-worth and esteem, and my perception of my place in this world.

I had to start by observing myself from the outside. I had to observe my fears and my limiting beliefs from outside. I had to become someone else to see the old me. I had to know the fear, and I knew now that this work needed to be done through self-love and self-acceptance. I had to start looking at fear as if it were a frightened little boy inside me. I imagined that fear was Little Morten when he was a young boy, and then I thought about how to calm and help him. And when I thought about my own two boys, it wasn't hard to start caring for Little Inner Morten. Just like I hug and care for my own two boys when they need support and guidance, I had to start doing the same with myself.

I thought about all the times I'd scolded myself over the last 30–35 years, and I realized what was wrong with my mind. It wasn't only my visual impairment that had caused my low self-worth and esteem. It was my perception of myself. The way I spoke to myself had created the person I was now. The way the inner critical voice had judged all my actions and my existence. How I thought about myself. It struck me that I never spoke to or about other people in the way I spoke to myself. When other people made mistakes, I showed them understanding and patience. I supported them, encouraged them, and wished them well. I gave my boys and Mette love, but what about myself? What did I say to myself? I had to be honest. I didn't always use kind words. I rebuked myself, blamed myself, and was a bad role model for myself.

This was where I had to start. I had to begin taking care of myself. I had to stop getting frustrated with myself, stop scolding myself and going crazy inside my head when I didn't live up to the huge demands I placed on myself. I had to start being happy and glad, love the world and my family and —not least— deserve their love. I had to re-invent Morten Bonde. Replace the old behavior that had controlled me until I was in my forties, and practice new habits for the future that could deal with the possible impending blindness, without becoming bitter and spiraling into self-pity, loneliness and inadequacy. The voice in my head was no longer going to be my enemy. It was going to be my friend. Viktor Frankl, who survived being a prisoner of the Auschwitz Concentration Camp during World War II, wrote in his book *Man's Search for Meaning*: "When we are no longer able to change a situation, we are challenged to change ourselves." I couldn't change going blind, but could I change the way I viewed going blind? Could I change my perspective?

I now had the will to rise from the role of victim that I'd assumed, take the bull by the horns and take responsibility for my future and my life. If I was going to realize my vision, I had to become wiser about myself and how we humans function. How we are motivated and how we can motivate ourselves. I had to become an expert in how the mind works and how we can influence it. I had to change my view of myself and the world we live in, and there was only one way to do that. I had to acquire new knowledge.

I now embarked on the most intense research phase of my life. I scoured the internet for knowledge. I read and listened to everything I could get my hands on; on anything that could point me in the right direction. Books on philosophy, psychology, religions, self-motivation, self-development, biology and quantum physics were absorbed. Each discovery led me to the next. I saw tons of lectures on YouTube and I sought out what intuitively caught my attention and curiosity. Almost as if something in me was drawing me toward finding the right knowledge. As though an unconscious force was controlling me. It might sound religious, and in a way, it is, but not in the way you may think. My research opened several doors for me, and behind one was the ability to have a perfectly open view of the world we are living in and the possibilities it offers. In my previous life, I had all too often had unyielding attitudes, and I was inclined to cling to old knowledge. If I had once accepted and memorized a truth about life and our world, it would be hard to shake it.

As I just mentioned, my words can easily sound like I had found God or some other form of religion. I've never believed in a miracle-creator-god who, with a magic wand, created the Universe, the stars, the earth, and the humans and animals on it. But I have discovered that there is probably more between heaven and earth than I was open to accepting before. My eyes were opened to the fact that ancient spirituality, knowledge and techniques are still practiced in the East, in the form of Buddhism and Hinduism, and by the indigenous peoples of North America—the way they view the world is fundamentally different from the way we in the West view our world. Their ancient philosophies stretch back thousands of years, and curious about some of that wisdom, I gained a sense of hope and joy that I'd lost or perhaps never had. Gradually, I discovered that we humans, with our highly developed consciousness, are unique creatures with far greater potential than we ourselves can imagine.

My belief in myself kicked in the moment I opened my mind to possibilities that I hadn't been open to initially. As I became able to look beyond my old core beliefs, a new world opened up for me. A world where I create my own life because I decide to. I discovered, through meditation, that I could reach depths within myself that enabled me to open doors that had never been opened before. Later, I will share my experiences with meditation and mindfulness with you. The key to my transformation from being a despondent, visually impaired version of myself, to becoming someone who believes that anything is possible, is the contact with my deeper self that I gained through meditation. I began to practice what the old Indian tantric master Tilopa from 988 CE once so beautifully wrote: "Have a mind that is open to everything and attached to nothing."

You've been hacked

Tuesday, September 26, 2017:
I had more than a hundred pages of the book written by now, and I was honestly surprised at how well it was progressing. In a way, writing down all my thoughts on what I'd experienced throughout my life, on what living with my visual impairment had been like, and on my outlook on life, on the whole, felt liberating. Discovering I had an

inner critical voice, whose existence I'd never really been aware of, was also surprising. "The Voice" as I now called it.

I was sitting on the bus on my way to work, listening to an audiobook, when I got an unexpected surprise. While I was looking at the screen of the cell phone, it flashed twice. Quite briefly, and it was pure coincidence that I even noticed. At first, I thought it was the phone, but that didn't really make sense—it was pretty new. I paused the audiobook and stared at the phone. It happened again. Three short flashes in perfect rhythm. Flash, flash, flash. It almost seemed like the phone was communicating with me. Nonsense! How could it do that? I stared at the phone for a few minutes, but it didn't flash again. I continued with my audiobook and 25 minutes later I was in Billund.

I didn't notice any more flashes during the day. But, that evening, as I was sitting on the sofa in the living room with my MacBook Air on my lap, reading through what I'd written the night before, it happened again—three quick flashes in the exact same rhythm as on my cell.

What is going on here? A strange impulse hit me. I opened the Notes program and typed a sentence: *Is anyone there?*

The moment I pressed the question mark, the screen flashed three times at the same tempo as before. Was the computer answering my question? No, that was stupid.

Of course, it wasn't. But before I could finish thinking that thought, a sentence began to form itself automatically on the screen under my previous question. The words appeared as though written by an invisible hand. *Hello, Morten. Don't write anything else. Wait.*

I was speechless! My computer was writing messages to me, and just for a moment, I thought about whether an updated Siri (Apple's built-in virtual assistant) was responding. No, it couldn't be. Siri doesn't contact the user. She only answers when actively asked, and I hadn't. I got a shock when a dialog box appeared on the screen that read: *Establishing encrypted connection.* I removed my hands from the computer as if it were on fire. A shiver ran down my spine. Had I been hacked?

The dialog box disappeared, and now another sentence appeared in the Notes file.

This is Mr. F. You weren't supposed to notice anything. How did you discover we are monitoring your channels of communication? It doesn't matter. What's done is done!

"What the heck?" I exclaimed, and Mette looked at me in surprise.

"What is it?" she asked.

I reassured myself and replied, "Nothing, I was just thinking something."

She returned to watching the TV, and I looked at my computer screen again. I slowly moved my hands toward the keyboard and began typing: *Are you surveilling me?*

A new sentence appeared: *I've set up an encrypted connection between our computers that the others can't detect. As I have warned you, this is a dangerous game you've started, and you don't realize how dangerous this project is for you and your family.*

My blood froze when I saw those words in black and white.

I started writing: *What do you mean "it's a dangerous game"?*

A moment passed, and then more letters began to appear.

I've read your description of the meeting at the municipal office, and if you share that story with others, you'll be a laughingstock. You absolutely can't write that you've been struggling with poor self-worth and esteem throughout your life. No one will ever take you seriously again if you fool around with such personal information. I know you trust Mr. P, but he hasn't told you the whole truth. Trusting him will be your downfall. Stop while you still can.

My heart pounded and my hands shook as I typed on the keyboard.

You have to tell me what is so dangerous about this. I don't understand, Mr. F. I need more information.

Mesmerized, I stared at the screen, but there was no response from Mr. F.

I was in a cold sweat; the thought of being watched

gave me an almost panic-like feeling.

"This is crazy, Morten," I said to myself, surprised to realize that I'd actually spoken aloud. Mette looked at me again, confused.

"What's crazy?" she asked.

But I just shook my head and said, "Nothing."

All evening, I sat in my own thoughts. Should I stop what I'd started? Could I even do it at all? Could *I* change? Could I write a book and was I really in danger? Right now, I felt that I was.

I brushed my teeth and crawled into bed. Thoughts were running through in my head and I was slowly coming to a conclusion. I'd write to Mr. P in the morning and tell him that I was dropping the project. I couldn't continue with this. I felt bad about that experience with Mr. F, and now I was lying in the dark, not able to sleep. My eye condition, my job, Mette and the boys. Were they in danger? And, if so, was it because I was about to reveal that my eyesight was worse than anyone knew? I couldn't handle it anymore! *I can't change, and maybe I don't need to change at all.*

Had this really been my idea from the start? It dawned on me that it hadn't actually been my idea. I'd come up with the idea to change direction in my life after Mr. P had called me up that summer evening many weeks ago. I'd believed him when he'd said that I could change my life of depression and stress into something else. I'd needed to believe it. It'd given me the push I needed to get started. Was it my idea at all, or worse: was I being manipulated? Had Mr. P planted an unrealistic idea in my head, and was I now putting myself through hell for something that couldn't be done? Was I deluding myself? Was I finally realizing that it was just wishful thinking? Yet another sleepless night lay ahead!

The next morning, there was a message on my phone from Mr. P:

I know you doubt yourself, Morten. I know you don't think you can do this right now, but I beg you—listen to your gut. I only want what's best for you. You won't regret deciding to continue with the project. You're making the right decision. There's no going back now and you know you don't want to either. You have to look ahead and find confidence. Trust me and trust yourself. Your friend, Mr. P

I stared at the phone for a long time, and despite me being in two minds about what to think and believe about what was happening to me, at that moment I was in no doubt—I had to finish what I'd started. There was no turning back now. Mr. P was right—there'd be no life for me if I was stuck in the past, and the only way to create a life for myself in the future was to do this *now*. To believe in Mr. P and the inner voice whispering: *It's now or never.*

I'd continue writing more of the book tomorrow. Whatever the cost. I wanted to write about the insights I'd had this past week through my research into the human mind. I'd made some interesting discoveries that I knew would change my view of the world and myself. I had to share it with anyone who'd like to hear about it. To help others and to help myself.

Come on, Morten — you can do it!

PART 2
HEADING FOR
POSSIBILITY ROAD

A new outlook on life

Now you know my story and some of the challenges I've faced in my life. I've shared the difficulties I have as a visually impaired person and the blockages I've struggled against. Perhaps you realized that you have blockages in your life too; blockages that you haven't given deep thought to. You may not even have been aware of them. So, take a moment to think about it. Can you name some of your blockages offhand? If you can't, it might be time for you to think about what they are, because you definitely have them. The purpose of me sharing my story isn't to win your compassion, sympathy or understanding, but because I know that we all have blockages in our lives that prevent us from living the lives we really want to live. When I discovered this, I became obsessed with the idea of exploring it in more detail, and that is where the idea to write this book came to me. Developing this book has been a way of bringing the philosophies and ideas I've learned about to my own subconscious, so that they would reflect how I would behave.

As we will explore later, there are several ways to do this. One is repetition, repetition and more repetition. By reviewing the material in this book again and again, the content became my new core belief and my philosophy for life.

Instead of realizing our dreams, we often invent reasons—or rather excuses—for why it's a stupid idea to go after those dreams. *I'm not good enough, I don't have time, I can't afford it, I have to do what's expected of me, I can't* and so on. But I know now that we can overcome every single one of these blockages. But you have to know yourself and know your blockages and limitations before you can challenge them. And you have to get to know both yourself and the world you live in much better. Here, in PART 2 of the book, I'd like to share the knowledge I've acquired that has helped me get ready to move from Hopelessness Street to Possibility Road and to become the creator of my own life. I'm not a doctor, a brain scientist, a psychiatrist or a psychologist, so what I want to tell you about now is MY understanding of the vast amount of knowledge that I have absorbed. Knowledge I have learned and discovered. I've rewritten what I've read, listened to and seen, in my own words, so that it makes sense to me, and hopefully will to you too. I've strived to describe how I've worked with my knowledge to bring about change in myself. It's my hope that you'll be able to use my story and my knowledge to realize that you too can become the creator of YOUR own life.

You become what you think about!

One day, while sitting on the bus, an old audio track on YouTube happened to catch my attention. It was a 1956 recording with radio host, motivator and writer Earl Nightingale (March 12, 1921–March 28, 1989). Growing up in poor conditions, he'd spent his entire childhood pondering why some people succeeded, became rich and the masters of their own lives, and why others lived in abject poverty, never fulfilling their dreams and aspirations. These were the same thoughts I'd had throughout my childhood. Maybe not so much on the difference between wealth and poverty, but I certainly wondered how and why people were so different. Why could some of my classmates do what I didn't dare to? Why was I never picked first when we played soccer during recess? Why could some afford big cars while we drove around in a rusty Lada? Why was my friend's bike always cooler than mine? In adulthood, the questions deepened: How could a man with no arms and legs teach himself to swim, walk, and become a phenomenal motivator for other people around the world? Nick! Why was I depressed at the thought of being blind when other people with terminal illnesses, that they knew they would die from, could inspire other people and love life? Why wasn't I the master of my life? Why didn't I do everything I dreamed of? Why is it so difficult for us to change our habits and be completely free?

Why did I let myself get thrown off course by the thought of losing my eyesight? We can certainly agree that most people would pale at the thought of losing their eyesight, and certainly go through a similar crisis to what I went through, but how could some people manage such situations without a crisis? Or was that a misunderstanding of people who had mastered their lives? Maybe they were doing so well PRECISELY because they *had* gone through a crisis?

One day in his twenties, Earl Nightingale had a revelation. While reading Napoleon Hill's famous book *Think and Grow Rich*, he realized that the six words he'd read were the answer to the question he had been asking himself all his life! His revelation was:

"We become what we think about."

He realized that he'd read the same truth over and over again in the New Testament. "We become what we think about" — "You reap what you sow." I've subsequently found the same assertion in other cultures and religions. For example, Buddha said, "What you think, you become; what you feel, you attract; what you imagine, you create." Ancient wisdom we don't seem to heed nowadays.

Earl Nightingale concluded that if you think about success and strive for success, you will succeed. Conversely, if you think negative thoughts and don't think you'll succeed, then you won't succeed. It's similar to the statement that's often attributed to Henry Ford, founder of Ford Motor Company: "Whether you think you can or you can't, you're probably right."

Why do we become what we think about? Why can some people become world champions in badminton and others can't? Is it just talent, or is there more to it? I think you know the answer to that question already. But to understand it, you need to think about the mind as a garden where you have the possibility of planting every single plant imaginable. If you plant pretty flowers and take care of the garden, the flowers will grow lush and beautiful. But if you plant and fertilize weeds, those weeds will grow big and lush.

There's an old tale that illustrates this perfectly. One evening, an old Native American chief was sitting beside a crackling campfire with his grandson, when he broke the silence between them with a little story:

The chief: "A constant battle rages inside you. Like two wolves fighting each other. One wolf represents anger, envy, sorrow, regret, arrogance, self-pity, guilt, hatred, haughtiness, lies, doubt and selfishness. The other wolf represents faith, hope, love, peace, humility, kindness, empathy, generosity, gratitude and truth."

His grandson sat for a moment thinking, then asked, "Which wolf wins, Grandpa?"

The old chief looked directly at his grandson and replied, "The wolf you feed."

We all have particular talents. The above anecdotes tell us that what we focus on is what we become. Instead of focusing on negative values and adverse aspects of life, instead of focusing on what we fear doing badly, we need to focus on what we want to do well. We become what we think and focus on! If we think limiting thoughts, we will be limited, and if we think thoughts of joy and success, we will be happy and successful.

We become what we think! Therefore, it's vital to focus on thinking positive and successful thoughts. Only when we focus on joy, possibilities and success can we achieve joy, possibilities and success.

After searching the internet and studying Earl Nightingale, I found these motivational quotes. They became the start of my understanding that I become what I think and focus on.

- *"You are NOW and you become what you think."*
- *"Learn to enjoy every minute of your life. Be happy NOW."*
- *"Success is the progressive realization of a*

worthy goal."

- "What you need is a goal, a timetable and the
  courage to press the start button."
- "Imagine you've already reached your goal
  and imagine how that feels."
- "When we fear, it's because we don't know enough.
  If we have enough knowledge, we won't fear."

Commuting on the bus between home and work, I listened to recordings of Nightingale, and the more I listened to the recordings, the more they resonated with me. "You become what you think!" Could it really be that simple? I realized how much responsibility that meant I had for my own life and my goal to be happy and to see possibilities. Despite it sounding banal and simple, this humble insight was life-changing knowledge. If I thought negatively, my life would be negative. If I thought positively, my life would be positive. I decided. Whether I would retire or whether I would continue to work with what I loved working with was my choice. It was that simple. Whether I wanted to focus on happiness or if I wanted to focus on grief was my choice. Both states were ever present in my life, but what did *I* want to focus on?

I realized that if I said my impaired vision, my surroundings, my childhood, my wife, my children, my job were to blame for my attitude and my life, as it were, or if I felt pressured, stressed, and depressed about the prospect of becoming blind, then it wasn't the fault of something in the outside world. No. It was entirely my own fault! I choose for myself how I want to think and how I want to live. My thoughts create my reality.

I recognize that it can be difficult to accept that your happiness and possibilities in life may depend on what you think about. But once I embraced and accepted that this is indeed the case, things changed for me. I'd like to share something with you that convinced me that my thoughts decide how my life will be.

The power of belief

As I described earlier, I suffered from depression, so I'd been on antidepressants for two years. That was fine and probably did make a difference to my mood, but when I came across a major Danish study, published on videnskab.dk, which questioned the effect of antidepressant drugs as a treatment for depression, I became curious to learn more about the effect of these drugs. The conclusion of the publication was quite simple: "The medicine has no noticeable effect on mild or chronic depression." Studies with results such as this frequently come to light, and the researchers don't always agree, but, as it turned out, the researchers behind this study believed that antidepressant drugs had no effect at all, but rather had a lot of side effects. Side effects I'd felt in myself. So I was motivated to be free of the medication.

If antidepressant medication doesn't work, how can doctors and psychiatrists prescribe it to millions of patients around the world?

It aroused my curiosity, because I was one of those patients. When I talked to my own doctor about this, she couldn't explain what exactly in the drugs helped treat depression. So, I did my own research and discovered from the patient information leaflet that the effect of the medication was unknown. That neither the scientists nor the developers behind the medicine actually knew how and why the medicine worked surprised me.

The "placebo effect." I'd heard about this phenomenon before, and you probably have too, but still it was new for me to read about cases where the placebo effect had played a role in people healing simply because they'd believed.

During clinical trials, patients are divided into several groups, where one group is medicated with a new drug for, for example, headaches, while another group is given a fake pill. When a large proportion of patients being treated with fake pills then report that their headaches are gone, it's called the placebo effect. The patients' belief that they were given a miracle pill to get rid of their headache actually caused the headache to disappear. Similar trials have also been conducted with patients suffering from depression, and the results were the same. Patients who believed they were given a new effective happy pill, which according to the doctors should work after fourteen days, were given a fake pill instead, and after fourteen days had passed, they got better, just like the doctor had told them they would.

The following examples are borrowed from Bruce Lipton's book *The Biology of Belief: Unleashing the Power of Consciousness, Matter & Miracles,* but I've come across similar examples in books by other authors.

Bruce Lipton, Ph.D. and former researcher at Stanford University's School of Medicine, is an American cell biologist who was among the first scientists in the world to clone stem cells. He's probably best known for promoting the idea that genes can be influenced by environmental factors (epigenetics), which means that people have a greater impact on their health than genetic research previously determined.

One of the experiments he shares in his book involved patients with knee injuries. Subjects were divided into three groups. The first group had the damaged cartilage in the knee removed; the second group simply had their knee joint rinsed and what was believed to be the cause of the inflammation in the knee removed. The third group tested whether or not the placebo effect would cause the patients' knees to heal on their own. The patients were sedated and three standard incisions were made. The surgeon then pretended to perform real knee surgery while the patient behind the screen was only anesthetized locally. Thus, giving the patient an EXPERIENCE of being operated on. The patient could hear the doctors talk about the surgery, but they didn't actually intervene surgically in the knee. They just pretended!

When the operation was over, the incisions were stitched and the procedure was completed. After that, all three groups received the same treatment: they were instructed in an exercise program to rehabilitate their knees, and the result was both fascinating and surprising. As expected, the groups that received genuine knee surgery got better, but the placebo group also got better. What had cured the patients of the osteoarthritis in their knees was the placebo effect. They believed they'd been operated on, therefore, they got better. It wasn't due to a doctor cutting away cartilage in the knee; it was because the patients themselves BELIEVED that a doctor had cut away the cartilage in their knees. The placebo group was subsequently able to go for walks and play basketball and do everyday things that they hadn't been able to do before their fake surgery. Only after two years were the placebo patients made aware that they had undergone a fake operation. One of the patients from the placebo group, who before the operation could only walk with the help of cane, was now able to play ball with his grandchildren

Bruce Lipton also recounts the 2002 article "The Emperor's New Drugs" from the American Psychological Association's journal *Prevention & Treatment* in his book. The paper, by Professor Irving Kirsch of Connecticut University, found that measurements during clinical trials showed that 80 percent of the effect of antidepressants could be attributed to the placebo effect.

A striking fact about the effect of antidepressant medication is that over the years, despite Kirsch's studies, the drug has actually fared better and better in clinical trials, probably due to well-devised marketing. The more advertising campaigns for the amazing effect of antidepressants, the more effective such medication actually became, which demonstrates that conviction is contagious. The people have been convinced; they believe that antidepressants work against depression, and that is precisely why they work! A widely known and accepted public belief is that if you suffer from depression, then happy pills are the solution.

Another convincing story about the power of belief on human psyche and physiology is the story of athletic runner Roger Bannister and his pursuit of the "unbreakable" record. Until the year 1954, no one had succeeded in running a (metric) mile in less than four minutes. Countless athletes had trained and struggled to do so in under four minutes for years. It was impossible, and so it was concluded that human physiologically couldn't exceed this limit. It was simply not possible for the human body to run a mile (1500 meters) in less than four minutes. It became a core belief of the world of athletics. That was until May 6, 1954, when Bannister ran 1500 meters in 3 minutes and 59.4 seconds. It was incomprehensible. An invisible barrier was now broken, and only forty-six days later that incomprehensible record was beaten by John Landy in Turku, Finland. It has subsequently been beaten many times.

The moral of this story is that given that it was widely known that no human could break the four-minute barrier, it was almost impossible for anyone to cross that barrier. But once the first man proved that it was doable, other runners were able to do it after him. The conviction that it couldn't be done made breaking that barrier an impossible task, and the conviction that now it could be done made it possible for others to run even faster.

Lipton goes on to share the story of Janis Schonfeld in *The Biology of Belief,* who participated in a clinical trial in 1997 to test the effect of a particular antidepressant drug. She was astounded when she discovered she'd been given fake medication. The pills had cured her of the depression she'd been suffering from for thirty years, and the brain scans taken during the trial showed that brain activity in her prefrontal cortex had significantly increased. It wasn't just "in her head" that she had gotten better. As the mind changes, so too does biology.

Just as positive thinking can pull us out of depression and heal an injured knee, negative thinking can, as you can now well imagine, have quite the opposite effect. If the mind is preoccupied with negative expectations, it can damage our health. These negative effects are called the nocebo effect.

The nocebo effect can be as strong as the placebo effect in medical treatment. Doctors who lack the appropriate bedside manner and/or are inconsiderate can deprive patients of hope.

When I received my Retinitis Pigmentosa diagnosis, I was told I would slowly lose my eyesight. I was informed that having RP is extremely exhausting. It was also suggested that many "of my kind" get placed on job-placement schemes, and I was slowly convinced that I was getting tired, should apply for such a scheme and that my vision was gradually disappearing. If our bodies are indeed influenced by our beliefs and thoughts, then I can better understand now how I ended up exactly with what the counselors and ophthalmologists had predicted I would. I often think about how I might feel today if I'd never been told I had an eye disease. Would my vision loss have slowed down or not changed at all?

In my research of RP, I came across several cases where people first became aware that they had RP at a late age. They had lived their lives ignorant of their condition and had never been in situations where they felt they were "sick" from a conviction that held them to belief that they were ill. Once, when I attended an RP course, I met a man who, after he had entered the health care system, lost his entire vision completely, and I met another man who discovered he had eyesight problems, so he consulted his ophthalmologist, who diagnosed RP. A week later, he was completely blind! I can't help but draw a connection to my new knowledge of what belief does to our organism.

A last story I want to share with you is the story of Sam Londe, who had esophageal cancer—a disease that in 1974 was one hundred percent terminal. Londe was treated for his cancer, but was told by doctors that the cancer would certainly return. Londe died shortly after he was diagnosed, which came as no surprise to the doctors.

However, an autopsy after Londe's death revealed very little cancer in his body. Certainly not enough cancer for him to have died from it. Spots were found on his liver and on a lung, but there wasn't a trace of the esophageal cancer that was believed to be the cause of his death. He died *with* cancer, but he didn't die *of* cancer. So, what did he die of, if it wasn't esophageal cancer? Was it because he'd been convinced that he was going to die? In some nocebo cases, doctors, parents and teachers can take hope away from us by programming us to believe that we are powerless.

These stories are reminiscent of my own experience when I decided to reduce the course of medication I'd been prescribed for depression. I tried diligently, but without success. I'd been told the medicine was making me feel better and that if I scaled it down, I'd probably experience a dark time again for a while; that these side effects would be noticeable about four days after stepping down the dosage. And rightly so—every time I tried to reduce the medication, I became pretty miserable about four days afterward. I felt anxious and stressed and sick to my stomach. I couldn't face continuing to reduce the dose. I didn't believe it could be done. I tried so many times; each without success. When I became familiar with the research project from videnskab.dk, which I found through a Google search, and read Bruce Lipton's book *The Biology of Belief*, it changed my view of what our thoughts and beliefs really mean to us and our lives.

With my new knowledge in mind, I decided to try to step down the dosage once again. I now understood more about how our cells work in our bodies, and with newfound determination I said to myself, "I decide! I become what I think about!" I kept repeating it to myself in my mind. I now knew that the antidepressants probably didn't have anything to do with getting better; it was more about me BELIEVING that the medicine worked. And if belief could do it, I could also convince myself that the side effects I was experiencing when reducing the dose were the result of my belief that they would come.

I decided to start the stepping-down-the-dosage project the day I went on a summer vacation so I could focus on it one hundred percent. As you've probably already guessed, there were no side effects this time. Not a single one! When the four days had passed, the point at which I used to feel strong side effects, nothing happened ... absolutely NOTHING! Not one side effect at all. It was astonishing. With my thoughts and my new knowledge, I'd changed a belief and, thereby, changed the outcome of an event in my physical life.

Something else I experienced was the insomnia that came with the stress and depression. The antidepressants were supposed to help with the insomnia too, and when I tried to reduce the medication, I couldn't sleep at night. Which was another reason I continued taking the tablets. After all, I believed the medicine was what made me sleep.

One night, during the period I was trying to scale down the dose, I was unable to sleep for the third night in a row.

It was around 3:30 in the morning. I kept thinking that the next day would be a nightmare if I didn't fall asleep soon; it would mean I wouldn't be able to do my job properly. I had meetings and presentations, and I couldn't cancel or let my colleagues down. That third night I broke down and decided that I wouldn't be able to reduce the medication and that if I took a pill, I'd be able to fall asleep. I tiptoed out to the medicine cupboard and swallowed a tablet, crept back into bed. A few minutes later, I fell asleep. Next morning, I thought about what I'd experienced and realized that the pill couldn't possibly have had an effect so quickly. It wasn't a sleeping pill; it was a "happy" pill, which in addition to making me "happy" also made me tired. It couldn't have worked that fast.

It's important for me to emphasize here that the above are MY own experiences. They are the result of my research and a goal that I was one hundred percent motivated to pursue. I don't encourage anyone to reduce medication without the help or support of their doctors. My scaling down was also the result of having the mental and physical drive to reduce the dosage wholeheartedly. It's perfectly okay to ask for and receive help in the form of medicines, friends, doctors or others—you don't have to do it all on your own. Taking antidepressants really is a step too far for many people because they fear it will change their personality. You may think you're weak because you need help. And if you are going through a vulnerable period, it may seem tempting to just stop taking the tablets and maybe seeing your psychologist and/or psychiatrist too, so that you can feel in control again. If you step down your medication, it helps to have a support system in the form of therapists, family or others who can help you observe if your behavior changes for better or worse.

My power of belief

With my experiences and new knowledge in mind, I put two and two together. It was the BELIEF that the pill would work that made me fall asleep. My subconscious needed the pill to fall asleep, because that was the program installed on my biological hard drive.

Now that I also knew that "I become what I think about," something struck me: What if my thoughts about myself were to blame for the depression and my suffering from stress? I could relate it back to the time when I was tired and thought my eye disease was making me tired; when I thought the only thing left for me was retirement and hopelessness. What I *thought* was my destiny, came to pass in reality. I thought that was the path I was to go down, and so my reality reflected that. When I realized in my epiphany in the municipal office that I needed to find Possibility Road, and really began to believe that it was doable, my reality changed too. That day in the cell-phone store, when I was twenty-four years old, and the feeling and idea to do something else with my life came to me, and I truly believed that leaving that industry was the right thing for me, it happened in reality.

And what about this audacious thought: When I started my career in the advertising industry, I told myself and Mette, time and again, that I wouldn't last a lifetime in this industry, but neither would I be able to find a job in another industry. I wasn't good enough for that! It was my firmly held core belief and, therefore, I may have given my subconscious an indirect order. A few years later, I developed a rare hereditary eye disease and I am the only one in the family who has it. A self-fulfilling prophecy, and in a bizarre and ironic way, this mysterious and rare eye disease "saved" me from my own doomsday prophecy of not being able to last a lifetime in the advertising industry.

I'm well aware that it's controversial and on the verge of what most people can accept as credible, but think about it. If what we believe in determines the reality we get—which many new research studies attest, and which the ancient religions and philosophies state—then, in reality, there's no limit to what can really *be* if we believe it one hundred percent.

A confrontation with Mr. N

Wednesday, October 11, 2017:

I read books on topics I'd no idea even existed. I read books on consciousness and the power of the mind over matter. I read about religion, philosophy, psychology, physics, quantum mechanics and biology. It was fascinating—there was so much I had no concept of, but it all made me look at life differently now. Topics were randomly selected, but the parallels were astounding. I felt like I was reborn. Every waking hour was spent listening to audiobooks, watching lectures on YouTube, writing my book, doing my job at the LEGO Group and being a dad and a devoted husband.

I don't think either my family or the LEGO Company viewed my intense research as something disruptive. They experienced a happier Morten. A Morten who glowed with energy, and whom they perhaps had been missing for a long time. I was motivated by my project and that energy oozed into my way of being with them.

Audiobooks were my travel companion when riding the bus and walking home. When the house was quiet in the evenings, I worked on my book, so family life was actually going really well, and I had just finished the chapter on the power of belief and the effect that our minds can have on our health.

One warm fall day, when out walking and thinking about what I'd written the night before, a weird feeling washed over me. Some pretty personal details had been shared in that chapter. I'd written about reducing the antidepressant medication and a thought struck me. But before I could think anymore, I heard a familiar voice behind me.

"THIS HAS TO STOP NOW!"

I turned around quickly. Mr. N was right behind me! How had he gotten so close to me without me noticing? He was furious, and he pushed me hard in the chest. Having no idea what was going on, I was completely speechless. He'd appeared out of the blue, just as I'd gotten the strange feeling. I hadn't even thought about what or how I was feeling.

"YOU HAVE TO STOP EXPOSING US! YOU CANNOT WRITE THESE THINGS!" he shouted, spittle flying out of his mouth.

I still couldn't say anything. Completely stunned, I stood passively on the bike path, unable to understand what was happening. I was in shock.

Mr. N was apoplectic, and I was honestly afraid for my life. I couldn't explain why, and I didn't have time to think about it, because now he was advancing toward me. I retreated, but Mr. N was faster than I was, and now he was very close to me. I could feel his hot breath on my face, and I had no idea what to say. Facing Mr. N always made me tongue-tied and paralyzed. He had a strange power over me.

He began whispering, "You cannot write what you have written, Morten. I will not allow it! You are compromising us and endangering our lives. I am only going to say this to you once: do not show what you have written to Mr. P. Delete the entire chapter when you get home. Do not ever show it to anyone. No one will take what you write seriously and no one will ever read it."

He pushed me and I wobbled backward. He turned and walked toward a car parked in the shoulder lane. How had that car arrived without me hearing it? My noise-cancelling BOSE headphones must have shielded the sound. He got into the car and, tires screeching, tore off in the direction of the city.

I was completely shaken. I didn't know what to think and had to take a few minutes to compose myself.

What the hell was that? I thought. My body was shaking all over as I just stood there, watching the car retreat on the horizon.

I'd gotten a feeling and before I could even think, Mr. N had shown up right behind me. What had I been thinking? I tried to rewind my thoughts, but the only thing I could remember was the sneaking fear that had crept over me as I'd had misgivings at what I'd written in the last chapter. My discoveries. The admissions I'd made. It was as though Mr. N feared my new discoveries. As if he felt threatened by them. That was it! He was afraid of what I'd discovered. He was provoked by the progress I was making. I suddenly felt sure again. He wasn't going to be allowed to stop this project. I was certain I was heading in the right direction and was keen for the project to succeed. I would write this book; I would publish it. I was going to see possibilities even where it looked most black. Whatever resistance I met. I was going to do it!

When I got home, I opened the computer and looked at what I'd written the night before.

"Mr. N isn't going to decide for me," I said quietly to myself. I pressed SAVE, and backed up my entire folder. I'd start the next chapter tomorrow. It was going to be about one of the most fascinating topics I'd studied so far—how the subconscious controls our lives and how we can consciously focus on what we want in life. Feeling motivated, I began to picture the book in front of me. It would come true. I was determined to do it.

The subconscious and the conscious

I was heading down the rabbit hole and there was no going back. I had to become more knowledgeable on this subject, because if it was all about BELIEVING, then I needed to know more about how I could change my mind to believe in science and techniques that could help me toward my goal. It amazes me today that we don't learn about this at a younger age—about how our subconscious works and about how it controls our lives. I was most definitely astonished when I discovered that I AM NOT ME! It's a strange statement and a strange sentence to write, but nonetheless, this statement encompasses an important insight that can change the way you face both people and challenges—and, on the whole, how you perceive yourself.

Works by authors, such as Bruce Lipton Ph.D., Dr. Joe Dispenza, brain researcher Peter Lund Madsen, Eckhart Tolle and many others, were pored over and absorbed. (You can see the complete literature list at the end of the book.) What follows is my wording and understanding of what I get out of comparing all the information I've obtained from these authors. It isn't a rehashing of these authors' opinions, and there may be details that are my interpretation. It's also possible that I haven't quite understood everything, but the essence is more important than the precise details. And professionals may challenge my conclusions, and that's quite okay. What I write is my understanding and now my core belief. I'm not trying to tell you a Truth. This is my truth as I understand it now, and it's up to you to interpret what I've written and decide what is to be your Truth.

Let me start by defining what the subconscious and conscious minds are. A simple Google search brings up this clarification: "The subconscious is part of your mind that notices and remembers information when you are not actively trying to do so, and influences your behavior even though you do not realize it."

The two minds exist as mutually dependent minds, which means that they work both independently of each other *and* with each other. The conscious mind is located just behind the forehead and is called the frontal lobe (the prefrontal cortex). Its primary function is to plan and provide for the carrying out of our actions. Areas in the frontal lobe direct our attention to our world, and they, thereby, effect how we create our conscious awareness. Your conscious awareness is your self-conscious, free and individual "I" that influences your brain to perform actions.

The conscious mind makes sure to keep an eye on the body, surroundings and time. *Do I have a pain in my back? Am I tired? Is it too cold, too light or too dark? Do I like the T-shirt the man next to me is wearing? Do I even like the man?* The conscious mind is the creative mind and is what sets us apart from most other forms of life on earth. Animals respond instinctively to their surroundings and respond according to what they have learned throughout their lives. Their reactions are habit-based; they will have the same response to the same impulse again and again and again. Their subconscious minds determine how they act.

The conscious mind is creative, and as a result of being

creative, we don't need to be limited to reacting based solely on impulses—just like with animals. We can have an impulse and, through our conscious mind, change our reaction from time to time. The conscious mind creates our personal desires and expectations for life. In other words, if you ask yourself, "How can I see possibilities instead of limitations?" your question and answer will, at first, come from the creative conscious mind. But, as you learn later, the answer will also come from the paradigm programmed into your subconscious. A paradigm is our view of the world or to put it another way: the perspective we have on the world in which we live.

The conscious mind can learn in many different ways—watching a video, reading a self-help book, attending a lecture or just getting an idea, but while our conscious mind is directed toward our goals, aspirations and thoughts, who do you think controls how you act on a daily basis? Who, in actuality, is making the day's decisions? It's the subconscious and it does exactly what it has been programmed for. Yes, you read that right—programmed for!

The subconscious works in many ways like a super-computer with a multitude of programs, and when the conscious mind is occupied by external events, we don't keep an eye on how the subconscious mind is behaving. We run on autopilot. When that is the case, we may not act in line with the goals and dreams we have because the majority of our basic behavior has been downloaded through observing other people's behavior and opinions.

For the first six to seven years of our lives, the brain has not yet reached an adult level of consciousness and is in a phase where the imagination is unfolding. This is why children under seven have such a fantastic imagination. You've probably heard the phrase "a child's brain is like a sponge, soaking up information," and that's exactly what it does.

During the first seven years of a child's brain development, behavior is downloaded from the environment, parents and teachers, and the child experiences their world in a form of hypnosis. When we are in the childish state of hypnosis, we learn incredibly fast, because there's no filter that judges, analyzes or processes what we learn. This is also how children can learn language and other skills significantly faster than adults do. Nature has created us in such a way that we learn quickly about the world we live in during the first seven years of our lives. In those formative years, the human hard disk is filled up with programs—but where does the brain download these programs from? The subconscious mind gets its behavioral programs by observing other people, such as mom, dad, family members and our environment.

In principle, these observations are recorded in the same way that movies are recorded on a hard disc. It's just, in this case, the hard drive is the subconscious mind. The conscious mind hasn't yet developed in the child by this time, so everything that is recorded during the first seven years of life is captured absolutely uncritically and without a filter. Try to think briefly about the programs you downloaded when you were younger than seven. Think about what programs you upload in your own children. Are these the same programs you got? This is key to understanding why we are the people we are, and it is why I wrote "I AM NOT ME" at the beginning of this chapter. I am the programming I've been given.

As behavior is created in the subconscious at an early age, it hasn't been controlled by the filters of the conscious mind. Thus, many people are surprised when they hear that they are exactly like their mom or dad—the people who from the beginning of their lives programmed their subconscious. But think about this: The behavior and core beliefs we get from other people, such as our parents, friends and teachers, may not be in line with the goals we have in our conscious minds and as adults. Our dreams and visions. The person we want to be.

The greatest obstacle to us realizing our dreams and aspirations are the limitations programmed into our subconscious.

When a child is older than seven, the conscious mind is so

developed that their being in the hypnotic state ceases. It's a bit like a great melting pot that hasn't had a lid for seven years, and now the lid is put on. The brain has gotten its basic programming, and the "adult filter" is now added to the mind. New programs can still be added to the subconscious mind, but now it happens via the learning process—habit formation—which means that we have to repeat actions over and over to learn new skills. *An old dog can't learn new tricks!* Yes, it can! They just have to be repeated and repeated and repeated. Repetition leads to the development of a habit, and habits are programs of the subconscious mind. So, when we get an impulse and there's a corresponding habit in the subconscious mind, then that program/habit is automatically put into play by the body, because the body and the subconscious are closely linked. The body responds via impulses from the mind or the outside world and then plays the programs that are programmed into the subconsciousness.

Take, for example, the smell of freshly baked bread. Your subconscious has a program that can respond to the impulse/scent you experience. The subconscious knows from experience that freshly baked bread tastes delicious and makes you happy, so it plays the program that sends neurotransmitters to the body that make your mouth water, so you're ready to eat the bread. And the desire for freshly baked bread becomes overwhelming. It all happens automatically—it's a habit, a program stored in the subconscious. Certain ways of reacting to everyday situations are similarly controlled by the habits of the subconscious—perhaps you always get upset if someone criticizes your work?

That's because the subconscious automatically plays a program, which was recorded earlier in your life. You may have experienced often being criticized by teachers, parents or friends in your childhood that left you hurt and upset. Well, every time you are criticized, that program replays here in your adult life. You probably aren't even able to explain why you get upset. Your conscious mind has long since forgotten that you were once criticized, but your subconscious never forgets.

The subconscious mind controls you. All it takes to activate a program is an impulse, some kind of sensory input, and the program will play itself—one hundred percent automatically and without interference from your conscious mind. The subconscious never sleeps and is always ready to react!

The conscious mind can easily change itself. New ideas come to you all the time, and you can change your opinions. The subconscious mind, however, is designed NOT to change very easily, and there's a very simple reason for that. Once you have learned an important behavior, it should preferably not be unlearned again. Learning to ride a bike is a program, and if the "riding a bike program" changes every day, then you have to learn how to cycle every morning before heading to work. That would be impractical—to say the least. Once you've learned how to ride a bike, you want to keep that program and don't want to change it. Therefore, the subconscious mind is resistant to change—it's designed to sustain and hold onto the learned programs. This mechanism ensures our survival. If we were primitive humans who have learned to run when a mountain lion arrives, it would be impractical for us to forget this vital piece of learning every morning. So, it's learned and stored on the hard drive of our subconscious, and there it remains.

The conscious mind can think thoughts. But while the conscious mind thinks, it stops paying attention to what is going on around us and inside us, as it now primarily uses conscious brainpower to process what has just been observed—or perhaps something that was observed last week—or something that might happen in the future. Thus, the conscious mind is comparable to a time machine that is always either in the past or in the future.

The average person thinks up to 70,000 thoughts a day, losing focus six to ten times a minute! Think about that the next time your mind wanders when your mother-in-law starts talking about her houseplants(!) You are legitimately excused! Try testing it on yourself. Make yourself comfortable in a cozy chair. Set your smartphone to ring after 60 seconds and get ready to press start. What you need to do now is close your eyes and focus all of your attention on your big toe. Every time your thoughts take your focus away from your big toe, note it and gently bring your attention back to your big toe. Are you ready? Press start and go.

Was it hard to keep your attention on your big toe? I'm guessing your answer is "YES!" And did you notice how long sixty seconds is when your mind has nothing to occupy itself? Sixty seconds feels like an eternity, and perhaps you also noticed your mind pulling you away from the stillness. The mind wants to be entertained and sitting still, boring itself with observing your big toe is not high on the mind's wish list. Not when it can amuse itself with Facebook, YouTube, Netflix, HBO, the news on TV, problems that may hit us in the future or the memory of those who have hurt us in the past. The mind would rather deal with "life's great problems"—the quotation marks are there because those problems are often things that we ourselves create. I read somewhere that scientists estimate that only 8 percent of the "problems" we experience in life are what can be called genuine problems. The other 92 percent of problems are problems we create in our minds, and they are strongly colored by our interpretations. So, what I'm saying is: We are preoccupied with problems that in reality don't exist anywhere else than in our minds!

When the conscious mind is absent because it is busy thinking and "solving life's great problems," the subconscious mind takes over. This is actually a good thing — what if it didn't and you're driving your car through the city during rush hour, changing gears, operating three pedals, tuning the radio and listening to what your passenger is saying while also trying to listen to what junior is telling you about his day from the back seat. You are focused on the outside world and the subconscious has taken control of your actions. Another scenario could be sitting alone in the car on your way to work, and all your focus is on "solving all your problems" by thinking about them as you drive. But you don't stop the car so you can think in peace and quiet. No, the subconscious takes over for you.

According to Bruce Lipton, your conscious mind can process about 2,000 bits per second. This is equivalent to keeping watch of about seven different things at a time. The subconscious mind can process 400 billion bits per second! Chew on that for a moment! That's a colossal amount of data. But keep in mind that not only does the subconscious drive the car and keep an eye on traffic while you are lost in your thoughts, the subconscious also simultaneously manages your breathing, your heartbeat, your metabolism — and it renews the approximately 70 trillion cells in your body that are constantly dying and need to be replaced with new healthy cells. Imagine if that was something you had to do with your conscious mind!

The subconscious mind ensures your pupils grow smaller when sunlight gets in your eyes—it really does take care of everything while you're thinking about buying an iPhone or a Samsung Galaxy. You know—life's really "important questions"!

The purpose of taking you through this description of the conscious mind and the subconscious mind is to bring your attention to an important insight I learned, when, in despair, I tried over and over again to force myself to think more positively and to see possibilities. When I tried to be like Nick Vujicic—a man who mastered his life and embraced his possibilities—it was so hard, because I kept returning to my old way of being and thinking. The situation was desperate, and if it hadn't been for the fact that my only choice was to hang in there (the alternative was stress, depression and a sad life), I might not have continued to challenge myself. But when I discovered the "secret" of the conscious and the subconscious mind, I was able to come up with another strategy to achieve my goal: "to see possibilities instead of limitations."

95% of life is subconscious

Science has discovered that we spend 95 percent of our waking lives thinking, "solving imaginary problems," pondering over the past and worrying about the future, which means that 95 percent of the time we are working through the programs of the subconscious. When we think, we're unable to control our body with our conscious mind. You probably remember that the conscious mind can only process seven different things at a time. So while our thoughts revolve around plans for what we should have for dinner; that we're late for the gym; that the presentation we're working on at work isn't ready; that we have to buy groceries for the visitors coming over at the weekend; that we have a pain in our backs; that we're unhappy with the extra pounds we're carrying around our middles; that the guy in front is driving like an idiot; that we're unhappy with our lives; our subconscious mind (our autopilot) takes over so we're not hurt, crash our cars or stop breathing as we ruminate and ponder on things we have to see to.

Of course, if the subconscious works 95 percent of the time, it means that the conscious mind—which is you, your desires, your aspirations and your dreams—only works 5 percent of the time! That's a crazy thought! This means that our conscious mind only controls the ship, so to speak, 5 percent of the time. Only 5 percent of the time is it our conscious "I" who is articulating our dreams and ambitions and controlling our body. The rest of the time, the body runs old programs, which were mainly written onto our hard drive when we were kids. Programs that aren't even our own, but our parents, their parents, their parents and so on. Programs from the core beliefs of our teachers, our family, the Cartoon Network, Donald Trump, our friends and the rest of the world.

Think about it. Maybe you're still afraid of spiders, even though you know perfectly well that spiders in Denmark are completely harmless. Or you are still afraid to speak to a crowd because someone told you in the third grade that you were really bad at it and you believed it was true back then. Perhaps you get upset when someone criticizes you because, as a child, you experienced one of your parents getting upset when criticized? You saw how they reacted, and their way of reacting became your way of reacting. It became a program. You may have heard your family complaining about certain politicians on television or heard certain opinions about particular topics at the dinner table. Maybe you repeatedly heard opinions on behavior that was thought to be wrong, or opinions that, when you reflect on it, impede you from accomplishing what you want to achieve today. Perhaps you would like to be successful or to view life more positively, but you may have grown up in an environment where everything was seen with pessimistic eyes.

I began this book by recounting my childhood with loving and caring parents, but I have to admit here, in love, that I didn't always have parents who exuded confidence and a "here I come" attitude. "You can do anything you want, Morten" wasn't something I often heard. This upbringing isn't unique to my family. It's something that has dominated our entire society: "don't fly too close to the sun," "don't get too big for your britches."

But something my parents truly mastered was teaching us that goodness is a virtue and that loving and caring for the ones you love is tremendously important. But believing that I could change the world and create exactly the life I wished for wasn't something I'd been led to believe from either my parents or the community in which I lived.

Your body remembers your old programs throughout your life and brings them back to life whenever they are activated by a feeling, a smell or another impulse from the outside world. But we don't have to live with these programs for the rest of our lives, because—and here's a bonus tip: having our awareness in the present means we can use our conscious mind's abilities to rewrite the old programs we have stored on our hard drive. It demands awareness, repetition, repetition and repetition, and later I'll tell how I did just that!

Thoughts are the language of the brain; Emotions are the language of the body

We don't think about these programs being played, because we rarely notice it. We're always focused on what is happening outside of us, our plans, our limitations, our concerns, our ambitions, the future or the past.

My dominant, subconscious programs were limiting, and the voice at the back of my mind kept telling me I wasn't "good enough"; that I couldn't do it; that "I'm going blind, so I have to stick to the safe and secure" and "I'm no use to anyone." It was a voice that scolded me every time I made a mistake, whenever I got an idea to take on new challenges or whenever new possibilities presented themselves. Saying no was safer than taking a risk — challenging the unknown.

I can see where these programs come from; that knowledge and recognition is vital if you want to change them, because before you can change the programs, you need to know that they are there and that they CAN be rewritten. That knowledge made all the difference for me. This was, to a great extent, the knowledge I'd gained from Bruce Lipton's and Joe Dispenza's books.

I'd convinced myself that this was who I was: "Morten, visually impaired, who never really took chances, who was mediocre, who would never amount to more than he was now, who should be grateful for even getting this far at all. Morten, who would be blind and who had now—if he was to be able to get through this life—left his fate in the hands of others. He who would have be placed into a job-placement scheme or retirement and be dependent— because that was probably the only thing he could do."

I didn't want it to be that way. I wanted to be someone who dared to take chances and challenge the world, so why couldn't I change? As I've described, the subconscious is a mind that can be affected through repetition. If we repeat the same messages to ourselves again and again, we slowly become the person we keep telling ourselves we are. "We become what we think about." And if we always focus on our problems and challenges, because we're trying to solve these problems in our minds, we program our subconscious with limitations. The subconscious doesn't care what you program it with. It's objective and does what it's programmed to. If you instead start to focus your attention on what you want rather than on what you do NOT want, then you'll have found the programming code for the subconscious. You become what you think about and focus on, so if you always think about what you want, then that's what you'll get.

In addition to the conscious mind being the subjective and creative mind in which we come up with our dreams and aspirations, it's also a filter that prevents unwanted information and programming from getting to the sub-conscious. Its job is to protect the subconscious mind from harmful impressions—from "dangerous" and new programming.

Imagine it's January 1 and you've just woken up with a thunderous headache after the night's festivities. While lying there on the couch, your body sore, you happen to look down at yourself. You see a pale walrus with black socks lying there. And, actually, the socks are a bit hard to spot thanks to the paunch that's protruding a bit too much. You think: *No more. This is the year I'm going to get fit. I want a six-pack. I'm not drinking beer, eating pizza or squandering my life away anymore. I'M GOING TO GET FIT!* You've had a vision. You can feel how the thought of changing your life fills you with positive energy and optimism. You want to change your life and the time is now. "YES, I CAN!"

You decide that you're going to exercise three times a week from tomorrow, and you feel strong, optimistic and full of energy.

Later that day, after clearing the house of empty booze bottles and removing all the candy, you walk around, still thinking about the impending lifestyle change and you're still positive about the idea. But it's moved into the background a bit now that you've taken a shower and you're looking a little more presentable. Your wife smiles at your ambition—thinking this is the seventh year in a row that you've made this New Year's Resolution on January 1. She smiles indulgently and thinks: *Let's see how it's going in a few weeks.*

The next day, you wake up and go to work—everyday life has returned to normal. You get up on the same side of the bed, put your feet into your favorite slippers and slowly shuffle out to the bathroom. You sit on the toilet and look at your phone. You check your Facebook profile first, then the weather app and then the sports news. You finish your business and put your phone in the same place you always do. You shower, and as the water trickles down over you, you think about all the meetings you have today and how this week could end up being a very busy one. You remember the project you are to present to management—it's not finished. *Oh, this is going to be a tough week!*

You dry yourself with your favorite towel and put on your favorite sweater and good old jeans—of which you have four pairs of in your closet. It works, so why change it? You walk into the kitchen, turn on the coffee machine and the news, and you half-listen to how Donald Trump has once again posted something embarrassing on Twitter and about catastrophes from around the world. You drink your coffee and eat your breakfast, and before you know it, you're sitting behind the wheel of your Skoda Octavia on the way to work (Oh, wait—didn't I have a

Skoda Octavia?). Your thoughts return to the day ahead of you, and you can already feel the approaching anxiousness over the presentation you are to give and which you haven't yet finished.

You arrive at work, meet the same colleagues, and you get through the day. You make your presentation, which, incidentally, went well—like it always does. When work is over, you drive home and you come to think of your boss's offhand comment: "Yes, that presentation went like always." What did she mean by that? Wasn't it good enough? Was it boring and predictable? Am *I* boring and predictable?

Before you know it, you've returned to the suburbs. You go inside, peck your wife on the cheek and start telling her how the boss said your presentation was predictable and boring. You're upset about how your manager judged your presentation and your humor is now quite low. You throw your bag down onto its usual spot and start helping with dinner.

While preparing dinner, you think about how you're going to handle your boss no longer liking you, and suddenly you realize the lasagna is ready to be put in the oven. You turn on the oven to heat and then bake the lasagna for thirty minutes. While it's cooking, you check Facebook on your phone and see that your neighbor is going on another trip to Bali. "How the hell can they do that?" you ask your wife, sulkily, who concludes that they must be mortgaged to the hilt—and then some.

You eat dinner while watching the news and everyone sits where they usually do. You drink from your favorite glass, with the grooves on the side, and, like always, everyone helps to clear the table and fill the dishwasher. You get cleaned up and soon you're finally ready for the couch.

You and your wife sit in your respective regular spots, and turn on the TV, while Facebook is checked just once more. You watch your favorite series, and at 21:46, your wife asks "Hey—weren't you supposed to go to the gym today?" You jump up out of the sofa, exclaiming "DAMN! I forgot!" You're annoyed with yourself, because you've really messed up by already forgetting your New Year's resolution, but how were you supposed to fit that in too, given the day you've had and life you have? Anyway, you don't have time for the gym, and now that your manager is considering firing you for your incompetence, you have to come up with a solution to that problem first. You'll have to devise a plan for how you can pay rent, because without a job you won't be able to afford to keep the house. But, well, you can't disappoint yourself and give up your New Year's resolution on the first day, either! "Damn, I'm a loser!" You promise yourself that tomorrow you'll think more about your resolution and not forget it. You'll think about it more, tomorrow. *Tomorrow will be different, but first I have to come up with a plan for how to keep my job!*

How did you lose focus on your new dream—"to change your lifestyle and get fit"—so quickly?

It's normal for humans to think and plan, but, as the example here shows, most people spend far too much time on routine behavior and worrying, and thinking, in general. When we think and worry constantly, it's almost impossible to keep our focus on what we really want. Getting the idea that you want to change your life isn't enough. There needs to be a focused mind behind that decision.

Did you also notice how, in the above example, the train of thought convinced you that your boss didn't like you and how, in the end, you found yourself wondering how you'd be able to pay rent after being fired? It was an unconscious thought that started with a random comment from your boss being interpreted as a criticism. In reality, your manager didn't say anything about you being boring and predictable. That was your own analysis and conclusion, and then it became the story you told your wife. And yourself! And so, on that note, let me share this nugget with you: researchers have found that 70 percent of our thoughts are negative. Seventy percent!
Should your day have gone better, then you should have decided to be one hundred percent present that morning before your autopilot started the day for you. Instead of

214

starting the morning by visualizing your goal, you let the old programs take over; you let yourself be sucked into your world of thought, and there was no focus on your new goal there; only the "old programmed problems" — the ones you've been brewing for the last few years. Scientists have discovered that 90 percent of the thoughts you have today are the same thoughts you had yesterday.

The subconscious is at play. You might have gotten a brief glimpse of your new goal in the morning, but your body didn't have any programs in the subconscious that supported doing what was needed to get to the finish line. Rather it sent signals to the brain that the "going to the gym" felt wrong. That wasn't a nice feeling, because we're conditioned to seek what is safe. That, which isn't dangerous. And, as a result of this feeling from the subconscious, the likelihood is that in the future you WON'T take the necessary steps to start that new life you want.

If you'd been able to keep your new goal in focus and thought of nothing but reaching the goal, you would have succeeded in sticking to wanting to exercise and gotten through the first few weeks of the new "programming" of your subconscious. Repetition would have ensured that, over time, the new "exercise program" would turn into a new automatic action. A habit.

When I was on sick leave with stress a few years ago, I discovered that I liked strength training, so I went training several times a week. At first, I didn't always want to go. A lot of excuses often popped into my head for why I should stay at home and lie on the couch. Despite the fact that I felt happy and encouraged every time I went to the gym, something held me back from the "new." Something held me back, even though the "new" livened me up.

I managed to get through the "programming time" and, after a few months, it became a habit that I haven't let go ever since. It feels wrong if I don't go at least once a week. I almost go into withdrawal. It became a habit because I repeated the action again and again for my subconscious. I couldn't stand thinking about work, blindness and problems, so strength training became my sanctuary. I kept going to the gym because the reward was being able to let go of my prison of thought, and eventually my new behavior was accepted, and my subconscious wrote a strength training program into my behavior library.

The same goes for our social behavior. The way we have practiced and trained ourselves to act in our everyday lives. That, which has become of our personality. Both positive and negative behavior are governed by the habit-controlled subconscious mind. In other words, if you are constantly negative and see problems, it's because thinking like that has become a habit. Your brain creates neuropathways and then neurotransmitters that cause your body to experience that particular behavior.

The same is true if you are always positive and see possibilities. Again, your brain creates connections and neurotransmitters that support that behavior. It may well be that you make a conscious choice to change a behavior, but, in reality, it's the subconscious that ensures that behavior is delivered in the long run.

Just think about that for a moment. If you've scolded yourself, for years, for being unable to achieve your New Year's resolutions, or you've cursed yourself for not being good enough at work or life in general, and you've created an inner core belief with your self-criticism and self-loathing, then try to think back on this example. We are too hard on ourselves all too often. We reproach ourselves for the inner visions and ideals that we are unable to live up to, and that self-reproach pushes us out of balance and even further down along Hopelessness Street. But what if I could give you some everyday examples that might make you realize you no longer have reason to "kick yourself" over everything you can't live up to? What if I could make you realize that you're a set of automated programs and all you need is new software and a little course in how to install it?

Imagine you just bought a new Apple laptop, unpacked it and hit the start button. You've gotten the idea to write a book about how you learned to reprogram your subconscious, and you can't wait to get started on the writing. You expectantly follow the little line on the screen growing longer and longer below the familiar Apple logo; finally, the computer is ready. You're about to start up Word and ... WHAAAT?! Word won't start! I can't write my new book because someone forgot to install Word on the computer. If that happened, would you then lift your new precious Apple up over your head and throw it at the wall? I guess not! But that's what we do to ourselves when we lack a program on our own hard drive—our subconscious. We kick ourselves and hear a voice inside our head say: YOU'RE USELESS. HOPELESS. THIS IS TYPICAL OF YOU. YOU'RE SO STUPID. We forget that we ourselves are precious hardware and that we are unique and beautiful creatures, but that not all programs come pre-installed on our hard drive.

When you discover that Word is missing from your new Apple computer, you know that there's no point in throwing it at the wall. No, you have to invest your money in the program. You have to install it on the computer and THEN you can write and achieve your goal of writing a book.

Let's take one more example: Imagine your body is a jukebox with a thousand songs in its music memory and it automatically plays them in the same order every day. Imagine that one day you'd like to change the order in which the songs are played. You're so tired of hearing the same humdrum songs. How are you supposed to go about doing that? What you may have done for years is kick and scold your machine hoping to stop playing the same annoying jingle that you can't take listening to anymore. You are sad and tired of that tune, because it has been played every day for the last 25 years and you want it to stop playing. You want to hear a new song, but the only way you think you can change the track is by kicking the machine. Has that ever worked for you? No, right? The machine just keeps playing.

If you're hoping to change the tune, then the following needs to happen:

1. You need to consciously realize that you're tired of the song being played (Mindfulness)
2. You need to find out how to reprogram the machine (Knowledge, action and repetition)
3. And once you've figured out how to reprogram the machine, you enter the new commands into the machine, based on a conscious desire for new music, and—ta-da—the machine now plays a new tune (New behavior)

Kicking yourself is not how you fulfill your heartfelt desire to change your behavior. You need to figure out how to reprogram your computer—your subconscious mind. How to install new programs!

I kicked my "jukebox" for years and years, hoping to

make it play new tracks, but it was futile. It worked some days, but we don't make lasting changes in our conscious minds. We do that in the subconscious. If you think you can bring about great changes in your life with willpower alone, you're going to have a hard time. Remember: your conscious mind, where willpower exists, is only a little computer compared to the gigantic subconscious.

Trying to chastise myself to change only made matters worse. I wanted to be better at taking the initiative, taking chances and letting go of my fears—better at dealing with my loss of sight—but I couldn't make the transformation, because I didn't know how to program my inner jukebox. With my inner judgments and hostility, I created imbalance and disharmony. I know that now, and you will know it soon, too. The day I sincerely realized that our most important task in life is to find balance, I got a tattoo on my arm with the words "There is no light, without dark" to always remind me that when I experience dark times, I must acknowledge them and feel gratitude for them, because without them I'll never really be able to cherish and appreciate the light times. To this day, I only have to glance at my arm and then this vital realization comes back to mind—to my awareness.

The conscious mind gives you the possibility of making a life decision. You can choose joy and health; you can decide to be friendly or you can decide to be unfriendly. You can decide to be co-operative and kind, and your outside world will respond to that behavior. Your thoughts, feelings and images you create in your mind, and the thoughts you have *about* your thoughts, feelings and those images, leave, through repetition, an imprint in your subconscious. And the subconscious creates that reality for you by changing your old actions and behaviors into new behaviors that reflect your new thoughts, feelings and inner images. To repeat: "You become what you think about!"

I'd like to give you one last metaphor to visualize the relationship between the conscious and subconscious minds, because it's vital that you understand this. Imagine a huge ship where the hull of the ship is your body. Up on the ship's bridge, the captain sits looking out his panoramic window. He is the conscious mind, watching the vast world outside. He has the full overview of the situation—he knows where the ship is and where the ship is going. He can get an idea for the ship to sail left, right, slow down or completely stop, but all he can do is give the order. He's not involved in how the ship practically fulfills his wishes. That's how our bodies work, too. I can have a wish—a thought—let's say to run fast—and then the body makes the necessary adjustments to the physiology so that the body can carry that out. The heart starts beating faster, oxygen is transported efficiently around the body via the bloodstream, and millions of other adjustments are made, without my having any idea what is going on. I just gave the order. I thought the thought.

The captain on the bridge is the conscious minds with goals and aspirations. He can decide that it will be good for the ship to turn starboard because there's a huge iceberg ahead, and if he doesn't turn, it'll mean that the ship will collide with the iceberg. That would mean the destruction of the ship (the body). But he can't turn the ship with the power of thought alone. He has a crew to blindly execute his orders and wishes. He had the thought/vision, but now it's up to the crew to do the work, and if the captain can keep the crew motivated and give them regular correct instructions on the desired course, then the captain can reach his goal of turning to avoid the iceberg and saving the entire ship.

The crew down in the engine room represent the subconscious. It's the crew that actually make the ship move. They make sure that each and every part of the ship works in collaboration with each other. The captain ensures that there's plenty of coal (nourishment/energy) in the engine room, and the crew ensures that the coal enters the right boiler, at the right time, so the ship is ready to sail faster should the captain impulsively decide it. They are the ones that can stop the engine if the ship is to stop. They are the ones who make the ship's pumps and hydraulic systems work, but they have no idea what's going on in the world outside of the ship's hull. There are no windows down in the engine room, so they are dependent on the captain giving the crew good commands from the bridge via the ship's intercom (the nervous system and neurotransmitters). The crew never doubt the captain's orders and instructions. They don't judge or question them.

You see, if the skipper isn't a very good captain and constantly sends confusing commands and instructions down to the engine room, which is comparable to the critical and doubtful *self-talk* and unfocused thoughts many people have, the crew, which is the subconscious, can't carry out the captain's orders in the way he really wanted and thought. Initially, he wanted to sail to Copenhagen, but somehow, he ended up in Malmö. And how did he end up there? He was preoccupied with Bobble Wars on his cell phone. He was too busy talking to the first mate (friends, colleagues, family) in the chair next to him, who continued to doubt whether or not the captain's command was the correct one. "Are you sure that we're on the right course? Why do we have to go all the way to Copenhagen? Are you sure you've thought it through properly? Why don't we just sail to Malmö like we usually do?"

If the captain is an indecisive and absent-minded leader, it will have consequences for the running of the entire ship. It's the same for us humans. If our conscious mind is too preoccupied with a stressful everyday life and we can't decide on a direction for our life or have no idea what direction to take, then the subconscious has no choice but to do what it always does. It exists to look after you and carry out your commands. If you, as the skipper of your ship, can be a good leader and send good, clear and positive orders to the crew in the engine room; if you are conscious of a clear course and destination, then you'll get a shipshape vessel and crew that will help you reach your destination and your dreams. So, it's really about being a good leader to and for yourself—giving the right orders and not constantly questioning them. Later I'll tell you how positive self-talk became my way of giving clear orders to my subconscious.

The story of the captain and the ship is, of course, a simplified metaphor, but I think it explains in an accessible and understandable way how a lack of focus and presence in the now can sabotage what you would like to achieve in life. And this is exactly how our body and mind work in principle. But the way the conscious mind communicates with the subconscious is different from a captain speaking into an intercom to his crew. And yet, this metaphor isn't that far from reality.

In the body, the intercom system is replaced with chemistry. Perhaps you've already heard of dopamine, serotonin, oxytocin, cortisol and so on? They're just some of the neurotransmitters. I'm not going to delve into neurotransmitters in this book, but if you'd like to know more, a Google search will bring up plenty of material.

Their role is described in detail in Joe Dispenza's book, *Breaking the Habit of Being Yourself*, but I'd like to share my paraphrased and simplified understanding with you here.

Every time you have a thought, you make neurotransmitters in your body, and if you have positive thoughts, you create neurotransmitters that make you feel happy. Whereas if you have negative thoughts, you make neurotransmitters that make you feel unhappy or upset. In other words, if you think you're insecure, then you feel insecure. The moment you start to feel insecure, you start to think what you feel, which, in turn, makes more neurotransmitters, so you can feel what you think and think what you feel, and suddenly you're trapped in a think-feel-circle. And what eventually happens is that feelings become a way of thinking. And what that really means is that the mind is now interwoven with the body. You no longer think with your conscious mind, but with your body (the subconscious mind), because the body now decides the outcome based on a feeling. In this situation, you can't think in any way other than how you feel. So, you wake up in the morning feeling unwell; you start to THINK negatively, and then you begin to FEEL negative, and you re-live this circle—based on a feeling you had that morning—all day long. This means you'll never break out of this cycle. And nothing new will ever happen.

For years, I had negative thoughts about myself and my future. I was running on autopilot 95 percent of the time; I sabotaged myself by running negative programs, programmed by my repetitive negative thoughts, but I discovered that I could rewrite these negative programs and change them into positive behavior. I realized that the positive programs could replace the negative ones, and, along the way, those positive programs began to become my new way of behaving.

A new understanding of the world

But it's one thing to have this knowledge of how we think and function. It's something else entirely to actually implement this knowledge into your life—to figure out how to really change your programs. I was highly motivated by a desire not to get stuck as a consequence of my future prospect as a blind person, and I was driven to do something active to be happy and find joy in life. To leave Hopelessness Street and find Possibility Road! I knew that if I didn't change my behavior and my way of thinking, I'd end up a bitter victim of my eye condition. So, you could say, that the prerequisite for my changed behavior was a heartfelt desire to change. If I couldn't muster this desire with my conscious mind, I wouldn't be able to change the behavior.

My goal for life became:
Despite RP, I want to live a happy life and see
possibilities rather than limitations.

It may seem, in this book, as if all the discoveries and learning I've experienced came in perfect chronological order. That is far from the case. My experiences came to me in a chaotic order and many of them at a time when I was unaware of their importance. In other words, when I was introduced to mindfulness, back in 2009, as part of a process to better deal with stress, I'd no idea how significant it would be for my life. It's one of the most significant discoveries I've made. But in 2009 I had no idea. Every day, we are bombarded with knowledge that can seriously change our lives and move us in a positive direction, but we can't receive these messages until we are ready to receive them. I am now aware of many concepts, mechanisms and tools that I clearly remember being introduced to or coming across before, but just wasn't ready to receive.

I have reflected on this a lot. How many times a day are we presented with opportunities or possibilities that could change our lives for the better? But we simply don't see them because they're not accepted by our critical conscious filters and, thus, aren't allowed to penetrate into the subconscious and become new programs.

I always end up thinking of the movie *Yes Man*, starring Jim Carrey, which is about a bank loan officer—Carl Allen—who always feels passed over and never feels like anything good happens to him. He says no to all the opportunities that come his way. Despite his best friends constantly trying to make him realize that the reason nothing good happens to him is because he doesn't let it, this information just doesn't seep into his mind. Only when he's randomly invited to an event where he meets a spiritual guru whose philosophy is to embrace all possibilities—to literally say YES to all opportunities that come your way— does something happen in his life. After the charismatic guru works his charm, Carl leaves the event with the conviction that if he says NO to possibilities and opportunities again, something terrible will happen to him. Thus, inspired by fear, Carl now says YES to all the opportunities that open up to him. It gets him into all sorts of weird and wonderful situations, but he slowly begins to realize, in all the challenges, that life smiles on him when he smiles on it. It's a great movie, and I often think of it whenever I get an impulse to say NO.

Something I didn't fully comprehend when I was introduced to it was mindfulness. I can clearly remember the first time I came across it. It was actually a pretty comical experience, and if you've tried to practice mindfulness, then you probably know how weird it can be to try to feel your big toe!

You see, before then I was programmed to only accept new knowledge and wisdom if I understood it. Without that understanding, I couldn't accept it. It was a massive impediment to my development. I always had to feel convinced about something before I dared trust it. This has been the case with many of the topics I share in this book. Can you remember the quote from the old Indian tantric master, Tilopa: "Have a mind that is open to everything and attached to nothing?" The concepts and techniques had to slowly grow on me before I could accept them.

I remember a stress coach who helped me at one point— she told me something back then that I only understand now. She said, "Morten, you have a need to always understand before you can accept. But, in reality, you have to try to accept before you can understand." Today I can see wisdom in that advice, but I didn't get it back then. I heard what the coach said, I understood the words well enough, but I didn't understand the *meaning* of the words. I had built up a behavior since childhood, to protect myself, which meant that I rarely really trusted other people. It was as though I had to see the evidence first before I could decide whether or not I would trust someone else's words and good intentions. I didn't openly express this behavior, but if someone, with a good heart, tried to convince me of something that, in their opinion, would be good for me or a project I was working on, then I needed evidence before I'd listen to them. I might manifest this by asking lots of questions, thinking through the consequences or carefully considering whether or not there were risks associated with following the advice. And if there was no evidence to show that the advice would lead to something good, I almost always thanked them for their help and went back to my own way of doing things. AUTO PILOT. I needed to understand before I could accept.

That way of acting is an expression of judgment of the perceived reality. We always judge what we are presented with, but when we judge, it's with the programs that are in our subconscious. At one point, I realized I needed to practice non-judging and getting better at accepting before I understood. Yep, you might say, I had to start practicing FAITH. And if there was anything that was difficult for me to surrender to, it was faith. Especially because I was a declared atheist. I didn't believe in anything other than we are born, live and die. It's up to *us* to make the most of our short lives while we can. Admittedly, I now feel a little different about this opinion of life. I don't believe in an almighty God who considers us from on high and whom we have to *deserve* to meet in the afterlife. But I do believe that there's far more to this universe than what we humans can understand and explain with our limited senses, brain and mind.

Your world is an interpretation

When we perceive our world, we have an experience that what we see is how the world really is. We trust what our senses tell us. We believe the stories we've told ourselves, and we are, on the whole, convinced that the world is how we perceive it. But when we voluntarily or involuntarily hold onto our beliefs, we lock ourselves into a mental picture and believe that is the only "truth" that exists. But if we can start letting go of those beliefs that don't serve us, we can begin to form new core beliefs. And to help you shift the core beliefs you may have, here's a scientific fact to shake perhaps your most fundamental belief: Your world is an illusion created in your brain!

When you look at the world with your eyes, the image that is created in your brain is only an interpretation of the data captured by your eyes. What we see is just the way in which our brain has translated the light that hits the eye and is then sent to the back of the brain where it is processed. The brain then creates a picture of what it "sees." Other sensory input, such as impulses, smells and tastes are interpreted similarly—again the brain creates an experience based on what the senses record.

The brain does this so well that you think you're seeing the real world directly, but you aren't. You're seeing it with your human senses. Take colors, for instance. You see a red sunset and think "the sky is beautiful and red," but there is no "beautiful" or "red" in the world. "Beautiful" is a word, a sound created by the larynx in a body, which tries to describe something that has just been interpreted in the brain—the so-called "reality." And the "red" that you believe is beautiful and that you think you see is just a certain frequency of light that we experience as red. No matter what information you get from the world, you never experience it directly. There will always be an interpretation in the brain. When you look at your world, you see only a small percentage of the light that hits your eyes. We only see a little spectrum of the reality going from violet to blue, yellow and green to red.

If we could have an intelligent conversation with a bat that navigates using its ears via high-frequency sound and not its eyes, don't you think that our "view" of "reality" would be vastly different? And if, at the same time, I met an alien who could see the full spectrum of light—even ultraviolet and infrared light—don't you think that we'd have very different perceptions of what the world "looks like" too? We interpret it differently, based on the senses we have.

With each new discovery, physicists have shown us that everything we once thought we knew about the world is constantly changing. The world isn't made of solid matter that we experience on the surface. It just feels like that. When we move down to the subatomic level, nothing is fixed or permanent anymore. Everything consists of moving particles—what we perceive as a chair are simply particles in oscillations, held together by a force field.

So, we can't even say that a spade is a spade anymore. A spade is just a name for a thing that, at the subatomic level, is a particular composition of atoms and particles oscillating at a certain frequency. And what's even more shocking is that when you take a closer look at these atoms, they are composed of even smaller particles, and the distance between those particles is so vast that, in reality, there's astonishingly more "nothing" than "thing." Physicists have found that the universe consists of 99.999999999 percent empty space, and thus our bodies also consist of 99.999999999 percent "nothing." This "nothing" is in quotes, because even this "nothing" is "something," but nobody knows what that something is. Right now, it's called energy, but that's also just a man-made word for something we don't quite understand.

But does the world really exist then? Of course it does, just not the way we think it does. Yes, there's a world out there that you can touch, and if you run into a wall, you can be sure to have a bump on your forehead. But the world is a representation of what your senses can perceive. We perceive only a small part of the process that eventually gives us the "reality" we experience. It may be a particular sound or taste that our internal computer—the brain—uses to create a perceptible experience, but which is actually only a representation or projection of the world. So, our understanding of the world in which we live may be quite different from everything that is out there in reality but which can't really be experienced with our limited senses.

And why this scientific tirade? I'd like to state for the record that everything we experience in our lives is an INTERPRETATION of reality. It's not reality itself. And if you can begin to see this, you may begin to discover that you can influence how you want to interpret your world and your life to a lesser or greater extent. And so, if nothing is as you thought it was—if the world isn't comprised of solid matter, but rather primarily of "nothing," then isn't it also reasonable to think that all the interpretations you've made about yourself and your position in life are truths that can be reinterpreted—by you? Couldn't you in reality think you're a winner instead of a loser? Who, in "reality," decides?

Try to view your life from this interpretation. This perspective. You're a winner. You've already won the wildest race you could possibly imagine, and you did it without thinking about it—with absolutely no butterflies in your stomach or pre-race jitters. You were shot out of the starting hole in a flash at an insane marathon, where only one in 300 million would reach the finish line, and you won, because you're sitting reading this book right now! You won a race over 300 million hard-pumped opponents who were all racing for their lives. You were the toughest and most persistent sperm! Just think about that for a moment. Let's try to put that story into perspective with something tangible.

You're at the starting line of the New York Marathon with 300 million other runners. The starting pistol fires and you run like crazy, and finally, after a hefty run, you spot the finish line in the distance. You increase the pace and then jump the last few meters through the air and ... YOU WIN! You win over 300 million other marathon runners. How often have you patted yourself on the shoulder for that? If you interpret it that way, can you avoid seeing yourself as a winner? I guess not! It's a different perspective, and it's just as correct as what you may believe today, because who decides what's right—for you?

We can again draw parallels to the now well-known phrase "you become what you think about." That, which we think and focus on becomes our reality. The way we decide to interpret our world gives us our life situation. But we humans have such a hard time focusing; our "monkey" minds are extremely active and almost never at rest.

There's an everlasting stream of thought, which takes me to my point from the book's foreword.

We have a monkey mind that we don't seem to be able to turn off. About 90 percent of our thoughts are repetitions and a large percentage of our thoughts are completely unnecessary. We seem doomed to live with a noise machine in our heads during every waking hour of the day. Some thoughts are fine and may even help solve a problem you have, but the majority of our thoughts are about problems that don't even exist right here and now. We quite often invent imaginary problems that only generate mental noise that creates more anguish.

I was constantly concerned about things that I often couldn't do anything about anyway—my eyesight, for example. But I also worried about things that I could do something about. My thoughts revolved continuously around the same issues, and the more I thought, the more worked up I got and then came the stress and depression. Much of the flow of thought that goes on has to do with who we think we are, who we think we should be and our problems. We use our thoughts to try to solve problems, and the more we think, the more we escalate the problems.

We think and worry because if we don't, we won't take responsibility for our lives and our problems—right? "I have to do something! If I don't do anything, my life will fall apart!"

The flow of thought and the "monkey mind" appear to

be a product of our Western culture. Not everybody in our world lives as much in their heads as we do here in the West. Do you remember earlier in the book when I talked about discovering ancient spirituality, knowledge and techniques that are still practiced in the form of Buddhism, Hinduism and of the indigenous peoples of North America?

In his book, *Memories, dreams and reflections*, world-renowned Swiss psychiatrist Carl Gustav Jung described a defining experience he had with a Native American chief in 1932. Having conversed with Chief Ochwiay Biano, "Mountain Lake," Jung remarked: "I was able to talk to him as I have rarely been able to talk to a European before."

Chief Mountain Lake described to Jung how the Native American people had perceived the first white people from the distant continent:

"See." Ochwiay Biano said, "how cruel the whites look. Their lips are thin, their noses are sharp, their faces furrowed and distorted by folds. Their eyes have a staring expression; they are always seeking something. What are they seeking? The whites always want something, they are always uneasy and restless. We do not know what they want, we do not understand them. We think that they are mad."

Jung asked him why he thought the whites were all mad "They say that they think with their heads," he replied.

'Why, of course, what do you think with?" Jung asked

him in surprise.

"We think here," he said, indicting his heart.

Chief Biano opened Jung's eyes to the limitations of western "Rational" thinking.

And it's in the midst of that flow of thought that we try to find ourselves. We search for our identity in our thoughts, and now I return to what happened to me that day in the municipal office one December day in 2016. I discovered that I'm not the thoughts I have about myself. I am not the story I've been repeating all my life. I'm not the roles I play in life.

When someone asks me who I am, my usual answer is: "My name's Morten Bonde. I'm Danish and I'm a senior art director, speaker and author. I'm a family man," and so on. I automatically begin to tell the narrative that has become my story through a lifetime of experience and repetition. The subconscious that has become my personality. I list all my identities, but there's something I then overlook: Namely that the "I" who now realizes that it is the same "I" who has always been in the background—deeper than thought. The "I" who has never really changed. The "I" that makes me *me*.

When you immerse yourself in meditation, you experience time dissolving and all that is left is the eternally present NOW.

Everything we will ever experience is happening NOW. Everything we will ever know, we know NOW. We think about the future without realizing that the day the future comes will also be NOW. The only thing that exists is NOW. It's the analytical mind that holds on to thoughts of the past and decides whether it was good or bad, and that very same mind makes predictions for the future that are either classified as worrying or liberating. But the only thing that really always exists is NOW.

In reality, all the experiences I gain in life happen inside me and I believe that it is the only Truth. I put myself at the center of my experienced reality, which is in reality an interpretation behind my eyes and between my ears, because it's from here I seem to experience the world. But really, it's all an illusion. And now I come to the point of this long philosophical account:

Meditation is about allowing the thinking mind, that eternal stream of thought, to calm down and be quiet. When that happens, we start to notice that there's a place of inner silence within us, and in that inner silence we begin to notice who we really are—not only our thoughts. We notice them too, and we can reveal them for what they are: thoughts. Just thoughts. We find peace in finally noticing what's going on inside us. We give ourselves time to feel our emotions instead of suppressing them; we stop constantly observing what's out there in the world and start to see what's going on in us. And then something magical happens: The mind becomes quiet.

Being mindful

Learning to accept before understanding was a key to my being able to change. And the way I learned to allow this to happen was to practice being present in the here and now. This was possible through mindfulness meditation. I actually don't think my transformation would have been possible without training in being mindful. My judgments were, in fact, the cause of my rigid state of mind: My judgments about myself, my situation, my visual impairment and about my limited future prospects.

When I was first introduced to mindfulness meditation, the thought of focusing on your toe or knee was ridiculously absurd. But that was because I was caught up in the behavior of needing to understand everything before I could accept anything.

I just want to debunk some myths. People's experiences of mindfulness are often made fun of. There seems to be a perception that people who practice mindfulness meditation are the "alternative." Or maybe it's just me. It's often the funny and weird character in a movie who, with incense sticks, crystals and a slightly ditzy behavior, is the one who practices yoga and mindfulness.

People often grin at the spiritual and the different and would themselves rather not associate—or be associated—with the "abnormal." And I can understand that, because it hasn't yet become mainstream enough to be an everyday thing. Sure, I was just as judgmental before I became confident enough in myself to accept and tell all and sundry that I meditate and practice mindfulness every day. Disciplines that have been practiced for millennia in other parts of the world.

I once tried to introduce the discipline to my colleagues, and during the session, two co-workers had to leave the meeting because they couldn't stop laughing. It was impossible for them to accept or to, at least, try to find out what mindfulness really was. I'm telling you this because now that you've come so far in the book try to make every effort to keep your mind open and throw aside your prejudices. Give yourself the opportunity to read the rest of the book with a completely open mind. *Have a mind that is open to everything and attached to nothing.*

And shouldn't we try to make meditation something that's super cool? Almost all the celebrities I can think of are diligent meditators who meditate daily. Many of them even justify their success with their ability to be mindful and focus on the present. Here are some quotes from famous celebrities—maybe they can tear down some prejudices!

"In meditation I can let go of everything. I'm not Hugh Jackman. I'm not a dad, I'm not a husband. I'm just dipping into that powerful source that creates everything. I take a little bath in it."

Hugh Jackman (Wolverine – X-Men)

"I am a great supporter of Transcendental Meditation. I have been using it for almost 40 years. I think that it is a great tool for anyone to utilize as a tool for stress."

Clint Eastwood

"If you just sit and observe, you will see how restless your mind is. If you try to calm it, you only make it worse, but over time it does calm, and when it does, there's room to hear more subtle things—that's when your intuition starts to blossom, and you start to see things more clearly and be present more. Your mind just slows down, and you see a tremendous expanse in the moment. You see so much more than you could see before. It's a discipline; you have to practice it."

Steve Jobs

"I heard a phrase, 'True happiness is not out there. True happiness lies within.' And this phrase had a ring of truth to me, but the phrase doesn't tell you where the within is, nor how to get in there. One day it hit me that meditation would be the way to go within."

David Lynch

"All of life happens in the present moment, right here, right now. If you are looking to change your life, change something right NOW. Then, repeat that change over and over until you get what it is you want. It might seem hard or scary, but it is much harder to be stuck in a life you hate."

Jim Carrey

Ninja warriors and Shaolin monks are masters of meditation—just look at what they are capable of and can master. Sports stars meditate and visualize and attribute their great success to it. It's like Goofy's Super Goobers. Without meditation, there are no Morten superpowers, and, thus, fewer powers to get through the day with all the challenges my visual disability gives me.

The father of modern mindfulness practice, Jon Kabat Zinn, defines mindfulness as follows: "The awareness that arises from paying attention, on purpose, in the present moment and non-judgmentally."

Mindfulness is the ability to be in the now. It's the ability to pay complete attention to what is in your life right now and here, right in this very moment. The ability to be present without being distracted by all the thoughts and feelings that constantly pop up in the conscious mind.

Do you see the connection to the chapter on the conscious and subconscious minds—where I told you about all the things that occupy us every day. Who's picking up the kids today? Did I remember to buy groceries? What groceries do I need to buy? I've a pain in my back. When do I need to be at the gym? I have to remember my wedding anniversary on Saturday ...

When you are mindful, you become better at listening to yourself and others. You are also better able to follow your intuition—something many modern people have lost touch with in our busy lives of careers, parenthood, relationships and all the other demands that the world and, not least, ourselves place on us. When you are mindful, you give yourself a break from your busy life. You quiet your conscious mind so you can observe your subconscious mind—and discover all the programs.

You gain peace to get to know yourself.

To be mindful, it's vital that all your senses are awake. You register your feelings and thoughts and experience them without assessing or judging them. You step out of yourself, observe yourself from the outside and, thereby, expand your awareness of yourself. You can see your patterns from the outside and respond consciously before your subconscious manages to play one of its automatic programs. In other words, mindfulness enables you to better guide yourself and to change your behavior. Training in being mindful was one of the first disciplines I needed to master before I could change my behavior and my life. If you're not aware of what behaviors or aspects of your life you would like to change, then you can't change them. Mindfulness is the tool for getting to know yourself on a deeper level. You could say that if you run on autopilot 95 percent of the time, then it's unlikely you know yourself at all, but rather react based on the programs of the subconscious.

Mindfulness isn't a new phenomenon like many in the West mistakenly believe. It stems from Buddhism originally and is several thousand years old. According to Buddhism, a life spent pursuing things, eternal youth and happiness will lead to lasting pain and suffering in life. By being present in the now, you give your mind its freedom and develop acceptance, gratitude, goodness and compassion for yourself and others.

I realized I had to become my own best friend and accept myself as I was—one hundred percent. This was where I had to start. So, once I was wiser about how the conscious and subconscious minds work, I resumed practicing being mindful every single day. It became a daily routine and it helped me with a few of my other challenges—stress and sadness.

Practicing mindfulness on a daily basis had a positive effect on my body and my mind. It was as if I could bring the peace and focus I created in my mindful moments into the real world. I started to notice what was happening in my body during the day, and I discovered that when I was at work, my pulse was constantly high and I was dizzy for most of the day. The conclusion was that the combination of always being on maximum alert—so as not to fall, overlook people or trip when going up and down the stairs—and looking for things I couldn't find effectively caused my stress. The behavior I'd developed during all the years I'd hidden my eye condition, meant that people couldn't ever discover that I was visually impaired, and so I was always on guard not to be "revealed."

As I began to notice what was happening in my body, I realized that I was always tensing my muscles and that there was a constant tense sensation right in the middle of my solar plexus.

I observed, too, how I dealt with different situations—like when you look at another person and take in their behavior. By being more mindful, I was able to see myself from the outside and I discovered that when a project manager or my boss gave me an assignment, my first thought was whether or not I was good enough to do the job. I automatically thought: *I hope I don't make a mistake.* I could feel how these thoughts triggered a reaction in my body.

As I explained earlier in the book, every time you think, the brain sends neurotransmitters to the body. When I thought that I wasn't sure I could do the job or that I wasn't good enough, they were the exact "emotional" neurotransmitters that the brain sent out to my body. And I now realized that every day was a tour on the thought-feeling-circle, which was the result of a limiting program in my subconscious.

My old "I'm not good enough" program was still playing—even here in adulthood. A program I'd had ever since childhood. The program had always been run in autopilot mode, so I was never aware of it. I could see that so clearly now. By being mindful throughout the day, I now noticed many of my limiting programs. I'd never really listened to my body when it tried to tell me it was exhausted. Negative and limiting neurotransmitters were constantly being sent around my body. I was often absorbed by negative thoughts. I didn't speak positively to—or about—myself, which only nourished the thought-feeling-circle. I'd now identified those aspects of myself that I needed to work on changing first. Because before I could change my behavior, something inside me had to be repaired. I had to start being a better captain for my ship. I had to start being the loving, motivating and inspirational leader of myself. Something I'd never been, and I had to start motivating myself.

Scanning yourself with your awareness

If you would like to practice being more present in the now and get to know yourself better, then *body scanning* is a good place to start. The technique simply involves scanning your entire body with your conscious awareness. You can do it lying or sitting down, though I prefer to do it seated so I don't fall asleep. You can actually do it anywhere at any time. I do this exercise while standing in the queue in a supermarket, on the bus, in a meeting room and when I'm strength training. It's a technique that teaches you to feel what is going on in your body so you can then respond appropriately.

In a body scan, you notice your body bit by bit. It's important that you don't try to change anything, but just register and accept what is. It can be hard to sense anything initially, and I first experienced my thoughts constantly focusing on events in either the future or the past. That's perfectly okay, because that's what you're practicing becoming aware of and discovering—to notice when your thinking mind takes your attention away from the present moment!

You practice becoming aware of your flow of thought. Instead of letting your mind take you on involuntary "catastrophe journeys" (which mean that negative neurotransmitters are being sent around your body), you practice observing your thoughts from a distance and sending them on if you don't want to fly with them. And you practice bringing your focus back to your body.

As I described at the beginning of the book, I've always been a reflective person—I discovered that my thoughts and feelings had controlled my life. Not the part of me who could visualize the life I truly wanted to live.

When doing a body scan, try not to change anything you notice in the body. Practice accepting it instead. That exercise will slowly influence the way in which you normally judge yourself. Instead of judging and criticizing yourself, you learn to become an observer of yourself rather than always being an involuntary participant in your own inner drama. Body scanning is a way to get comfortable in your own body. It's not about having to relax or achieve anything—no, it's about feeling what's happening in your body RIGHT HERE AND NOW.

I quickly became quite good at it, and so, I also became really good at noticing what was happening in my body during the course of the day. I got better at saying no to myself and others. I got better at accepting myself exactly as I am, and I became less focused on what others thought of me. I got good at calming myself and the noise machine in my head.

When you bring your focus back and into your body, and keep an eye on your breathing, and breathe more slowly and deeply than you normally do, you tell your body that everything is as it should be. For me, it's kind of like pressing the body's reset button.

If for some reason I've been in a state of stress, sadness or worry, I now know that this condition is often caused by thoughts centered on episodes of the past or worries about the future. I allow myself to feel the emotions evoked by the thoughts, and by bringing my focus back to my body and my breathing, I bring my body back into balance, back to "right now," which, in reality, is the only thing that exists. It works almost every time! I say "almost" because all of this is still relatively new to me. I often forget my new knowledge and let the old programs take over, but I now quickly notice that I'm playing the old programs.

I'm not saying that you should no longer have feelings that are sad, worrying or that make you angry, but I am saying that you don't have to remain in those feelings. Feel them when they are there, without fighting them, and then acknowledge that they're often an echo of the past. We're human, and these feelings are part of our nature, but the intention was never for us to wallow in our own stress chemicals. We weren't meant to live our lives with long-term worries and fears. That's something invented by modern humans, and it's why stress has become such a common phenomenon in the Western world.

A Letter Man disappears

Thursday, October 26, 2017:

I'd now written a large part of the book in a few months but hadn't yet read what I'd written in its entirety. When I looked at my outline, I felt apprehensive about how the book would be received. I was writing about some pretty deep topics. Topics on which I was in no way an expert or trained to understand. How could I presume that someone would take me seriously or even bother to read the book? It was a book about ME after all, and what was so special about me?

It'd been a few weeks since my unpleasant encounter with Mr. N on the road, and although it probably should have scared me enough to give up the project, I hadn't stopped reading, learning or writing. It was impossible for me to stop now. I'd gained so many new insights into the human psyche and into my own, and there was so much I understood now about myself and the way in which I'd reacted in many situations before. I'd now learned and understood that my attitude to life, my visual disability and the world around me were something I had created myself, and that my attitude had been characterized by negativity, worrying about the future and stress. I'd taught myself to meditate and be mindful, and I could feel a difference between the old Morten and the Morten I was in the process of creating.

As I sat reflecting on the book and on what I'd written in it, I picked up the envelope I'd received earlier that day in the mail. I hadn't opened it yet. There was no sender on the envelope, so I'd presumed it might be from the Letter Men. I was waiting to open it until I was alone, because it was impossible to know what it would contain.

I took a deep breath and reached for the gold-plated letter opener that stood in a cup on my desk. Carefully, I opened the letter, half-expecting something toxic—or something equally as terrible—to fall out. But inside the envelope was just a single piece of paper. I pulled it out and unfolded it. On the paper was written: *Meet us at the lodge tomorrow night at 10pm. Bring your latest chapters.* Mr. N must have sent it. Short, cold and precise.

I closed my eyes for a moment and took notice of how I was feeling. Whenever I'd received messages or inquiries from the Letter Men in the past, I'd always been nervous, gotten palpitations and become anxious. But there was less worry now and that was liberating. This time I felt ready to enter the old library at the Letter Men's headquarters and present my latest chapters to them. This time I'd arrive at the lodge standing tall and look the Letter Men directly in the eye. Especially Mr. N, who time and again, had tried to discourage me. I was determined to win over Mr. N and show Mr. F that I wasn't afraid to reveal those sides of myself that I'd kept hidden for so many years. The extent of my vision loss and the fear of being discovered. I was tired of all the hiding.

At ten o'clock the next evening, I found myself standing once again in front of the old door of the Letter Men's headquarters. After knocking the ancient door with the rusty demon, the door opened, and the old butler appeared.

"Welcome, Mr. Bonde. My masters have asked me to relay a message." He handed me a small envelope. "You are to read this and do as described."

I rolled my eyes at how the Letter Men were trying to intimidate me. It was ridiculous and their methods no longer really affected me. I was more prepared for them now and I wanted to show them that they couldn't rattle me. Mr. N had aggressively attempted to make me delete a chapter from the book, but I'd resisted the pressure. Actually, I hadn't done anything when Mr. N had come at me on walk home. That dawned on me now. I hadn't let him provoke me, and I hadn't fought back. It seemed as if that was exactly what he'd been trying to incite from me, but my surrendering had made him back off.

I opened the letter and read the contents. *Meet us at Koldinghus Castle*, it said. I frowned. What was I supposed to do there? The last time I had been to Koldinghus Castle was ... I couldn't remember, but it was a long time ago. Should I do as they ordered? I wanted to prove to them— and especially Mr. N—that they didn't have any power over me, but also to show Mr. P that I'd come a long way with my project. That I'd found the ability to challenge the difficult situations that had arisen in my life.

"They are waiting for you, Mr. Bonde," said the old voice behind me.

I nodded at the old butler and walked toward Koldinghus Castle. The streets were dark, and the drizzle made the city resemble a scene from an old crime drama set in 19th century London. All that was missing was a fog, and Jack the Ripper on my heels. The instant that thought flashed through my mind, a blanket of mist descended on the street. *I'll be damned!*

I walked down the wet pavement of the main street, the old cobblestone road that led up to the medieval castle, and I began to feel the nervousness creeping up my spine. Everything was gloomy and dark, and I began to doubt my intention to obey the Letter Men. But I continued, as if my legs were obeying someone else's brain. And before I could think another thought, I was standing in front of the old arched entrance to Koldinghus Castle.

It was murky and sinister, and the more than 750-year-old fortress seemed extremely inhospitable and ominous in the dark rainy evening.

I looked around and couldn't immediately see where I was supposed to go. Just then my phone hummed in my pocket. I took it out, and there was a message on the screen: *Meet us in the Banqueting Hall.*

The Banqueting Hall, I thought. *Where the hell is that?*

It'd been so long since I'd been to the castle, I couldn't remember it. I typed "Koldinghus" into the phone's browser and added "banqueting hall" to the search field. A map appeared in the search results. The banqueting hall was on the second floor in the north-west corner of the castle, beneath the nearly 250-feet-high tower, which offered a beautiful view over all of Kolding. The castle courtyard gave access to the banqueting hall via a staircase, and I began to walk toward the entrance to the old stairs. I had the manuscript in my bag, which was hung over my shoulder. I was both nervous and excited about how this meeting was going to go. I was pretty sure the Letter Men had already read the manuscript, given that they had access to my computer and had followed the progress of my work word for word. But for some reason they'd decided I should meet them in person this time. And in this unusual place. Why?

I found the entrance and walked slowly up the stairs and through the old hallway that led to the banqueting hall. It was dark, so I was glad I had my flashlight. The only light in the passageway was from the flames of oil lamps hanging on sconces. The farther I went, the more light I could sense ahead. It had to be the light from the Banqueting Hall. I reached the end of the hallway and carefully entered the old grand hall.

In the middle of the hall was a large round table, and around the table were four high-backed chairs, where there seemed to be two figures in the dark, and I assumed it was two of the Letter Men. But which one was missing? I hoped it was Mr. N, but feared it was Mr. P. I slowly approached the round table and said quietly, "Is it you?"

I stopped and waited for an answer, but no reply came from the dark figures sitting less than twenty-five feet away from me. I moved steadily closer, and when I reached the table, the silence was broken.

"Yes, it's us, Morten," said Mr. P, and I felt the relief in my stomach.

Thank you for being here, Mr. P, said a voice inside my head.

"Who is that sitting next to you?" I asked, hoping it was Mr. F.

"It's Mr. F," replied Mr. P, and then there was silence again.

"Where is Mr. N, and why are we meeting here?"

I was now very close to the table and I could faintly make out their faces. I could tell from Mr. P that something was wrong. He looked at me, expressionless. Mr. F had a horrified expression on his face and seemed almost reproachful. "Where is Mr. N?" I asked, nodding toward the empty chair, but no one said anything.

After a long pause, Mr. P spoke. "Mr. N has been gone for a while now. No one knows where he is. We called you here this evening to ask you an important question, Morten: Do you have anything to do with Mr. N's disappearance?"

"Eh, what?" I exclaimed, totally perplexed. "ME?" The question left me completely speechless.

"What does Mr. N's disappearance have to do with me?" I retorted as I sat down on the fourth chair.

Mr. P looked at me intently and then over at Mr. F who still looked terrible.

Mr. P replied: "You're the last one we know of who saw Mr. N, and so we're now asking you if you know where Mr. N is or if you had anything to do with his disappearance?"

I was shaken. I thought I was supposed to present my book. But this meeting was about something else entirely.

"I have no idea what you're talking about, and I don't understand how you arrived at the thought that I would know something about what Mr. N is doing. Why do you think I was the last person to see Mr. N? And when was it?"

Mr. F broke his silence. "The last time anyone saw Mr. N was that day, out on the road, when you and he quarreled. D-d-do you claim you didn't have anything to do with his disappearance? W-w-we know that you had a very problematic relationship, and were, well—almost downright hateful to each other."

Mr. F was absolutely right, and I had no idea what to

say.

"Your silence is worrying, Morten," said Mr. P, rising from his chair. "I know that Mr. N was a problem for you, that you couldn't stand each other and now he's gone. That seems a tad convenient for you. I've always supported you in this project and I still do, but you have to tell me if you know anything about Mr. N's disappearance. You may not understand this, but Mr. N, Mr. F and I are a team. We are, in a way, inseparable and it's crucial for the success of the project that we're together at all times. This is how it has always been. It won't work without us being together. This has always been the case, and it's how it should be."

Mr. P sounded quite moved as he spoke. Mr. F sat nodding eagerly.

"Listen," I said. "I have no idea what happened to Mr. N, okay? He practically attacked me on the road, and when I wouldn't give up and delete the last chapter of the book, he just turned around and disappeared. Now that I think about it, he seemed almost panicked and obsessed with the idea of me giving up the writing project. Actually, to abandon my entire project of changing my mindset to see possibilities. IS THAT WHAT YOU WANT?!" I roared. "*You* were the one who contacted me and wanted me to start this project. You said it was my only way forward, Mr. P."

I was fuming. I'd been bossed around the past few months and had done what they'd asked me to do. I'd read, I don't know how many books—and they'd certainly given me a whole new perspective on life—and I'd written my book despite being unbelievably busy with my job at the LEGO Group and being a family dad. But now I'd had enough.

"Do you want to know what I think happened to Mr. N?" I shouted out into the vast hall, so it echoed off the ancient walls. "I think Mr. N couldn't accept the person I'm becoming, and so he quit. He couldn't stand watching me develop and when he felt his power over me growing weaker, he could no longer be part of the project. HE ABANDONED YOU!"

The words rang around the old room. The two Letter Men remained silent.

"Now I'm going to tell you something. From now on, I won't accept being bossed by anyone—do you hear me? Mr. P—you have been instrumental in this process. I can't understand how you are on Mr. N's side when you want me to advance and become another person. Someone who can see possibilities, even if I am to lose my eyesight. Mr. N can't be part of this project if I am to complete it. Don't you understand that?"

Mr. P looked completely discouraged, but I could see he was thinking over my words.

"And you Mr. F, pull yourself together. You're always

telling me that things will go wrong and that I shouldn't continue with the project, but I intend to continue—to go all the way. You can't stop me! And I don't think you want to stop me either. If Mr. N is gone, it'll be even easier for me to reach my goal. Come on, friends. We don't need Mr. N."

I looked at Mr. P and could see that he was listening to me intently. It was as though he was thinking over my words and actually considering if there was any truth in them. He looked at Mr. F.

"I believe that Morten is correct in his theory. I think Mr. N disappeared when he lost his power over Morten."

Mr. F looked down at the table and didn't say anything. He remained silent for a long time until he slowly lifted his head. There was a whole new expression on his face and, slowly, he said, "You're right."

Brainwaves and stress

For years, I'd battled with stress. A word that has gradually become as common as *happy, upset* and *angry*. In the short run, stress is an important state for your body that can save you from all sorts of trouble, such as escaping a predator or a threatening assault down a dark alley. These kinds of experiences cause your brain to trigger a chain reaction in your body so as to save your life from the imminent danger. This is a good thing—it gets you ready to *fight, flight or freeze*. It could start with your eye spotting something that your brain interprets as a threat. The brain then quickly sends fear or anger neurotransmitters, such as cortisol, around the body, which results in the organs and muscles used for fighting or fleeing getting the greatest supply of fuel and oxygen. Your heart pumps faster, your chest expands, and your breathing gets faster and deeper. Your muscles tighten and your pupils grow larger. Your mouth gets dry and the sweat starts to ooze. You know all these signals yourself.

Remaining in this state for too long is a problem for the body because it isn't designed for it. However, the truth is that many people are in this state most of the time. We're often drawn into this condition when we focus on everyday problems, career problems, worries and fears. If we stay in the *fight-flight-freeze* state, we'll most likely end up with long-term stress or depression, which is what happened to me. But I'd never experienced an attack from a predator—just an overheated brain that was focused on all my problems.

My great inspirational writer, Eckhart Tolle, describes the cause of stress in his very famous book *The Power of Now*:

Are you stressed? Are you so busy getting to the future that the present is reduced to a means of getting there? Stress is caused by being "here" but wanting to be "there" or being in the present but wanting to be in the future. It's a split that tears you apart inside. To create and live with such an inner split is insane. The fact that everybody else is doing it doesn't make it any less insane. If you have to, you can move fast, work fast, or even run, without projecting yourself into the future and without resisting the present. As you move, work, run—do it totally. Enjoy the flow of energy, the high energy of that moment. Now you are no longer stressed, no longer splitting yourself in two.

When I realized I was suffering from long-term stress, I repeatedly tried to practice mindfulness, but I often couldn't find peace and that frustrated me. I knew it could help with stress, but I couldn't get it to work. Palpitations and an out-of-control stream of thought made it completely impossible for me to stay focused on my body for more than a few seconds at a time. I'm telling you this because I wish someone had explained to me why this is the case. I only found out later on and it would have saved me a lot of frustration. (But isn't that how we always learn?)

"Life can only be understood backwards; but must be lived forwards."
— *Søren Kierkegaard*

When the frustration and suffering become so unbearable

that it can no longer be endured, we can choose to perish or find solutions to the problems. I chose to look for solutions.

"When we are no longer able to change a situation, we are challenged to change ourselves."
– *Viktor Frankl*

To understand why I couldn't find the peace that I sought, I needed to understand more about how our brain and body work. I learned that the basic substance of everything in our universe is energy in the form of waves, and that the way in which our brains work is via energy and waves. You probably remember the chapter on how the world we experience is limited by our human senses.

You may remember from movies, seeing doctors in hospitals scanning their patients with a device that can measure brainwaves. Neuroscientists can measure the electrical activity of the brain, and this process is called electroencephalography (EEG).

Researchers have discovered several different frequencies of brainwaves in humans: delta waves, theta waves, alpha waves, beta waves and gamma waves. Delta (1–3 Hz) is measured in the state of deep sleep and glides into theta (3.5–8 Hz), which is measured in the in-between state between deep sleep and being awake; to the creative, imaginative alpha state (8–13 Hz); to the waking, conscious, and thinking beta (12–33 Hz), to the higher and rarer gamma frequencies (25–100 Hz) that are measurable when humans are in elevated states of consciousness or in bursts of highly advanced insight or motivation.

By understanding that our perceived reality is created by our thoughts and core beliefs from within, we can transform our lives on the outside. Knowing the different states of consciousness can open up your subconscious and enable you to create the reality you want, but first we need to understand both the different brain frequencies and why we sometimes experience stress, and sometimes calm. When I learned what these different stages were doing to me, I became better at managing my emotions and thoughts, and I became better at switching between the different brainwave states.

I'm elaborating on this for several reasons:

Firstly, to make you understand that "normal" people can only switch one level at a time on the brainwave ladder. This was the useful knowledge that I needed to understand, when I was trying to explain why I couldn't always gather enough focus to practice mindfulness and, thus, not manage my stress. So, when psychologists and friends recommended practicing mindfulness when I was stressed, it was frustrating to find that mindfulness meditation almost caused me more stress because I couldn't relax. I was too wound up. I was mostly in a high-beta frequency (racing thoughts) and needed to dive into the relaxing alpha level, but no psychologist ever told me anything about that. The significance of this will make sense to you a little later when I tell you about brainwaves. Hang on in there—this is important stuff.

Remember, this is my way of understanding "brain research for beginners." So, there may be professionals who disagree with my simplifications but, again, I believe that the essence is most important and this knowledge has worked for me. It was important for me to understand this before I could break through the filter that exists between the conscious mind and the subconscious mind. Fair enough—I hadn't completely gotten rid of the old habit of needing to understand before I could accept, so this knowledge was helpful. It had to make sense before I could accept sitting still and focusing on my big toe!

Secondly, to prepare you for how you can shift between the various states with meditation at will. Through meditation, I taught myself to explore these different states, and I'd like to share my experiences with you later in the book (when I tell you how I actively came to work with all the knowledge I'm telling you about now). So, if you think I'm jumping around between lots of heavy info right now, hang on in there, because it will all make sense—later. Keep in mind that PART 2 is about the course toward Possibility Road, and PART 3 is about arriving there. Don't worry—we'll get there, and when we get there, you'll hopefully believe that YOU can change your view of yourself and YOUR life, too!

As you remember, I told you about the conscious and subconscious minds earlier, and I gave you the example of how we, as children, receive programs from our parents and our outside environment. Now I'd like to delve deeper into this area, because herein lies the secret to why we have become the people we have become. This knowledge helped me realize that I don't have to keep running old limiting programs. I can write new programs to replace the old ones.

As you grow up, brain frequencies that are your brain's electrical activity develop from delta to theta to alpha and then to beta. When you meditate, the goal is to be able to "lower" the critical beta waves by moving the brain's state from beta to alpha to theta to (for the ultimate meditation) gamma. Realizing how brainwave development occurs during human development can help you understand why meditation can make such a difference in our lives, as it did in mine. Ironically, the knowledge I've acquired means that my "understanding-before-accepting" behavior has been slowly changed to "accepting-before-understanding" behavior. I started meditating before I really understood what it was doing to me.

When I discovered that meditation was changing many

of my fixed patterns of behavior, I was motivated to understand why it was happening. Accept and understand! In the next chapter, I try to give an overview of how brainwave states can affect our lives. Again, my understanding has been gained through studies, such as Bruce Lipton's and Joe Dispenza's research in the field, so my understanding of the subject comes from these books: *The Biology of Belief, Breaking the Habit of Being Yourself* and *You are the Placebo*. I highly recommend you read these books if you find the topic exciting and my review leaves you wanting more. At the back of this book, there's a list of all the books I've listened to so as to gain the knowledge and understanding that I'm sharing with you here.

Delta-Theta-Alfa-Beta-Gamma

Delta brainwaves

When we are born, the only electrical brain activity measurable in the brain are delta brainwaves, and when, as adults, we sleep deeply, there is only delta. New-born babies are in delta and, therefore, they sleep most of the time. And by the time we are the age of one, we're still primarily in delta. Information from the outside world enters the subconscious unedited without any critical thinking and assessment.

In delta, there is little conscious awareness, and as the

body moves into slower brainwave states, we move deeper into the subconscious. The reverse is also true. The more we move up into higher brainwave states, the more we become conscious and participate in the external world.

The more you become aware of this, the more actively you can use this knowledge. Gradually, I was able to identify the various states, so when I noticed I was analyzing or thinking too much in beta (a state I've often been in for too long if I've been brainstorming uninterruptedly for a full day at work), I could gear down before my brain "burned" out. I was able to register and observe when I wasn't present in the NOW in a situation at work or at home, perhaps because of being stuck in memories and emotions of the past or trying to anticipate and solve problems in an unknown future.

Theta brainwaves

From about the age of two to five, we begin to develop a higher level of consciousness. In theta, we are in a trancelike state, primarily connected to our inner world. Children at this age live abstractly and in a fantasy world and exhibit little critical, rational thinking. I explained earlier that children go through childhood in a state of hypnosis—well, theta is the precise brainwave measurable in hypnosis. This is the state in which there's direct access to the subconscious. Thus, young children are likely to accept whatever you tell them. The tooth fairy comes at night and replaces the milk tooth hidden under the pillow with a coin. Santa Claus can bring presents to billions of children in a single night and comes down the chimney with gifts, even if the house has no chimney! Adults in hypnosis can be "programmed" to believe that they're enjoying a hot tub while in reality they're bathing in ice water. The hypnotist has "persuaded" the person under hypnosis to accept a truth that isn't actually real, and the body responds to what the hypnotized person believes.

At this age in a child's development, the following repeated statements play a major role in the development of their personality: "Real boys don't cry," "Girls always play with dolls," "You'll never amount to much if ..." "If you get cold, you catch a cold," "Be careful! If you fall in water, you can drown," "You're useless." These types of statements go directly into the subconscious mind because the theta brainwave state is the subconscious.

Had I known this when my two boys were this age, I would certainly have been more conscious of what I said to them. Not that I think Mette and I did anything wrong or devastating during their formative years, but I realize that my son's challenges with anxiety and worry may be a result of how we programmed him when he was very receptive to our programming. This was during a period when I had a lot of focus on my own limitations as a visually impaired person, and I think that during that time much of what came out of my mouth started with "I can't

..." or "It's hard ..."

Today we have an important doctrine in our home. We only use the phrase "I can't" when absolutely necessary, and both Mette and the boys agree that those three words never bring anything good to them. Instead, we say "I'm worried about ..." or "I'm thinking a lot about ..." I'll go into more detail on why later—it's about the power behind what you tell yourself.

Theta waves emerge in adults when we're in a drowsy state, that half-awake/half-asleep state. It's important to mention here that your subconscious never sleeps. It's always working, because if it didn't, you'd die—it's that simple. When you sleep, the subconscious works: lungs breathing, heart beating, hair growing and so on.

In theta, we are in a hypnotic state and programmable because there's no filter between the conscious and the subconscious mind. And bingo: here comes the secret to your reprogramming. When in theta, you can reprogram and affect your subconscious mind with minimal interference from your conscious mind. Remember: it's in the conscious mind that you judge the ideas that come to you. And when you get a new idea that you really believe in, you can subsequently begin to work your subconscious long-term.

But what if you DON'T believe that your new idea is realistic to execute? What if you decide in your creative brain that your new idea is a goal, but due to experience you don't believe it's feasible? What do you think will happen? The idea will be rejected somewhere between the conscious mind and the subconscious mind. *No room for any crazy ideas here!*

For an idea to be accepted, there must be agreement between the conscious mind and the subconscious mind, OR the conscious and judgmental mind must be deactivated for a time. That time is when we are in theta. Your conscious mind has stopped analyzing and interpreting, so new ideas can pass into the subconscious unimpeded. Can we use this knowledge? The answer is a loud and resounding "YES!" I call it LIFE-HACK. It's the back door through which you can sneak new programs onto your biological hard drive. I'll tell you how I did it later! And to be perfectly honest: The advertising industry does it all the time! Be careful of falling asleep in front of the TV, because you may wake up early in the morning with an uncontrollable craving for soft drinks!

Alpha brainwaves

Between the ages of five and seven, the brain develops to accommodate alpha wave frequencies. This is the beginning stage of the adult analytical mind. Here, the child begins to interpret and think about how the world works. At the same time, the inner world of fantasy still tends to be just as real as the outer world of reality. So, at this age, you typically have a foot in both worlds. That's why you're so good at role-playing at that age. This is the exact age group that I've communicated with in my years at the LEGO Group. I've been fortunate to work deeply with my own inner five- to seven-year-old boy that I can easily get into the mind of this age group. Which is probably also why I find it fairly easy to reach this state when I meditate.

At this age, your child may be pretending to be a LEGO City police officer or a firefighter who extinguishes wildfires, and hours later they're still in that role. Try to do the same yourself. It's unbelievably hard and it's difficult keeping up with their imagination, too. You have to use your thinking, conscious mind to imagine that you are a police officer in LEGO City. And, the illusion is continuously shattered because many of your "real problems" are waiting to be solved. But your little six-year-old has no trouble being a police officer, because they live the majority of their waking hours in an alpha state and you live in a beta state.

Adult alpha brainwaves are present in deep relaxation and usually also when your eyes are closed as you slip into a lovely daydream or during light meditation.

In alpha, the brain is in a slightly meditative state

Beta brainwaves
From the ages of seven to twelve onward, brain activity increases to higher frequencies and, thus, higher levels

of consciousness. From this age and up, you are in beta during your waking hours. This is the adult brain's area of work, and this is where conscious, analytical thinking takes place.

After the ages of twelve to fifteen, the door between the conscious mind and the subconscious mind closes. A lid is placed on the subconscious mind; childhood is over and adulthood can begin. You've received your programming and are now ready to use your programs. From now on, you no longer learn through hypnosis. All learning is now usually done through habit formation. So, if you need to change the programming you received, it has to be done via repetition.

The programs stored on the biological hard drive, the subconscious, are locked, and if you want to change these programs, it's going to require either hard work or mental tools—tools I'll share with you later. These are the very tools I used to reprogram my subconscious. In my research, I discovered methods for how to reopen the door to the subconscious mind and, thus, allow conscious ideas and visions to pass through to the subconscious. I gave myself four challenges that were to teach me new ways of thinking and responding. I'll tell you more about this in PART 3 of the book.

As you develop and become a teenager, you tend to move from low-frequency, up to mid-, and then high-frequency beta waves, which are seen in most adults.

When you read or hear what I'm telling you now, you're probably in the everyday waking state of beta brainwave activity. Your brain processes the sensory input and tries to make sense between your outer and inner world. All impressions are processed by your thinking, conscious brain. Beta brainwaves are vital for the way we work and address the challenges we face, but they can also result in stress, anxiety and restlessness if the frequency is kept at a high level over a long period of time. Here, the brain runs at high speed and it isn't possible to mentally gear down.

Beta brainwaves can also be described as the "inner critical voice" that speaks louder and louder the more focus it gets. In my lectures, I call this inner critic "the Voice."

High-frequency beta waves are for short-term survival situations, but, unfortunately, they have become a source of long-term stress and imbalance in many people.

Unfortunately, many people are in a high-beta state far too often. We're occupied with thoughts or tasks we don't think we can accomplish. We don't feel well, are chronically tired, anxious or depressed. Due to the need to constantly solve our, often, self-created problems (that are frequently only problems because we are unable to put them into perspective), we're kept in this high-beta state, which we can also call stress.

I spent several years trying to THINK myself out of my vision problems because that was the only way I'd learned to solve problems—the "power of thought" that we've grown up quoting when we talk about willpower and mental strength.

But there was no solution to my problem. At least not a solution that involved the power of thought. I thought and thought, but no solution ever came to light, because my eye disorder didn't disappear when I tried to think it away. This constant "thinking" became my way of existing, and one day the system crashed. It was, in fact, the slightly alternative stress coach who took me for walks in the woods and asked me to walk heel-to-toe who taught me that lesson. A few years had to pass before I realized this, but I'll get back to that.

During my research, I came across this quote by Albert Einstein: "We cannot solve our problems with the same thinking we used when we created them."

Einstein wasn't only a scientific genius, he also had great insight into the human mind. Here, Einstein is telling us that we ourselves create our problems in our minds via our thoughts, and that we have to learn to think differently to get out of the self-created problems.

If you could stop analyzing for a moment and return to the NOW, you'd probably find that there are no problems—RIGHT NOW. You sit peacefully in your favorite armchair on a calm Sunday afternoon as birds chirp cheerfully in the garden, the sun is high in the sky and life is wonderful. But there's no room to acknowledge this momentary miracle of life, because you're already solving the problems of the coming week based on your knowledge of the past. But these future problems aren't real. They're just one potential future, and trying to predict that is what is driving you crazy.

When I realized this simple truth, I couldn't help but be amused every time I briefly let myself be lulled by future worries. When I was to give my first lecture at Novozymes (a global biotechnology company), we agreed a few months beforehand that the lecture should be done in English. I was okay with that, but it was, of course, a greater challenge than doing it in Danish. I decided to be aware of whether or not this challenge would create worrying thoughts for me in the months leading up to the lecture. It did—every now and then—so I used mindfulness to notice the worry so I could create a new environment in which to think. *Everything will be all right.*

When the day came and I arrived at Novozymes, the lecture poster in front of the auditorium said: "The lecture is in Danish." I pulled the organizer aside and asked for an explanation. He looked at me slightly confused and said he'd forgotten our agreement, and had, therefore, assumed we'd probably agreed on Danish. I couldn't help but be amused by this surprise. Just think if I'd spent months worrying about having to give a lecture in English, which ended up being held in Danish! We can't predict the future, so why keep trying?

This is a good example of how we often worry about the future, try to form strategies for how to solve problems that might arise and then experience a completely different future to the one we imagined. In my case, the "problem" solved itself, and I thanked myself for not having wasted energy worrying. Think about how often you worry about things that it doesn't make sense to worry about!

I also stumbled upon a video on YouTube. It was of an Indian Hindu monk, Gaur Gopal Das, giving a lecture. He presented this slide, and he promised that if you lived according to the message on the slide, life would be much easier to live. The slide looked like this:

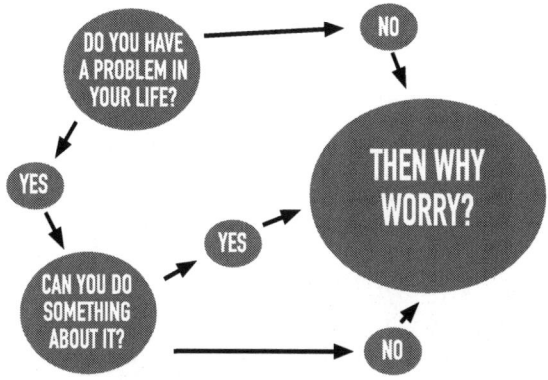

This is such priceless wisdom that I always recall this little thought experiment whenever I think I have a problem. Often, it's something I've escalated in my mind myself.

When you're wound up, you don't feel balance. Your brain isn't in a creative state but is fixated on survival, obsessed with possible disaster scenarios. When everything feels like a crisis, the brain is in survival mode and it can't waste time learning new skills.

The solution to this has to be found outside of the emotions you're fighting against and the thoughts you're bombarded by. What you try to analyze/think about keeps you trapped in the past—the familiar and "safe" past. The solution to the problem is, as Einstein says, found in new patterns of thought—not in old ones.

A gateway to the subconscious

Are you often in a state of high beta? If you constantly analyze everything you see and experience, judge it and decide whether it's good or bad, you're probably in high beta.

If we want to transform our lives, we need to become familiar with our thoughts, feelings and reaction patterns. This realization brought me closer to knowing everything I needed to in order to move with my journey. My journey from Hopelessness Street to Possibility Road.

The reason I'm taking you through this review on the significance of brainwaves for our lives and ways of thinking is because this information was crucial for me to understand before I could challenge myself and make internal changes. Before, I didn't really understand why I should spend time being mindful, why I should meditate and why it sometimes didn't work when I tried it. I didn't know that years of high-beta activity in my brain had created a mind in imbalance. When I learned that you can't go directly from high beta to the desired state of alpha/theta, which is the meditation stage, I had to understand why. Or, rather, how I could practice getting myself into alpha and then theta.

Here's a good simple tip: When your brain is in high beta, activate it with sensory input for the body. Whenever my thoughts ran wild, whenever I tried to think my way out of my problems, they only got worse. But walking barefoot in dewy grass, stroking my arms with my hands or balancing on one leg worked. This is actually a form of yoga. You distract the brain to stop the racing thoughts. The conscious mind can't cope with more than six to ten things (2,000 bits), and when you "interrupt" your thoughts with sensory input, the mind has to let go of its excessive thinking. That's how I was able to stop my runaway thoughts when they became too extreme and prepare myself for entering into alpha/theta. This is also a very effective way of dealing with insomnia. It's often worked for me. Walking in dewy grass so that your mind can have a break.

Gamma brainwaves

I've spent a lot of time and energy describing beta brain waves, because these are the frequencies we most often experience in our waking hours. But, now, we've reached the last category of brainwaves that have been measured in the human brain: gamma waves. Gamma is usually associated with elevated states of mind such as happiness, compassion, and even increased awareness, which usually results in better memory formation.

Gamma is a higher level of consciousness that people describe as "having a transcendent experience" or "breaking through." I've read about Tibetan monks who can bring themselves into a "whole brain" state, as it's called, on command. This state is often described as a total happiness, and it is because almost every center in the brain lights up on a brain scan when humans are in the gamma state.

If I were to guess, I'd say that was the experience I had back then in the cell phone store. While daydreaming, I had a suddenly crystal-clear realization that I should change career. There was no doubt in my mind that it was the right thing to do. Similarly, I may have had a gamma experience the day I sat in the municipal office because I got an unexpectedly crystalline insight that I'd been driven too far down the wrong road—Hopelessness Street—and I needed to find the way to Possibility Road.

Meditation: A path to change

You may perhaps be thinking that what I've spent so much time and energy telling you has little—if anything—to do with my eyesight, but is more general knowledge on the psyche and stress. And you'd be right, but I realized that if I was to master my fears and worries about going blind, and if I was to train myself to see possibilities rather than limitations, then I'd have to become the master of my own body. I had to make myself greater than my problems. I had to understand what mechanisms triggered certain emotions and what mechanisms caused stress, because I'd gotten into a situation that could only end one way: my downfall. If I didn't actively do something to stop the direction my life had taken, my life was going to continue as an endless marathon on Hopelessness Street.

As I told you before, the discoveries described in this book aren't written in the order that I made them. I chose to tell the story this way as I felt that was what would make most sense to you. For instance, meditation was one of the first and most important reasons that I was ever able to open myself up to the various possibilities offered without them being rejected by the filter in my analytical mind.

Now I'd like to tell you about meditation and what it has meant to me.

When I mentioned mindfulness earlier, it was to make it clear to you that I couldn't see new paths for my life if I couldn't learn to accept it as it was then—one hundred percent and without trying to blame and despise my life as it was. It was only when I could accept and love the life I was living—just as it was—that I could move on and change it. Once I'd gotten good at experiencing and accepting the present as it was, and could do so almost on command in everyday life, I began to seek out more information on spirituality and the mind. So, before I tell you more about how I rewrote my old programs with meditation, I'd like to give you an overview of what I've told you up to now.

1. I discovered that if I was going to maintain my joy for life while living with blindness, then I could no longer continue my life as it was.

2. I discovered that I'd been managed and controlled by excessive thoughts, fear and low self-worth and self-esteem and that my focus had been on my limitations for most of my life.

3. I discovered that I had an inner voice that always spoke negatively to me, and that I didn't accept my situation. I fought against it.

4. These discoveries came on the back of a life crisis of stress and depression, which, in turn, enabled me to see myself from the outside.

5. One day, in the municipal office, I had a

revelation: I realized I had to do something if I wasn't going to perish.

6. I defined a life goal that was greater than myself. One that was deeply felt and accepted by both heart and mind: *Despite RP, I was going to live a happy life and I would see possibilities instead of limitations.*

7. I taught myself to be mindful every day, which empowered me to identify my old limiting programs.

8. I learned about how the mind and the body work, and I was able to observe what brainwave states I was in, and, thereby, I became better at understanding stress.

It was now time to find out how I could change the old limiting programs, and meditation and positive self-talk were key here. Like I told you before, mindfulness is about being in the now and accepting it as it is, without trying to change it. Thus, it's a present, objective and non-judgmental way for you to relate to what you encounter— your physical state, your emotional state, your life, your thoughts and your surroundings. Emotions and thoughts are observed, neither ignored nor judged. This makes it easier to see what drives you and what you react to.

Mindfulness came to affect my everyday life in situations where I usually responded based on my habit-driven subconscious, which was built on the programs I'd installed throughout my life. By starting to observe the NOW, I was able to tell whenever the subconscious (autopilot) kicked in, such as in situations like these:

A project manager or my manager makes a comment about embarking on a huge new project next week. Normally, my subconscious mind would do everything to "protect" me; my subconscious had been trained for years to protect me and keep me from getting into situations where my RP was challenged or exhibited. My habit-reaction was to think: *Can I do that? Am I good enough? What is it? Will my eyesight be a problem? Will I be able to deliver?*

Now that I'd practiced being more aware and present in the now, I was quickly able to stop my autopilot with the following inner counterarguments to the subconscious. I would say to myself: *Of course I can do it! I've done it hundreds of times before! I am a master of communication! I believe in myself; I can do ANYTHING!*

I'd take four deep breaths, feel my body and magically take myself out of the control of the old programs. I experienced that it was now ME who decided how I would react in a given situation. Not my old programs. But I wasn't able to do it all the time. Certain situations made me forget my new insights and my progress, and that was when the fear managed to take a hold of me before my conscious focus could take control. It's as though once we end up in a state of mind, it's extremely difficult for us to get out of it again. I had to become even better at managing these mechanisms, and I had to start activating the knowledge I now had even *more* in my life. I had to start BEING what I knew instead of just knowing what I knew. I had to start DOING instead of just THINKING. British-American philosopher Alan Watts put it like this: "You can't get wet from the word 'water'."

For me, meditation was a way to move forward in this process. Meditation became a deeper step into my exploration of myself, and it was in meditation that I trained myself to keep a sharp focus on what I decided I wanted to focus on, and kindly and determinedly sustain that focus.

Meditation with theta —Reprogramming the subconscious

And what was I supposed to do with all that? Well, you see, all too often in my life, I'd experienced being driven around in the spiral of my own destructive thoughts—often without even noticing. A circle of feeling and thinking and feeling and thinking. Mindfulness taught me to realize it. Meditation taught me to control it. For me, meditation is maintaining focus in your mind to a such an extent that you stop sensing the body and what's going on around it. Meditation is knowing yourself!

The way I did it is completely self-taught and maybe

not how others will do it. I started by listening to guided meditation exercises on YouTube. Without ever thinking about it, these guided exercises were accompanied by music and theta sound waves. The purpose of meditation is, as I said earlier, to forget the body so that the mind can focus 100 percent inward. I'd absolutely no inkling of that when I started, but after giving it a try for a few weeks, I saw changes that surprised me. I'd listened to some guided meditations that were about programming yourself with joy, self-acceptance and self-worth, and I have to tell you this: IT WORKED!

It was a weird experience, because I didn't understand what was happening at first. But, later, I discovered that a combination of being in theta state (hypnosis) and being fed with messages that were happy, encouraging and self-affirming left deep marks on the subconscious. I actually started feeling what the audio files encouraged me to feel. It was amazing and I couldn't grasp it. But now both you and I know that when we're motivated by a deep desire for change and in a hypnotic state of theta at the same time, then we're in the process of reprogramming the subconscious.

The more I noticed the positive effect this was having on me, the more I practiced it. The more I practiced, the better I got at diving into the theta state. Now I discovered that I'd never been as relaxed as when I was in this meditative state. I learned what it was like to really relax all my muscles simultaneously. Even when I thought I was relaxing before, my body was always a little tense, which means that I always felt tension in some way in my body. Once I learned how to completely relax in my body, I learned to forget it for a while. That is the ultimate antidote to stress, because you get time to look inward.

An idea came to me. The self-motivational meditation audio files that I listened to were fine, but they were general and not created specifically for me. What if I created my own audio recordings with my own messages for myself? That would have to work even better.

As I mentioned earlier, you and I "hear" an inner dialogue commenting on our actions in various situations every day. That voice is our critical and analytical filter. It guards the entrance to the subconscious. Each of us has inner voices (thoughts) that speak to us again and again in our minds. This unconscious, internal dialogue controls how we react and, thus, vast parts of our lives. And this voice is a learned pattern, a program that we play time and again. One way to acknowledge, encourage and maintain optimism, hope and joy is to consciously fill our thoughts with positive, conscious self-talk. I discovered that I'd automatically and involuntarily told myself things that kept me down. My voice said: *You can't, it's stupid, you're not good enough, people will laugh at you, you're visually impaired, and when people discover it, you're finished*

... and so on.

All too often, our self-talk is negative. Researchers have found that 70 percent of our thoughts are negative. We remember the negative things we were told as children by our parents, siblings or teachers, because these messages are stored in the body. We remember the negative reactions of other children that made us feel of little worth. These messages have been replayed—repeatedly—over the years, thereby fueling feelings such as anger, fear, guilt and hopelessness. They became unconscious programs.

We become what we think and focus on most, so I had to practice focusing on what I wanted rather than on what I didn't want in life. I had to try to teach myself to think more positively than negatively, and, one day, I made a list of the negative thoughts I kept hearing in my head.

I'm revealing myself now, but it's okay, because I'm fine with sharing these innermost and deepest limitations that I had and sometimes still have. The more open I am about them, the more liberated I am from them. The more I expose them, the harder they find it to survive. In reality, the light of conscious awareness dissolves all unconscious patterns.

I noted the negative thoughts that the inner voice repeated in everyday situations, and opposite each one, I wrote a positive contradiction. The positive side of the list was the state I would like to experience more often, and the negative side was the behavior and thoughts I wanted to change and master. The list looked like this:

I can't	I can do anything
I am sad	I am happy
I am afraid	I am fearless
I am weak	I am strong
I am limited	I am unlimited
I can't see	I see perfectly
I am no good	I am amazing
I am ill	I am healthy
I hold grudges	I forgive
I feel insecure	I feel confident
I am fearfull	I am brave
I am negative	I am positive

In addition to writing down these opposites, I made up several self-reinforcing and motivational affirmations that I would like to identify myself with:

- I am brave and I believe in myself
- My thoughts are filled with optimism and my life is amazing
- Today I'm creating new, more positive habits
- Many people look up to me and acknowledge my worth—I am admired
- I am blessed with an incredible family and

wonderful friends
- I acknowledge my own worth—I believe in myself
- I am invulnerable, I am strong
- I am a skilled writer and speaker
- I come up with great ideas every day and carry them out
- I reject negativity and exchange negative thoughts with positive ones

I read these sentences aloud and recorded them on my cell phone, edited them into meditation music containing theta waves, and embarked on my experiment. I knew how to meditate, how to stay focused and I knew the amazing effect it would have on—and for—my mind.

So, I meditated thirty minutes every morning just after I woke up and thirty minutes before going to sleep. The result was astounding. My ability to find peace and inner strength in everyday life was significantly enhanced. I felt stronger, happier and in good balance, and the fear of "catastrophes" was significantly reduced. It all became self-reinforcing. The more I experienced these effects of my meditation, the more diligent I became about practicing it.

My meditation

Let me try to describe my meditation. I start by finding somewhere that's peaceful and quiet. That's not always possible—such as when I meditate on the bus—but closing out the outside world is a matter of practice.

My starting point is being awake and in a state of low beta. If I'm in high beta, I need to come down to a state of low-beta first. I do this by stimulating my body either by touching or shaking it. I create a situation where the excessive thinking in the brain has to stop so it can register the sensations the body is experiencing. When I can feel the thoughts subside, I settle into a comfortable chair and start my voice recording. Now I'm in low-beta.

Let's say I want to meditate for forty minutes, and I have a recording of that length. I spend the first twenty minutes trying to relax my body completely. This is done with the aid of the guiding voice that helps me make my body grow quieter and quieter and relax more and more.

This is where something amazing happens. Before I started meditating, I was never able to relax my body the way I can in this process. I go from coming from the waking beta state—where the focus is on the thoughts that constantly appear in the mind—to becoming aware of my body and feeling it from head to toe. In this process, I become aware of everything that's actually going on in my body. At first, I couldn't feel anything, but then I began to feel buzzing and vibrating sensations, and, over time, I began to feel waves of energy move through my body. One way to achieve this condition is through breathing.

Focusing on that enables me to turn my awareness to my body. If you're focused on breathing, your mind can hardly focus on your thoughts of the past and the future. If you can remember, this way of getting started is similar to the previous description of mindfulness, and it is my experience that mindfulness behavior is important to master before you can delve into deeper meditation.

Once I've gotten my body to be completely still for 20 minutes, it has been deeply relaxed for a period of time, and I begin to forget my body and focus my awareness inward. I'm now ready to dive into lower brainwave stages, and my meditation can begin to move from being focused on my body, to focusing on just being. I forget about time and place and afterward, when the meditation is over, I always wonder where the time went. The fact is the mind forgot about time because it was no longer tied to the body. It was no longer concerned with having to deal with the outside world but could focus its energy inward.

When I'm in this state of "forgetting time and place," I step into theta, and now I'm in the domain of the subconscious without the judgmental filters of the conscious mind. I can't remember this phase afterward, but I'm not asleep either, because I'm sitting upright in a chair. If I fell asleep, I'd immediately notice my head dropping. This is where my self-talk can begin. The conscious mind is sleeping, but the subconscious is very active, so now I "program" it with my new messages. And without any analytical filter judging whether or not the messages are consistent with old habitual behavior, these new programs are snuck in through the back door. I hack the system with new software that I want to install on my hard drive.

As this process happens in a state of theta which is light sleep/hypnosis, I don't experience this with my thinking mind. It's silenced and just IS.

After about fifteen minutes, this process is over, and the voice (my own or a YouTube clip) gently begins to bring me back to an awake state. I sometimes experience complete bliss during this part of the process. Something happens to me when I've been in this state. It's as if my body and my mind have been reset and are in complete agreement on what I want to accomplish and do in my life. Nothing worries me. Seen from this state, life is an immensely happy place to be. It's almost indescribable. This is just my simple attempt to explain something that can only really be understood experientially. Words are only the signposts; they are not the experience!

When I open my eyes and get ready to return to reality, I have a whole new outlook on problems and the turmoil of everyday life. After meditating, I often experience heartfelt gratitude for my life, my happiness and my beautiful family. I appreciate my children and my beloved Mette, and I am happy that I am healthy and strong and have my whole life ahead of me. Poor eyesight doesn't mean anything in these moments. It's a tiny problem when compared to the enormous gift life is. Imagine being in this state and then imagine it continuing for several hours after the meditation. That is what has really changed my way of seeing my life and my role in it. I've learned to focus on what is happening right NOW, because if I do that then I can't be subjected to thought torture in the form of extensive focusing on the past or a potential gloomy future. In that moment, I'm in the present; my eyes serve me well and I'm as happy and content as I decide to be. I'm not a product of my past or my future. I'm NOW and I'm right here. I've become better and better at bringing myself into that state. In meditation but in everyday life, too.

What happens in the long run is that I become more and more aware of the thoughts that don't do me any good and that I want to distance myself from, and the better I know them, the better I get to know the desires and dreams that I wish I could focus more on. Once I become aware of that mechanism, I'm no longer the programs, but the consciousness that lies beneath those programs. I'm now the consciousness observing the programs. And now I have the energy to ask some simple questions:

- What kind of life do I want?
- What are my desires, my dreams and my visions?
- What can I contribute to this world?
- How can I live the good life that I want to?

If I keep focused on what I want instead of what I don't want and call forth the right neurotransmitters, my body will start to think that it's living in the future I want. And if I repeat loving kindness, self-love, compassion and strength every single day, then I cultivate the right neurotransmitters and slowly begin to become more familiar with the new "SELF/I" than I am with the old.

The process of learning and re-learning is now seriously underway. Old familiar habits are broken down. Old emotions stored in the body are "forgotten" and the body is rebuilt with a new mind and new emotions. Energy is drawn from the past and focused on what I want to happen in the future. I change course from Hopelessness Street and steer directly onto Possibility Road.

Secret mission

Thursday, November 30, 2017:
Mr. N had disappeared! It'd been weeks since my somewhat dramatic experience at Koldinghus Castle, and I hadn't heard from the Letter Men since either. I'd gone

home after stating to Mr. P and Mr. F that Mr. N had disappeared because I'd finally reached the point where he no longer had power over me. I was now going to try to concentrate even more on transforming myself into someone who could see possibilities instead of limitations. My visual disability was no longer going to be an excuse for not living the life I wanted. And with my goal of living a happy life, I finally had something to move toward that wasn't just materialistic. It was an ideal. Something greater than myself. I'd made some great discoveries for myself during the last month and I'd described the entire thing in the book. I finally realized that it was my way of thinking that had created the stress and depression I'd been fighting against. Gaining insight into how the brain can change wave states, depending on how I thought and used my body, was sensational for me. Everything made sense now—even meditation and mindfulness.

Finally getting an overview of my own history and putting it into perspective was also a huge step for me. I was now aware of what kind of a person I'd been and what kind of person I wanted to be, and that this discovery was a prerequisite for change. Knowing where you come from and where you want to go.

I'd discovered that I could reprogram my subconscious. I'd started this process and no longer needed Mr. P to encourage me. It was as though he'd become part of me. He was, in a way, the Letter Man that I resembled least initially, but he was the one I needed to resemble most. Mr. N and Mr. F were, in a way, more like the old Morten. Always wary of the new and the unknown and always worried about the future and chained to the past. But now Mr. N had completely disappeared, and Mr. P and Mr. F were silent. Despite me convincing myself that I didn't care about Mr. N, I was also, in a weird way, concerned about what had happened to him. I felt a strange connection to him. As if we were connected in some indefinable way. Now that he was completely gone, there was a part of me that regretted the struggle I'd been party to keeping alive. I felt as though I missed what Mr. N represented. His personality and his way of seeing life. I couldn't explain why. That's just how it was.

As I sat thinking about this, one dark night in my study, my mind wandered to my experience at Koldinghus Castle. Why did we have to meet there? And how exactly had the evening ended again? I couldn't really remember saying goodbye to Mr. P and Mr. F. How had I gotten home? It was all a blank. As if the evening had ended abruptly and then I was home. It was reminiscent of a similar experience from a previous encounter with the Letter Men. I just couldn't remember when and under what circumstances.

I was typing away on the keyboard when a brief text box appeared on the screen:

It's time for you to tell us and the readers what you omitted to tell us at our meetings.

It had to be Mr. P who was writing to me. I knew well what he was talking about, but I wasn't going to share it with anyone until I'd seen through what I'd decided to see through. I wanted this experience for myself, to test whether what I wrote about and what I read and learned about could be implemented in my everyday life. Were these just good ideas and philosophies, or could I change myself by teaching myself to think new thoughts about myself and my role in this world? Could I turn my knowledge into action? I'd learned that new experiences create new neuropathways in the brain, and the only way to train your mind to think new thoughts was by having new experiences and establishing new daily routines. I knew this was extremely difficult because once a habit had become a habit, the subconscious was programmed and I'd programmed my subconscious to be mediocre and limited.

So, just a few weeks after my first conversation with Mr. P, I decided that I'd continuously implement my new knowledge into my everyday life. I hadn't shared this with the Letter Men—I didn't dare to discuss with them whether they agreed or disagreed with my approach. Deep down I knew, of course, that they knew what I was doing—they knew everything. But this was the first time they'd mentioned it. And it's the first time you're hearing about it, too. And I apologize for keeping this secret from you, but I wanted you to have all the knowledge I'd acquired before

I told you how it could be used in everyday life. I hope you can forgive me—after all, we're each other's confidants now.

I replied to Mr. P:

Yes, I've been on a mission over the last few months. You knew that already, didn't you, Mr. P? It's time for me to share this story with the readers, too.

Mr. P answered immediately:

Tell your story. It will inspire many.

PART 3
ARRIVAL ON POSSIBILITY ROAD

"You can't get wet from the word 'water'"

I'd started a course of research and I'd already learned a lot about myself and about how the mind works. I knew right from the start that if this project were to succeed — reprogramming my subconscious mind to see possibilities rather than limitations — then I had to start taking action. I had to DO instead of just THINK. Alan Watt's famous quote came to mind again: "You can't get wet from the word 'water'."

I knew what was holding me back from living my life the way I wanted to. It wasn't just the prospect of losing my eyesight; it was the fear of losing myself, losing my life, losing who I was, and the fear of my visual impairment being revealed. That fear had created a mind that worried about the future, which continuously conjured up all sorts of thought-created scenarios.

As early as summer 2017, it dawned on me that if I wanted to overcome fear and create a version of myself that could see possibilities rather than limitations, I'd have to put a plan in place.

And so motivated, I got an idea that could take me further on my mission. I experienced that the more I focused on positivity, the happier I became, and the more I influenced my surroundings in a positive way. The more positivity I gave to my outside world, the more joy and positivity I got in return.

"If you want to be happy, practice compassion." – *the Dalai Lama*

So, one summer evening in 2017, I got this idea: I was going to set a series of challenges for myself that would confront NEGATIVITY, FEAR, WORRY and the feeling of being LIMITED. I was going to act instead of just think. I was going to move from my stagnant position and seek out what I wanted. I was going to teach myself to think new thoughts. New experiences would lead to new thoughts, which would lead to new feelings, which would lead to new programs, which would, in turn, create a new version of me. I was going to reprogram my subconscious mind!

Challenge #1
30 days with STOP! SWAP THOUGHTS!
Mastering NEGATIVITY

My first challenge was an exercise in changing my automatic negative thoughts to positive ones. I was going to test what I practiced in my meditation out in the real world. The state of focus I reached in meditation was going to be brought into my everyday life. My negativity wasn't directed at my outside world *per se*, but at myself. In my mind, I complained about my life situation and about how shitty everything was. The idea of practicing being the positive version of myself came from Earl Nightingale's famous recording, *The Strangest Secret in the World*, where he challenged listeners to spend thirty days intensively changing a habit. I was now accepting that challenge.

For thirty days, I was going to be AWARE of my negativity when I noticed it, I would focus on its positive opposite. Once I realized I'd fallen into the habit of negativity, I was going to pat myself lovingly on the shoulder for noticing, and then I was going to try to let feelings, such as GRATITUDE, COMPASSION and FORGIVENESS dominate. I would like to make clear that thinking and acting positively doesn't exclude feeling angry or frustrated or negative. You can't do that. And neither is it advisable to try to do so, because fighting against these emotions makes them grow in intensity. Believe me! You give life to what you fight against and what you focus on. As Carl Gustav Jung put is "what we resist persists." This wasn't going to be an exercise in suppressing negativity, but in becoming CONSCIOUS of it. As part of the exercise, I realized that if I was feeling frustrated or angry, I needed to be aware of the cause and process it right now, right here. I couldn't drag it around with me for days on end.

Thirty days was manageable. My goal was to train myself to focus on what I *want* instead of what I don't want. Possibilities instead of limitations.

I came up with a little game to play for the rest of the month: the STOP! SWAP THOUGHTS game. Quite simply, every time I experienced something that had a negative tone—that is, when I decided something was bad, wrong, stupid, annoying, irritating or shitty—I was going to notice it, and within five seconds do a 180: turn my view of the situation around from being something negative to somehow being positive. I had to practice turning my focus toward positivity.

For example:
On the way to the canteen: *Ugh, it's raining.*
STOP! SWAP THOUGHTS! 1-2-3-4-5.
Better a light drizzle than a thundershower.

"WAAAIIIIIT," the bus pulls away from the stop three minutes early. *Damn! Now I'll have to wait half an hour for the next stupid bus.*

STOP! SWAP THOUGHTS! 1-2-3-4-5.

Hmm great! Now I have half an hour more to enjoy the sun and listen to my audiobook before I get home. I'm actually really grateful that there IS a bus from work to home at all.

It's so shitty that I can't drive anymore!

STOP! SWAP THOUGHTS! 1-2-3-4-5.

Ah well, at least I can always drink myself under the table at parties — I can't be the designated driver.

Ugh, he sounds like an idiot!

STOP! SWAP THOUGHTS! 1-2-3-4-5.

He's not an idiot. He just has a different point of view on the situation than I do.

You get the idea. I quickly discovered that there's always something positive to be found in the negative, and I amused both my family and several colleagues with this way of responding. My boys started calling me their "Hippie Dad!"

Several people have asked me how can they suddenly decide to look positively at situations if that's not how they feel? Make no mistake, that is what it was like for me at the beginning of my thirty-day STOP! SWAP THOUGHTS game. It felt wrong at first. It was artificial and awkward, but I'd arrived at the realization that I could wait all my life for happiness and joy to come along, but they never would if I didn't take the first steps toward them. So that's what I was doing now.

If you think you're going to have a bad day and you immediately feel sad at that thought, your day will most likely be bad. But if, using your focus and your will, you send a clear and direct order to your subconscious mind that today you feel strong, powerful and full of energy and joy, your brain will secrete neurotransmitters that can make you feel just that. Your body language and your attitude can help you become an alchemist of your mind, influencing which neurotransmitters your brain releases. This allows you to greatly affect your mood, help yourself forward and not drag yourself down.

I have many experiences and examples from my thirty-day STOP! SWAP THOUGHTS game, and I'd like to describe a few of them for you. When I embarked on this challenge, I was sad and bitter that I had to spend three hours every day on a bus. It was so frustrating, and I complained to myself every morning about no longer being able to drive. I felt humiliated, standing there in the pouring rain, waiting for the bus with a bunch of teenagers, while my neighbors drove by us in their comfortable cars.

My ego had taken a hit. But I'd started my STOP! SWAP THOUGHTS month, so I had to figure out how to activate my STOP! SWAP THOUGHTS game! *1-2-3-4-5. Morten, you have an hour and a half before you get to work and until then you can relax and enjoy your own company. When do you ever have time for that? Almost never!*

A-ha! I could use this precious bus time to listen to audiobooks and meditate. Something I had difficulty finding time for. Wow! Taking the bus became a gift and an advantage, and when colleagues or neighbors offered me a lift, I actually declined, because my bus time was now my best time of day. I changed my perspective; turned a negative judgment of a situation in my life into a positive one. I hadn't changed the situation itself. I'd changed *my view* of the situation! I had that power and the choice was mine!

I started to notice something else. When I waited for the bus, and it was twelve minutes late as usual, the voice appeared again: *Stupid bus. It's always late.* I stood, constantly checking my watch and *STOP! SWAP THOUGHTS! 1-2-3-4-5: new thought.* It wondered: *Morten, do you have a magical ability that enables you to summon buses by staring at your watch?* Yep, I was permanently watching the clock because I couldn't stand just waiting here. After all, I had something to do, damn it, and staring at my watch every twenty seconds was my solution to the restlessness.

So, I made a new rule. From the second I left home

each morning, there was no checking my watch. After all, I knew that if I left at the right time, I'd arrive in time for the first bus, and then there was NOTHING I could do to affect the flow of public transport. It just happened and nothing I did would make any difference to it. *Can you do something about it? No. So why worry?*

I began to observe the world around me instead, and one day when I was just observing, the wind caught hold of a small pile of withered leaves that'd been lying on the sidewalk. They danced around in a beautiful spiral, swirling faster and faster, as if carried by an invisible force. They took off from the ground and . . . then . . . then . . . the bus came! I no longer waited for the bus—I *experienced* the world until the bus arrived. It was a choice. The situation could be seen from a different perspective and I decided the perspective. Wait or experience?

Another positive effect soon emerged one day as I was *waiting* for the bus—a twenty-minute wait. The voice began to grumble again: *waiting here is such a stupid waste of time. It's below my dignity. Why aren't there more buses? It's ridiculous! I could be in my car if . . .*

Woah, said another voice. *STOP! SWAP THOUGHTS! 1-2-3-4-5. Hey—why are you actually waiting here, Morten?*

I'd been on antidepressants for a year and had gained about twenty pounds. I wanted to shed the weight, so I could turn this situation to my advantage. I could start walking and then hop on the bus further down. I headed off, feeling the wind in my face and the warmth of the sun on my bald head, and it was . . . it was wonderful!

When I got to the next stop, I looked at the bus stop and all the people standing with their noses in their cell phones. *Hmm*, I thought. *Why don't you just keep going, Morten?*

I decided to walk on. It was about four miles—a perfect way to lose weight. It was amazing. I felt in control of my situation and that I was seeing possibilities where before I saw limitations; that I wasn't defeated by negativity and sulking. I felt lucky to have discovered so much quality time in being cut off from my car. I got better at seeing time as something I needed to make the most of—not just as something that had to pass by.

I now understood this passage in one of Eckhart Tolle's books: "Whatever the present moment contains, accept it as if you had chosen it." I decided how to judge the situation in which I found myself. How I'd immediately assess it and how I'd act.

Due to my situation, I got better at enjoying the time here and now. I didn't wish I was somewhere else or walk faster to get home quickly. I just let time be and walked at the pace I wanted to. It was pure bliss, and I began to notice things I'd never noticed before. I noticed houses that I'd never seen before, even though I'd rushed past them in my car a thousand times. I noticed the fields and how the grain billowed in the wind; I noticed clouds forming fantastic shapes in the sky. I felt that I loved being where I was—NOW. I was able to feel what it was like to be here.

It began to lash on the walk home, and the "voice" moaned at the rain: *I'm going to get wet now; this would never have happened if I didn't have this stupid condition that's making me blind.*

The thought frustrated me for a moment, but I was also frustrated at having had the thought in the first place—that shouldn't happen this month! Then I remembered that the mission of this month was to NOTICE when negative thoughts started a chain reaction. I gave myself a loving pat on the shoulder instead for having noticed my moany thoughts. *STOP! SWAP THOUGHTS! 1-2-3-4-5. Walking in a refreshing rain shower is so nice after being cooped up inside all day. Good thing I brought my raincoat.*

We don't need to react to the voice of complaint. Instead, we can accept it's there. And the moment we accept it, it stops moaning. It begins to rely on the observer, who is the true "SELF"—the conscious awareness. And the decisiveness that the voice is now feeling, due to the positive neurotransmitters, which the new positive thoughts have activated in your brain and, thereby, your body, makes the voice feel safe and secure and so it starts to relax. *You are the captain of the ship. You give the orders.*

Can you see how this way of perceiving and reacting is a choice and that it can be applied in every situation we encounter? Do you see how practicing being consciously aware and present in the moment can make you discover the automatic, inner complaining voice and stop the limiting and automatic programs that the subconscious mind plays faster than you can consciously respond to? It's a new and different mindful way of life.

This is mindfulness in action. *"But Morten, I don't have time to practice mindfulness and meditation in my busy everyday life!"*

I often hear this when I talk to people about meditation, so I'd like to give you a tip on how to implement mindfulness in your everyday life without having to sit on a meditation mat and chant "ooohhm." That's still not such a bad idea, but I'm going to give you another option. I call it *Mindfulness on the GO*. Rather than just being mindful a few times a day on a meditation mat, you create moments of mindfulness in everyday life.

One day, when I was about to enjoy an afternoon bread roll with a cup of coffee, I decided to turn it into a mindfulness exercise. It was a tip from Eckhart Tolle's book *The Power of Now*. I buttered my roll and sat down at the table. I was going to be completely present as I ate the roll. But my autopilot had other plans. Four seconds after I'd settled down, my hand reached out automatically for the TV remote control. I stopped the impulse and regained my focus. The next impulse came just seconds later, when my other hand reached for my iPhone. Again, I stopped the autopilot and regained my focus. I smiled and took a deep breath, picked up the bread roll and noticed how weird it actually felt. I'd never thought about it before. The crust was crunchy, crispy but a little soft at the same time. I lifted it up to my mouth and took a bite.

I now had a large piece of roll in my mouth and started chewing. I chewed and chewed, and a thought came to me. I'd never before thought about the huge lump of flesh in my mouth—my tongue—spurting around in my mouth as I chewed, right next to an army of razor-sharp teeth that could bite the lump at any time! But it never happened. My tongue was in complete control of what it was doing without my conscious mind needing to interfere. Now that my conscious mind was interfering, I could feel that if it kept interfering—if it thought it could do better than the autopilot—it'd probably go horribly wrong at some point. My body was in complete control of the process—it'd done it a thousand times before. I suddenly felt gratitude for my amazing body that could do all this automatically.

Now came the next discovery. Another little miracle. My tongue did something else, too. I noticed that one side of my mouth ran out of bread every so often, and then what? Yes, my tongue rolled automatically from one side of my mouth to the other, carrying the bread with it. Now there was an equal amount of food on each side again. It happened automatically and I was absolutely intrigued by the ingenuity of the body.

Then came the next phase of the experience. The first bite of the roll had been chewed into a clump that now needed to be sent further along the system. So, my throat automatically made a swallowing movement, and the food moved further back in my mouth and—what?—it just slid slowly down my throat. For a moment, I was quite worried about whether the food would slip down the wrong hole and into my lungs, but again the body knew what it was doing. The food slid slowly and safely down the right tube, and into my stomach. I could feel it!

And so it continued, and when there was no more bread roll on the plate, I came out of my trance. My intense encounter with the NOW. I looked at my watch in amazement—almost ten minutes had passed with this exercise. I'd forgotten the time for a while and, thereby, all my everyday problems. I'd turned my focus from my thinking to focusing on the very moment. I also noticed that my head felt "lighter." I'd gotten a break from thinking, and it was a relief.

This is a way for you to bring mindfulness into your life.

You can do it at work, too, when you want a cup of *coffee*. From the moment you crave coffee, try to decide that you're going to experience the entire process of getting the coffee. Normally, you have a thought, coffee (from the conscious mind), and then you get up and return to your thoughts (autopilot). While getting your coffee, your thoughts continue to solve your "imaginary problems": *How am I going to get that presentation finished? Will they fire me if it's not good enough?*

Instead of getting lost in your thoughts, try to take note of every step out to the coffee machine. You realize that your shoes are really soft to walk in and that they make a fun little "clip, clap" sound as you walk. When you get to the coffee machine, you notice the aroma of good coffee. You reach for a cup and observe how it's quite heavy but smooth and cold at the same time. You put it in under the nozzle on the coffee machine and examine the control panel. You decide on an Americano. You press the button for Americano and notice that it makes a small click. In that same moment, something happens on top of the machine. You can see the coffee beans through the glass; they move, leaving a little crater in the pile of coffee beans. You notice the grinding sound and, suddenly, the nozzle splutters. Hot steam sputters out and then hot coffee. You notice the sound of trickling liquid and feel the hot steam. The fragrance of fresh coffee hits your nostrils and you take a deep breath. The coffee nears the rim of the cup and the machine stops. You reach for the cup and notice that the cold cup is now hot. You lift the cup and feel how heavy the cup now is. You lift it to your face and feel the hot steam against your skin. You carefully sip the coffee and feel the warm liquid in your mouth. "Ow, that's hot." You taste it and wonder why you really like this bitter drink at all.

This is another break from the thought prison. Again, ten minutes have passed in which you've forgotten "the real world." But can you now see that you actually forgot the "imaginary world" and experienced the real world? The only thing that was real when you had your coffee and bread roll experiences was the experience in the present. Thoughts were the "unreal world," but this is what we most often call "reality" because problems often arise in thoughts. Can you remember my experience of giving my lecture at Novozymes? The reality I'd predicted never came to pass.

After these mindfulness breaks, it's as if your system has restarted. Your inner-interpreter is reset—I've often found that problems that seemed unsolvable before taking a break from thinking were suddenly mere trifles afterward. They were something that occupied my thoughts, and when I viewed them from a different angle—a different perspective—they suddenly weren't so problematic after all.

You can create these moments of mindfulness for yourself throughout the day. Make it a habit to never wait in a queue. Instead of "waiting," you can decide to EXPE-RIENCE. Notice what's happening in your body; smell, see and listen to what's happening around you. Experience the moment instead of complaining about the long queue. Maybe you'll develop the same relationship with queues as I have—and experience them as fantastic possibilities to be present in the NOW and, thereby, silence the inner complaining voice cursing the supermarket for not having more checkouts open. Whether a situation is good or bad is your choice. You decide. So, why not create a positive situation?

Well, to get back to my walk. When I arrived home in rain-soaked clothes an hour later, I was on a total high. I skipped through the door and gave Mette a big kiss and both of my boys a long hug. Life was amazing, and I'd completely forgotten to appreciate it! It dawned on me that I'd spent my entire life in the fast lane. I'd never stopped to look at life. There was always something that had to be done and I always had to be somewhere—preferably quickly. I wasn't experiencing life—I was rushing past it.

I experienced changes at work, too. When I found myself in situations that I'd been stressed about before, I was able to take a deep breath and look at the situation from a distance, rather than get lost in impulsive worries. I also discovered that I could influence the culture at work with my new way of behaving.

One day, for example, I entered a meeting room where a black cloud seemed to be hanging over everyone. There was a pressurized atmosphere and when I asked why everyone looked so bleak, a storm of curses hit me. The campaign we'd been working on for months was to be drastically changed. Completely overhauled in fact. And then came a string of profanities over how stupid management was and how everything was shit. I stood for a moment and took notice. I could feel the resentment at this news brewing in me. But then I stopped and brought my attention to my body. *STOP! SWAP THOUGHTS! 1-2-3-4-5.* Then it was as if a stream of energy was flowing through me, and my whole body was restarted—and so was my perception of the problem we were now facing. In a moment, I could feel my breathing, my heart, my feet against the floor, and I felt happy that I was standing here and experiencing this.

I understand this is hard to fathom—it was as though rejected campaigns and those at fault made absolutely no difference. I was here right NOW; I loved this place and was just so happy that I was able to work here and do what I loved. I was grateful! A campaign that needed to be redone was insignificant compared to not being able to make campaigns again at all.

My genuine happiness evoked huge excitement in me and I exclaimed, "THIS IS GREAT!"

The room fell completely quiet and everyone stared at me.

"Eh, what do you mean?" someone dared to ask, after a few seconds of silence.

"We love doing campaigns," I replied. "And now we're being allowed to do it again!"

After a moment, a few people couldn't help but giggle, and before we knew it, the negative cloud that had filled the room was dissolved, and people were chuckling. It took just one person with positive energy to change a whole room full of negativity. One person who thought STOP! SWAP THOUGHTS! It was magic and I was the magician!

Another way to experiment with this new role was by trying to look and smile at people I came across. It was ironic, to say the least, because I'd learned that for years, I'd been ignoring over half of all the people I passed by. In my defense, I couldn't see them, but they couldn't know that by looking at me. It just looked like I was ignoring them. I wanted to try to compensate for that, so I began to greet everyone I met with a smile from ear to ear. It really confused some of my colleagues.

I was amused to arrive at work in the morning and greet my work-partner with the biggest smile I could muster. The effect was so funny.

"HEEELLO SIMON," I said, making Simon look at me

in wonder at first, not quite knowing what to say. I'd never done this before, so he eyed me uncertainly and then he looked himself up and down, as if there was something with his clothes.

"Eh, what's wrong?" he asked.

"Nothing," I answered. "It's just a beautiful morning and I'm glad to see you."

He hadn't a clue what was going on, but he couldn't help but smile broadly back at me. Discovering the effect I could have on other people simply through my behavior was yet another *a-ha moment* for me.

Yet another new routine or habit was formed during this month. I noticed that every night when I crawled into bed and tried to fall asleep, the "voice" was extremely active as it reflected on the day. *Today was a bad day—I didn't see the full glass and knocked it over, spilling it all over my MacBook!* My stupidity upset and annoyed me. *I'm a damn fool!*

Woah! STOP! SWAP THOUGHTS! 1-2-3-4-5. Does thinking like this help you, Morten? How do you feel?

I could feel I was saddened by the thought of my stupidity—but it hadn't really been a bad day! Then I had another thought: *Why am I worrying about this? I have insurance that pays.*

I thought of Mette's reaction when I told her about my accident. She'd said, "Stop thinking about it, Morten. It is what it is, and I think you're handling your disability really well!"

I thought about how lucky I was to have her. *She's amazing and I am so lucky to have her in my life.*

From feeling stupid, I suddenly felt lucky. Once again, I'd changed a thought, and thereby changed my view of the day I'd just had. I now felt love instead of sadness. Now that I thought about it, it had actually been a good day. *I decide!*

When you direct your focus to where you want it before you fall asleep, something happens in your body, too. When you give your body a positive thought and feeling before sleeping, you take that chemistry with you into your sleep. It's the signal you send to your subconscious mind and it's what it ruminates on during your sleep.

You can do another thing, too. Before you fall asleep, you can make a decision. Ask yourself, "What's the first thought I'd like to have tomorrow morning when I wake up?" You may decide that your first thought should be to have a great day with your colleagues because you're going to brainstorm a new campaign. You could imagine how you all enjoy yourselves as you come up with a cool idea for the campaign. You could imagine what it feels like when you get the idea and how your boss exclaims with delight. This is then the command you've given your subconscious mind for when you fall asleep; it'll continue to work on it while you sleep. Because the subconscious is always working. Normally, when you wake up, you may think: *"I can't take another day of sitting on that bus,"* but now you wake up with a goal for your day instead. A fantastic day is ahead of you: developing a campaign with your amazing colleagues. You jump out of bed because you know exactly how it's going to feel when you crack it. Nine times out of ten, that is the day I end up experiencing because I've programmed myself to create it. I create it with my intention and my decisions in the present. I create my day!

You may be thinking: Isn't there a risk of disappointment and feeling defeated if all these ideas and good intentions fail to materialize? There is, but only if you haven't made the deal that I made with myself before starting the 30-day challenge. I convinced myself and promised myself that I'd ALWAYS be my own best friend during this process. I was going to accept myself exactly as I was — I put myself in a position where I couldn't lose. I could only win — the attempt alone already made me a winner. It was my safety net and so, I'd nothing to lose and everything to gain.

Quite simply, I found a new best friend this month. Myself! With a mindset focused on thinking positively and a mentality that it would go well as long as I did my best, the inner voice began to change how it spoke to me. Instead of scolding me and speaking derogatorily to me, it spoke encouragingly and appreciatively to me. It didn't just happen by itself. No, it happened because I was aware and observed my self-talk, like a kindergarten teacher keeping an eye on the tone of the playroom and gently and kindly reminding the children to talk nicely to each other as they play. I reminded myself to speak nicely to myself in my mind in just the same way.

I was mindful of my own thoughts and self-talk; I no longer tolerated the harsh tone my inner voice used toward me. Now the inner voice said: *"Well done, Morten, you're so good"* and *"I'm so proud of you for what you just did."* And when I talk about a voice speaking to me, it is, of course, the good old ego, formed by years of habitual negative thinking.

My experiment created a new breeding ground for a new mentality in me, once I discovered that focusing on the positive helped me in every aspect of my day-to-day life. Life became more fun and easier to live. I stopped imagining disaster scenarios and I worried less about the future. I also put an end to drawing too much on past experiences. The entire experiment was self-reinforcing. The more affirmative experiences I had in thinking positively, the more it encouraged me to keep going.

At one point, I came to think of Ole Henriksen (the famous Danish skin cosmetician), who always seemed overly happy. I remember thinking that level of happiness had to be put on—no one could possibly be as happy as he always seems to be. And then I realized: that was probably how my colleagues experienced me, when I kindly and definitely tried to STOP! SWAP! myself to positive shortcuts in so-called "crisis situations" at work. My old core beliefs were battling with my understanding that I could be positive and happy because it meant changing the way I saw the world.

All behavioral changes are an attack on our habit-fixated ego. An ego shaped by the past that, over time, affects the subconscious mind. You probably remember that the subconscious mind doesn't voluntarily change its old programs. Repetition or solid awareness is needed to change them. And, in those thirty days, I felt I was able to challenge my old core beliefs as long as I kept my resolve and focused on it.

The thirty days also taught me that I always have a choice. Whether something is good or bad is my choice. I'd never realized that before. I was always quick to decide whether something was good or bad, and once judgment was passed, that was the end of the discussion. Now I experienced that I myself decided how to categorize a situation, and I also discovered that it's me who decides whether my life is bad or good—whether losing my eyesight is good or bad. It's all a matter of perspective!

"When we are no longer able to change a situation, we

are challenged to change ourselves."
   – Viktor Frankl

The world isn't created around us but rather within us. As I changed the way I experienced the world, the world changed.

Signs we miss

I had now opened my mind up to a new, more positive way of looking at the outside world, and something else was happening, too—I was beginning to understand events that had occurred earlier in my life, but which I couldn't see or understand at that time.

I thought back to an experience I'd had in 2016 with a really good colleague at the LEGO Group, who has since become a close friend. During the summer vacation, I'd been told by the doctor that I was now legally blind and could no longer drive. And being back at work after three weeks of vacation was a whole new situation for me—no one at work knew that I'd been given the title "legally blind" during the vacation.

Most people were still on holiday and, in my diary, I could see that I was due to work with a colleague for a few weeks. But I wasn't exactly myself. My thoughts revolved constantly around my new "status" as a legally blind person, and I ruminated on what the future would bring and how I'd be able to do my job. What was going to happen? My colleague helped me through those two weeks by continuously reminding me of all the things she could see that I could still do. I was over-focused on everything I thought I COULDN'T do.

After the two weeks passed and the project was handed over, I realized that maybe I could do something other than depend on my eyes. I could write, I could come up with ideas, I had a lot of experience, and I could motivate and mentor others. My colleague made me realize and believe this. Not right away, but over the next year.

I had another significant episode with the same colleague six months after we'd worked together on the design project. We met one day in the canteen over lunch, at around the time I had my epiphany in the municipal office that I had to find Possibility Road.

She had a book with her, and she told me that the book belonged to a close friend back in India and that it might be good for me to read it. By this point, I'd started listening to books on philosophy and spirituality, and I had a list of audiobooks that I wanted to listen to. So, I put my colleague's book on the office shelf, thinking I'd get around to reading it one day in the future. I'd more important books to listen to for now.

One day—several months after lunch with my colleague—I discovered, on the internet, a book that supposedly inspired readers around the world with its message, and I decided it was to be my next book. I got started and quickly acknowledged that this book was a life-changer. The book, written by German author, Eckhart Tolle, is called *The Power of Now* (I have mentioned it several times in this book), and its endeavor to end our negative thought habits blew me away. In the book, Eckhart Tolle introduces the concept of the "pain body": the negative emotions that accumulate throughout your life. The book paves a way out of our often self-created psychological pain by advocating living in the present; neither in the past nor the future.

I listened to *The Power of Now* as an audiobook, and one day on my walk home, a fleeting sense of déjà vu came over me. There was something familiar about the author's name. Where had I heard of him before? I couldn't place it, but I had a niggling suspicion. Once I got home, I strode purposefully into my office and looked at the shelf. I took down the book I'd borrowed from my colleague many months before, and on the cover was *"The Power of Now* by Eckhart Tolle"! Goosebumps washed over my entire body. Of all the books I'd read and listened to, this book had changed my way of seeing the world most of all. It dawned on me I'd been offered this book to read several months before, but I'd decided it wasn't important enough!

The moral of the story is that throughout life we're often presented with possibilities and situations that can change our lives without us even realizing it. I hadn't seen that the book, which was to become my most important tool for insight and change had been served to me right under my nose. I had to discover it for myself!

The same thing happened to me when the stress coach took me on walks in the woods. Can you remember that story from PART 1? I've been teasing it throughout the book and now you're finally going to get the story, because now it'll make sense to you too.

I went to her to be "fixed"; to get rid of the "nonsense" I was dealing with—the stress and the depression—but she just brought me for walks in the woods. What was the point of all that? Well, allow me to tell you (and the stress coach was probably quite aware that she never could have made me understand back then). I guess the insightful stress coach had immediately spotted that she was dealing with a client who was completely lost in his world of thought. In his prison of thought. That she was dealing with a client who lived only in his head and made all decisions and conclusions in his life based on his thinking mind. She knew I was someone who slowly had to realize that the life I'd been living, which was happening in my head, had to be rediscovered through my body.

Can you remember the Albert Einstein quote, "We cannot solve our problems with the same thinking we used when we created them"? Einstein knew this and solved many of his thought experiments precisely when he *stopped* thinking and was just present in the NOW. The basis for Einstein's famous theory of relativity came to him from staring thoughtlessly out the window of a patent office in Switzerland's capital. He often found solutions to intellectual conundrums in the gray zone between the worlds of thought and dozing. In the gray zone between low beta, alpha and theta.

Many of my good ideas, that I'd come up with over the years in the advertising industry, came to me when I'd given up on ever finding a good idea. Strangely enough, an idea flashed into my mind when I was in a state of surrender, as I urinated in the office's bathroom. The idea came out of nothing, totally unexpectedly; I hurried back into the meeting room to share the idea with the team — and yes, I remembered to wash my hands! And since then, whenever a workshop stalled, someone from the team jokingly asked: *"Morten, don't you need to pee soon?"*

The stress coach from the walks in the woods knew I'd never be able to solve my problems because they couldn't be solved with my thinking mind. In fact, they couldn't be solved at all. I had to accept that the problems were part of me and that I needed to discover my deeper "SELF" in order to live in harmony with these "problems." She was undoubtedly aware that the thinking machine standing in front of her would never be able to accept such a proclamation. And she was right. I discovered that through a deeper dimension, and I found the entrance to that dimension through the NOW. Through the body and through surrender. Through the death of my identities that I thought were me. I was to learn through my body, which I'd completely ignored and tormented for years. My body that was constantly trying to make me stop and discover a dimension other than the one of thought.

She showed me that not everything could — or should — be solved in our thoughts, but I didn't understand that. I think I slowly did start to realize it. But it's only after the process I've described to you in this book that I genuinely understand that the wise stress coach was trying to talk around my head and directly to my body and my essence.

I discovered a glimpse of it when, at our last session, she asked me — like she always did — what I'd gotten out of the day's session; about how I was feeling, and I made some smart remark about feeling a development and being able to put my experiences into perspective, blah blah blah. I thought and thought, trying to find a good answer. Surprisingly, she interrupted me and repeated her question, "Morten, what are you feeling?"

And then it dawned on me. I had no idea how to feel feelings. I'd cut myself off from my emotions years before. I'd let my intellect and my thoughts control my ship, and they didn't allow anything as ridiculous as emotions to get in the way of my "hide-my-eye-disorder-from-the-outside-world" project.

I stopped my excessive talking and just sat there, staring at her for a moment. It became apparent to me that she'd been trying to get through to this layer of me ever since I first sat with her. Understanding came to me at last.

"How am I feeling?" I repeated, finally seeing through my own mind's attempt to have control over everything in my life. I closed my eyes and said, "I'm just happy," and when I heard the words come out of my mouth, I couldn't help but smile. Talk about a banal and simple answer. Completely unworthy of my otherwise eloquent and articulate repertoire of words, preferably spoken in long and cleverly formulated sentences, so I can intoxicate my audience with the exuberance of my vocabulary.

But I WAS just happy. It was so liberating and effortless! I couldn't understand what she was trying to show me, and it was only several years later that it dawned on me. She was trying to make me realize that in my self-created, thought-based prison I was missing out on life and that all my problems were going around in circles. Can you remember how I described the feeling of my upper body being separate from my lower body that day on the bench in the woods? My head was separated from the body. I had no contact with my body. My body tried to tell me, but I didn't understand it. I didn't listen to what my body said. I didn't see the signs.

I can now see—and understand—that denying and fighting against the NOW that's present right here, right now, is the same as denying life itself. Only by accepting what is right NOW do you realize how futile it is to fight it. It is what it is. And yes, you can decide you want to change something or create something else based on your learning. But denying and fighting the present is pointless.

Challenge #2
Jump!
Mastering FEAR and WORRY

Thus informed by the realization that I often overlooked signs and signals, or said no to possibilities that came along, and armed with my experiences in my thirty-day challenge, I was now inspired to continue with my experiment. And, in reality, that's what it was. I was the guinea pig, and the world was my lab.

By now, I'd experienced with my own body that it was absolutely possible to change deep-rooted patterns and habits. To change old programs. It was possible, as long as you *made a firm decision* it really was going to happen. In just one month, I'd altered my perspective on my life, and it'd resulted in huge positive changes. In a way, I'd just gotten happier; I'd rediscovered the amazing world I actually do inhabit. I felt uplifted and almost like a new person. I was, at the least, aware that I'd discovered something significant and that I couldn't stop trying to create new beliefs. It could be done!

So, here I was, on a Friday night, contemplating the discoveries I'd made as they echoed in my mind. When I looked at my own behavior throughout my life, it'd been characterized primarily by self-control and by betting on the safe side. Rarely had I done anything that pushed boundaries. Could this behavior have lulled me into the mental state I was in too? I'd arrived at the belief that I should just accept that I was now visually impaired and that a direction had been set out for me, which I simply had to follow. That I should slowly wind things down and prepare myself for retirement. Now it dawned on me that I needed to step out of myself completely and change my way of thinking. *How do I do that?*

I had to break some of my old limitations and push myself further. I had to do something new. I had to enable my brain and my heart to perceive *me* in a new way. There are three vital ingredients that need to be present if you're going to reinvent yourself:

1. You have to change your thoughts about yourself—which is what I'd worked on in my thirty-day STOP! SWAP-THOUGHT challenge.
2. You have to learn new knowledge. Without

new knowledge, you won't know how to move forward.

3. You need to give yourself new experiences and change your old routines. New routines and experiences lead to new thoughts, which lead to new emotions, which lead to new subconscious programs, which lead to your new "SELF."

Based on experiences and sensory input (tastes, smells, sounds, sights and feeling/touching), the body sends constant feedback to the brain via neurotransmitters, and when it does, it makes you feel something. In other words, the end result of a new experience is a feeling, and if we're constantly experiencing the same things, then we always have the same feelings. I had to start creating experiences for myself that could help me have new thoughts, which could give me new emotions, which could make me feel strong, actionable, and like the master of my own life. It's the same as taking responsibility for yourself and your life.

Another thing that dawned on me was that I was always waiting for disaster to strike. I always expected something would go wrong. It might have had something to do with my visual impairment, because when you can't see, you try to compensate by always being prepared for every conceivable and unthinkable situation. And as 70 percent of our thoughts are negative (like I mentioned earlier in the book), I was now aware that I was spending far too much energy worrying.

One Friday night, while watching TV, I zapped past a documentary about parachutists, and a thought hit me: *What about doing a parachute jump?*

No, no, I hated heights, and I hadn't been in an amusement park since I was fifteen years old. Standing on a ladder or scaffold always made me feel as if the earth was pulling me down to it. But another thought came to me: If I did a parachute jump, I'd show myself that I could do everything I set out to do. I knew it was a powerful experience that would leave me with a great sense of victory and strength. And once that idea was formulated in my head, I decided that it should be implemented shortly afterward.

I wondered what the jump could do for me. Firstly, it would be a kind of rebirth; secondly, it was an opportunity to try out the techniques I'd learned through meditation and mindfulness. I was going to practice living in the NOW until I did the jump and focus solely on how great landing in the field, surrounded by my family would feel. What it would be like to feel intoxicating VICTORY.

I knew from earlier on in my life that excessive thinking and worries would feature prominently in the run-up to the jump, and via meditation and focusing on the NOW, I was going to try to observe the thoughts and not let them control me too much until the jump.

Thirdly, I was going to use this new experience—after all, a parachute jump is the ultimate challenge to FEAR—as an example for my everyday life, when I faced a challenge that seemed insurmountable. Once I'd jumped out of an airplane at an altitude of nearly three miles, other "big" problems would seem insignificant. I was going to use my experience as an antidote to trivial everyday problems that had so often occupied too much space on my worry scales.

The more I thought about this event, the more it became real to me in my mind's eye. Once again, I'd come up with an idea, and this time I was smarter about myself and my psyche. I wanted to go ahead with this craziness that would most definitely push and challenge the absolute limits of most people—myself included—and I was going to pay close attention to what was happening in my body while carrying out the idea.

It was clear from Mette's body language what she thought when I told her about my project—that I'd lost my mind. And I may well have if you were to compare my mind to the constant stream of thought in my monkey mind. I had lost my mind—the one that was identified with the flow of thought! It made complete sense to me. People could think whatever they wanted. However, Mette quickly changed her mind and supported me and my project.

After making the decision, we went to my parents for dinner, during which I told them about my idea. Horrified, my mother exclaimed, "You can't!" While my father exclaimed, "I'll do it with you!" And so, he did. I would just like to say that, at this point, my dad was seventy years old but still as agile as a forty-year-old, so the jump wasn't a physical challenge for him. He'd always dreamed of parachuting, and now the opportunity had presented itself. That very evening, I contacted the Skydive 2000 Parachute Club. Everything was agreed.

In the weeks leading up to the jump, I noticed how many times the "Voice" would try to talk me out of my mission—it was far more often than I'd imagined. But I spotted it immediately, because I'd learned from Challenge #1 to observe what the voice said. One day this thought came to me: *SHIT, my ears always pop on landing. What was going to happen when I jump out of an airplane nearly three miles up in the air and plunge to the ground at about 135 miles an hour?* I imagined my eardrums exploding in slow motion as I crashed to the ground screaming!

STOP! SWAP THOUGHTS! 1-2-3-4-5. Hmm, should I rewind that and rethink this scenario? Instead, I imagined it was going to be the greatest experience ever. I visualized the entire process from arriving at the airport, greeting the instructor, greeting my family, taking off in the airplane, slowly climbing up to the right altitude and, finally, jumping. And during the entire thought process, I made sure to associate only positive and happy thoughts with the experience. I created the whole experience in my mind and, thereby, created my reality. I decided this was one of the best experiences of my life. I vividly imagined the parachute jump had already happened and I tried to feel the feelings I wanted to have when I landed on the ground.

This was an entirely new way for me to prepare for future challenges and plan my reality. As opposed to always letting life happen to me at random, which meant letting my negative, fearful or prejudiced filters determine the outcome of my actions, I created my own reality for myself. I even imagined what the weather would be like. With an unpredictable summer, there was a huge chance of rain, but I imagined big fluffy clouds and blue skies.

Using my imagination, I visualized a picture I could remember from my childhood that had left a great impression on me. It was from the Walt Disney classic *Peter Pan*, where Peter and the Darling children are flying across London, and far below them, fantasy-like clouds hang like cotton wool in the sky. It was an enchanting childhood memory and now it had been brought back to life by my parachute jump.

Jump Day came, and the butterflies announced their arrival in my stomach. I tried to just observe and accept all my anxious thoughts and feelings instead of letting them control me. Whenever I registered a negative thought and feeling, I tried not to judge or evaluate it. I just registered it, hugged it with my thoughts and let it quietly pass out of my mind, like a cloud floating effortlessly by.

Feeling that I was in control of my mind was a fantastic experience. That I was better able to handle my thoughts and let them just be what they were: THOUGHTS. Fear never really took hold, because I saw fear as just a potential reality and *I* decided what my reality should be—not my feelings and thoughts. *I* could choose if I wanted to experience this jump as something to be afraid of, or as something to be excited about and look forward to. So, of course, I chose the latter. After all, the choice was mine. My thirty days of STOP! SWAP THOUGHTS had taught me that. I choose my perspective on the world: it can be dangerous and confusing, or it can be exciting and unexplored.

So now we found ourselves at the airport, where most of my family had turned up to see us jump. We were briefed and thoroughly instructed on how to do a tandem jump, and after twenty minutes we took off in the small airplane.

All day long, black clouds had been gliding threateningly across the sky, and there'd been several downpours. You may remember that I'd imagined a Peter Pan-sky and had replayed the movie many times in my mind while imagining the jump. And so, like magic, the weather changed to exactly what I'd imagined.

The weather was really glorious. There were amazing fluffy white clouds in a clear blue sky, and when we reached the three-mile altitude, we could see the Danish islands of Rømø on the right and Als on the left. Or rather, I took the instructor's word for it! He signaled that we should get ready to jump. My dad's instructor warned us that he was opening the door, and when he did, an ear-splitting noise and icy air blasted into the cabin. My dad was to jump first: one-two-three and he was gone. The butterflies started flapping in my stomach; I registered it immediately and just smiled at it. I thought, *this is going to be absolutely amazing. The experience of a lifetime.* We made our way to the opening and swung our legs out of the airplane. So now I was sitting on top of the instructor, with my legs over the edge, staring straight down at the clouds about a mile and a half below us, and the ground about three miles down.

Knowing that I could keep calm in this situation was an amazing experience. The instructor gently bent my head back and woosh—we were skydiving freely in the air. For the first few seconds, I alternated between seeing the airplane above me and the earth below me, but we soon leveled out to a stable position in the air, and now . . . WE WERE FLYING—as free as birds. Or as Buzz Lightyear exclaimed in *Toy Story*: "I'm not flying—I'm falling with style."

It was different to how I'd imagined. I'd thought it would feel like riding a roller coaster. That my stomach would do somersaults and maybe feel uncomfortable, but it was an entirely different experience. My body quickly got used to what was going on inside it. And once that happened, it was the ultimate feeling of freedom and happiness. I could see the clouds below me, and for a moment *I* was Peter Pan, flying over London. It was magical. It felt like lying softly on a big comfy pillow of wind with the whole wide world stretched out below. It was astounding. We were falling to the ground at a speed of nearly one hundred and forty miles per hour, and the dominant feeling was BLISS.

After fifty seconds, the instructor signaled that he was going to release the parachute. He supported my head again and pulled the cord. The speed stopped, as though an invisible handbrake had been pulled. This experience wasn't unpleasant either. Everything was quiet. From feeling the forceful wind resistance and the violent noise of the wind, everything now fell quiet and we hovered like eagles being carried on the wind. A sensory orgasm. One minute it was intense speed and noise, and the next, gentle gliding in complete silence; not a single thought filled my mind. It was an experience of being completely present in the now.

We descended through the clouds, large white balls of cotton wool floating gently in the air. A unique and exceptional visual encounter, which can only be experienced by falling freely with a parachute. With the help of the instructor, who patiently turned my head in the right direction, I caught sight of my father a little beneath me. It's a minor miracle that I even saw him in the vast atmosphere. Having only four degrees of vision means searching for things in the sky for a long time, but luckily, I managed to spot him quickly. He was hovering gently in the air, when his parachute suddenly pirouetted and plummeted in a downward spiral. And before I could think anymore about it, my parachute did the same. It was, of course, a controlled descent, and naturally, it gave an extra bang for our bucks, too. We rushed down in a spiral at forty-five miles an hour, and again I didn't experience any discomfort, just total freedom.

The ground rose to meet us, and we made ready for landing. My instructor yelled to me that he was going to let me go.

"WHAAAAAT?" I screamed in panic. Let me go? Was he mad?

"WHAT DO YOU MEAN LET ME GO?" I roared, slowly recalling the information we'd been given before the jump. He had actually explained that when we got close to the ground, he'd release me and let me hang a little further away from his body so that we wouldn't be tangled when we landed. I'd forgotten in my rush of adrenaline.

"OOH, YEAH. OKAY," I shouted back, trying to sound as calm as possible.

He pulled a strap and I dropped about five inches, wishing I'd thought a little more about this part of the jump when I was still on solid ground. In my confusion and lack of experience, I hadn't arranged my crown jewels properly, so when I landed hard in the harness, there was a tight clamp on my nether region. Ow, poor me. The instructor immediately spotted that something was wrong and thanks to HIS experience, knew straight away what was wrong, he shouted, "LIFT ONE LEG AND PULL THE STRAP . . ."

I interrupted him: "I'M NOT PULLING ANYTHING!"

He had to be crazy! Given the considerable height, I wasn't going to risk pulling anything that might send me plunging to the ground. It probably couldn't have happened, but there was no way I was taking any chances. I'd just have to live with pinched crown jewels for the next ten to fifteen minutes!

We'd practiced what was called "a sitting landing," and yes, it's exactly as described: a landing whereby you land on your rear end with your legs out in front of you as you glide across the grass. We approached the ground, and 1-2-3, solid ground under my bottom again. All the family present came to meet us, jeering and cheering as they filmed and took pictures. I had the greatest goofiest smile on my face—it'd been a truly amazing experience. Exactly what I'd imagined beforehand. I stood up, ready to manifest the next part of my visualization. The victory cry! But the manifestation project burst abruptly. Tremendous amounts of adrenaline were coursing through my body and I couldn't control my knees. They shook violently and felt like jelly. So, my victory roar was accompanied with wobbly knees and must have looked rather comical. About twenty seconds later, my dad got ready to land, which he did perfectly on both legs with a smile as big as mine. He looked like a small child who'd just gotten their first blue bike with a squeeze-bulb horn, chrome bell and twenty exterior gears on the cog.

Parachuting was an incredible experience, and instead of it being something I'd a reason to fear, it ended up being one of the greatest experiences of my life. The jump taught me a vital lesson: the body will almost always resist experiencing what is new and pushing beyond your limits because the subconscious mind will try to direct you toward the safe and the predictable. And so, we miss out on many possibilities and experiences in life. If we let familiar thoughts/feelings win—the "this-doesn't-feel-right-thought"—then we'll never experience anything new, and we'll never create new lasting neuropathways in the brain, which are the prerequisite for new behavior.

And so, we continue living according to old well-known programs that feel secure because these programs give you the neurotransmitters that you've become familiar with and addicted to.

Based on my research, I now knew that the only way I could change the routines and habits of my old "SELF" was to challenge them constantly. I learned that I could overcome the resistance in myself by, first, lovingly deciding to and then actually doing it. In reality—not just in my mind. *You can't get wet from the word 'water'.*

Similarly, I learned not to let past experiences slow me down in pursuing new goals and ideas in the future. Worrying about a potential future that may never come only hinders my ability to freely do what I really want. If my old self's prejudice against new, unknown challenges had been allowed to decide, I'd never have jumped out of that plane. I would have allowed caution and fear to triumph and I'd have told myself that it was probably for the best. That I could just do it next year. That it was just a stupid idea. This is what the body/voice makes you think every time you consider possibilities that aren't supported in the subconscious. If I'd let the fearful body decide, what would I have learned and experienced as a result of that decision? Zilch! The only outcome would have been the confirmation of my own inadequacy. I realized I had to seek out more of these kinds of experiences and start teaching myself that I can do everything I set out to do as long as I decide to.

Challenge #3
It's embarrassing to be visually impaired!
Mastering LIMITATION

"Having a disability and having to ask other people for help is embarrassing. It's humiliating and exposes my weakness."

That was one of my limiting beliefs. This is how I felt about my visual disability. It was a belief that often kept me from jumping into new experiences—what if I got myself into a situation where I needed other people's help? So, the next challenge was to tackle that limitation and demonstrate that I can do exactly what I want and that the only thing it demands of me is to decide to do it and resist the urge to seek safety.

Whatever exercise I came up with had to be something that many people would consider crazy and that would break the norms of ordinary behavior. It was to teach me not to be so focused on what other people think about me, which is the underlying limitation. The fear of standing out and breaking with the norm evokes a feeling of insecurity, and that uncertainty keeps us in our old patterns, which are, in turn, determined by societal norms. Social norms, which are perhaps just waiting for someone to be the first person to decide to break! Reinventing yourself and venturing down new paths will always be associated with some insecurity because we can no longer predict the outcome with certainty.

But what was I supposed to come up with? Inspired by a guy on YouTube, I decided that the boundary-pushing action was to lie down, flat on my back, on the sidewalk in a crowded city area and quietly count to thirty, while people crowded around me. They'd surely start to wonder what kind of a strange man was lying down in the middle of the pavement, and it was my job to be completely indifferent to what the "Voice" would yell at me during those thirty seconds. For example: *They think I'm weird! Will anyone call the police because they think I'm dead or mentally ill? Will anyone recognize me?* and so on.

It was an outrageous idea that sounded very innocent and simple, but I discovered that it pushed the limits so much that several attempts were needed before I was able to get myself to actually carry it out.

One day, when I was standing at the station waiting for my bus, I decided now was the time. The waiting room of the train and bus station was crowded with people, milling around the large waiting area. When I thought, *"I'm going to do it now,"* a chain reaction of old, unconscious programs started to automatically play out in my body — as I knew they absolutely would. Now I could observe how I reacted so that I could learn from the experience.

The thoughts started: *You can't, Morten. People will think you're weird. Some people might think you've fainted or that you're a drunken madman, sleeping off the stupor. Maybe someone you know will see you and what will they think?*

And, of course, these fearful thoughts unleashed the familiar release of neurotransmitters in the body to make it feel in line with the thoughts going through my head. So, my body now responded by vigorously protesting my plan. The subconscious started its program: "You-must-not-stand-out-or-make-yourself-a-laughing-stock-Morten." Adrenaline and cortisol began to coarse through my body, making my hands clammy.

I felt the same way I did heading into an oral math exam back in 1993 (which I failed), and it wasn't a nice feeling. The body remembers! But I wasn't in 1993 right now, despite that being what my body seemed to believe. I was at a bus station in Vejle in 2017, and my body was about to give everything to spare me from yet another humiliating math exam. But there was no danger. I was standing completely still in the waiting room, THINKING only that I was now about to do the exercise. I thought only about lying down in the middle of the hall and counting to thirty. And it was the thought alone of doing it that sent my body into a state of panic.

When you think about it, it's an inappropriate, exaggerated and, often, limiting reaction we get from the body when we plunge into what is boundary-pushing, challenging and/or different from the usual. And that is why we don't tend to seek out our limits. It feels wrong. Yet it makes sense at the same time. The body tries to take care of itself by avoiding problems that threaten its existence. But this defense mechanism often obstructs and hinders our dreams and desires. We wish we could just jump into new adventures and challenges, but a plethora of sensations stop us. It's the body's defense mechanism against unforeseen and "dangerous" events, and they impede our free development.

This exercise was an excellent example of when the activation of the body's defense mechanisms is completely unnecessary. The deeper meaning of this was, of course, that involving other people in my vision problems and asking someone for help when I needed it, pushed my limits. I always reacted the same way: my body resisted and refused to renounce its secret—the secret that I'd been training it not to reveal for years! Asking someone for help to solve problems related to my disability was the same as admitting that I was disadvantaged and disabled. Just thinking about asking other people for help always resulted in sweaty hands and coursing adrenaline. This defense mechanism was so distinct and integrated into my personality that it also applied to other areas and times of my life. Despite my job at the LEGO Group entailing frequent presentations and having to speak in front of assemblies, it was a challenge to my limits every single time.

The symptoms were always the same whenever I had to ask someone for help. I had to show my body and, thereby, my subconscious mind that together we could easily overcome these challenges. With my new program of being my own best friend and my inner voice now supporting me and motivating me instead of scolding and despising me, I was going to try to overcome the subconscious mind with the proper amount of self-love and inner motivation.

But why did I think it was embarrassing to reveal my disability? Exposing yourself pushes boundaries! One day, I was contacted by the University of Copenhagen, who, in collaboration with Oxford University in England, was developing special eyewear for people with visual impairments. This eyewear was particularly suitable for people with RP. It had a little camera and could project an image on the inside of the two lenses. My challenge is often that when objects and people get too close, I can only see a little of what is in front of me because my field of vision is so limited. If I look at a person from the distance of a foot and a half, I can see only one eye or a nose. If I could "zoom" the person further away, I'd be able to see more of their face.

Sure, they'd be smaller, but I'd better be able to form an

overall image. These glasses could do exactly that, so when the University of Copenhagen called and asked if I wanted to be a guinea pig, I immediately said "Yes!" The trial run was to take place in a huge supermarket. I had to go around the store with the glasses on, shopping as I normally did—which is pretty hard for me as I can't see such a large area. While I was shopping, a university researcher was going to film me so later they could study both my and other people's behaviors and reactions.

It went well. I managed to pick up a few things and went to the checkout line. I placed the items on the conveyor belt and waited. In front of me was an elderly lady, and in her boredom, she now turned her focus on me.

"What are you wearing, young man?" she asked outspokenly.

I politely replied: "They're glasses to help the visually impaired . . ."

I wasn't allowed to say any more. A strange expression came over the lady's face. It was as if the word "disabled" had flicked a switch in her. She turned and stood directly in front of me, stretched out her arm and lay a flat hand on my chest—perhaps to signal "HERE I AM."

Then she practically shouted, "IT'S GREAT THAT THEY'RE DOING SO MUCH FOR YOU DISABLED PEOPLE!"

I was not only blind to this elderly lady—she seemed to have concluded I was also deaf.

It wasn't a pleasant experience, which is why it's hard for me to accept having to use a cane or wear a badge. I don't want to attract attention.

I stood in the waiting room, took a deep breath, and closed my eyes. *You can do it, you can do it, you can do it.* I felt my knees starting to bend, but at the same time, my legs refused to obey. Instead, they started to shake, and my heart galloped like a racehorse. The entire drama played out in my head. I'm sure no one could see this inner drama if they looked at me. Well, damn it—the drama I experienced was just a phenomenon in my own mind. It wasn't a real problem. And here is a crucial discovery that you should try to mull over.

As I've explained several times, we often believe that we are our thoughts and that our thoughts are our reality. They can be so powerful that they make the body think that our imagined catastrophes are real, which is why we experience these disasters as real. But they're only real because our thoughts send neurotransmitters to the body signaling a dangerous situation. Can you remember the story of the captain on his bridge? He is the only one who can see the world out there and he gives orders and information to the crew (body/subconscious). If he's confused and guided by his thoughts, his emotions, and his past, he'll continue to confirm his bad decisions for his crew, and the ship will end up in the wrong harbor. That's what happened to me right there in the waiting room. So, if, as a captain, I can learn to keep my head cool and respond realistically to the challenges I face, I can make my crew do what I would like them to do.

Well, back to the waiting room at the station. I was sweating and my heart was pounding, but *yeeaah, do it, Morten, do it.* I was ready. It was now and . . . and . . . and then the bus came! Rescued by Line 43. I immediately stopped my knees from carrying out the mission and started walking quickly toward the bus. Ha ha—I had to admit being saved by the bus there, and as I sat on it, reflecting on the experience, I thought: *You couldn't do it, Morten.* It was shocking to discover how hard it was to lie down on the floor just because it would be considered abnormal and people might look. And because my body had a built-in mechanism that stopped me from doing embarrassing things that could damage my image—my ego—the constructed identity that was to be preserved at any cost.

It was an important lesson and something I came to ponder for a while. How often did I say no to new possibilities just because my body sent unconscious signals that they were "dangerous"? Think about that for a moment before you read my—probably predictable—answer to that question. The only way to notice these unconscious reactions is by being present in the now; by observing the subconscious mind with your conscious awareness. And do you remember that we're only consciously aware five percent of the time? So, 95 percent of the time, you never realize you're letting your autopilot—your learned programs—decide how you act in the present, which affects the future you create. If I were honest, that it's certainly what happened every time something challenged my eyesight issues, and I was going to put an end to that. Once and for all!

Once on the bus, I hurried to remind myself that I was just practicing for now, and that every attempt, thought or action, would be rewarded with inner acknowledgment and love. So now as I sat on the bus heading to work, I patted myself on the shoulder for having "failed" in my attempt. For, just the thoughts and experiences gained were proof that I was now embarking on an important process in my attempt to reinvent myself and become happy in my life situation as a visually impaired person. I was now regularly and lovingly challenging my own old limiting beliefs.

In fall 2017, Mette, Mikkel, Rasmus and I went on a four-day trip to London to experience the big city together. Before leaving, I decided that when we got to London, I was going to do the challenge in a heavily populated area of the capital. I told the others my idea and everyone thought it sounded both fun and ridiculous.

Mikkel, my youngest son, decided he was going to do the challenge with me. And, one day, while visiting Westminster Abbey, Mikkel and I decided it was time. In fact, it was Mette who reminded us of our project. So, there was no way around it. We looked at each other and said, "it's now or never," and then resolute, we walked out into the middle of the pavement on Parliament Square in Westminster, in central London, at two o'clock in the middle of a busy afternoon. Before we could think anymore about it, we lay down smiling, and looked up at the big gray-white clouds above us and began to count.

It was fun this time because I'd no danger signals in my body. I'd used the experience from the bus station at home to convince myself that this was completely and utterly harmless and my body now seemed to accept it. Maybe because my determination was strong. Deciding to do something abnormal and a bit strange, and then experience the feeling that it was fun and totally okay was a fantastic rush.

We counted to thirty together as people walked around us to get past on the sidewalk. There were people with dogs and prams, and afterward, in the video Mette recorded, we saw that no one had paid any particular notice to the two strange people from Denmark who'd come in on the four o'clock train and were now lying on the pavement in their city. Just think. This boundary-pushing act, which was what I'd thought lying on the sidewalk in a populated area was, turned out to be only "dangerous" in my head. When I carried out the "dangerous" act with my son Mikkel, it turned out that people were completely unaffected and indifferent—which begs the question: how often are we constrained by limitations that exist solely in our minds?

As I lay there on the sidewalk, I could hear the voices of my parents and elementary school teachers saying, *"You can't do that, Morten, get up now."* I just smiled at the admonishing remarks and stayed where I was.

I can do, whatever I want to, said my inner voice in resolute answer to the admonitions.

Twenty-seven, twenty-eight, twenty-nine, thirty . . . We got up laughing and gave each other a high-five for completing the challenge and continued on toward the London Eye. I smiled to myself. In reality, the only limitations I encounter in life are the ones I create in my mind!

Challenge #4
Morten Bonde: Motivational Speaker

The fourth challenge was, in fact, something that had been resonating in my mind for months. It was actually the first challenge I thought of. The new knowledge I had gained from listening to books from amazing authors and watching lectures on YouTube was so motivating and overwhelming.

Their ability to convey their knowledge in an exciting and captivating way motivated me, too. I was intrigued by how words and ideas could inspire and develop other people. What a skill and positive influence to have on people and the world. I experienced that I was able to change my old firmly established limiting beliefs and my old programs, and I really wanted to share my knowledge with others. Share with others that what we think and focus on becomes the reality we experience. *We become what we think about.* I felt like I'd discovered a secret that everyone should know: that the subconscious mind and our autopilot control our lives, and that a lack of awareness and focus prevents us from living the lives we want. Becoming super aware of these "secrets" was key to my development and transformation. At first, it was just fascinating knowledge and philosophy; later, it became the belief that I could put that knowledge into practice in my own life. Having read quite a few books, I knew that I could only complete my project if I practiced what I'd learned. Not just as a philosophy, but as deeds in my own life.

If I was going to teach my body not to panic and react to my old learned habits and patterns every time I faced a sight challenge, it was going to require practice and plenty of repetition. I'd taught myself to motivate myself with positive self-talk, I'd taught myself to meditate and be mindful and I'd learned that the subconscious mind needs to be influenced through repetition. So, I needed a project to put this into practice.

I'd experienced time and time again in my career as an art director that if I wanted to learn a new graphic program, just reading the manual was of no use. I might be able to learn many of the features off by heart, but that never taught me how to use the program creatively and freely. There was only one way for me to get to know a program: I had to have a concrete project to try it out and practice—a project where I learned through repetition and my mistakes. This is how the idea of the four challenges came to me.

I thought: *Morten, kill two birds with one stone. You're encouraged by speakers who motivate and inspire people, and being able to do that, too, has become your dream. And you know, Morten—if you're going to implement this new knowledge in your life, then you need to put it into practice.*

Actually, I had to do more than practice. The idea of wanting to see possibilities instead of limitations needed to become an obsession. I had to be obsessed with the idea of leaving Hopelessness Street and finding Possibility Road, and I had to be obsessed with the idea of becoming a speaker.

I don't think anyone else quite understood why I was so obsessed with the idea of giving lectures and writing a book, but that mission was my way of teaching myself to see possibilities through a goal that could be accomplished in my real life. Not only that, though. Every waking hour —and even when I wasn't awake—I was going to dream about it. It was going to be an obsession! And it was!

Challenge #4 went as follows: "Give a lecture at the LEGO Group in English to all my colleagues, about how I moved from Hopelessness Street to Possibility Road." And notice how the phrase is formulated. It's worded in such a way that it sounds like the transformation has *already happened*. It hadn't actually happened by this point in time. I hadn't yet completed any of my challenges. I'd only just started consuming piles of books on HOW to do this, but I still hadn't implemented it in my life. I was still ON Hopelessness Street. But I phrased the sentence that way, so it was clear that I'd already reached my goal.

I created the feeling of having achieved my goal before I'd accomplished it. It was about creating the feeling in the body and "becoming familiar with" (the Tibetan definition of meditation) how it would feel to have achieved the goal I'd set for myself. Once I was able to create that feeling of success and nourish my mind with thoughts that could evoke this feeling, the subconscious would, at some point, think this was actually the new reality and then it would start working *for* me and not against me.

The subconscious mind always obeys what you suggest it should obey, but it only does so if you really implement it. And it does it objectively—so it doesn't judge whether or not it's a good idea or is right for you. When you can create the reality that you want to be in with your thoughts and feelings, then the subconscious mind will work to achieve that reality.

And if you tell your subconscious mind that you've already accomplished the goal every day in meditation, it'll slowly become your new reality. "YOU ARE WHAT YOU THINK ABOUT!"

I decided that within the next four months I was going to give my first lecture on my great transformation and my journey there. I didn't put any pressure on myself, and I allowed myself to make mistakes in the project. If I failed or didn't have the lecture ready in time, the attempt and all my efforts would still be a success in themselves. And nothing I'd learned in the process would ever be taken away from me again. Just having a goal and working toward it was a success.

It was all about training my subconscious mind to accept new programs and to see possibilities where before I saw only limitations. While executing my first three challenges, I used my new tools. I meditated and was as present in the now as I possibly could be. And I trained myself to overcome myself as I documented the entire process— in this book and the lecture I developed, It was a way for me to remember and store all the important information I'd gathered. I kept thinking that, at some point, I'd have to tell people about all my learning and experiences, so it was important for me to remember them, to record them and to think about how to convey them. So, I spent many of my walks formulating sentences and explanations of my discoveries and experiences. Thus, the four months became an intense, fun and inspiring time of preparation for Challenge #4—though all this groundwork was really just training to be a new version of ME. The pending lecture became a way of motivating myself to persist in changing my habits and thoughts.

Something else that I experienced over the four months was that my colleagues and friends were very inspired by and interested in what I told them when I shared my project with them. Again and again, I experienced that my knowledge of our subconscious and conscious minds—the idea that we become what we think—was really something that got people thinking. It was something many people had never thought or heard about. Whenever I talked to colleagues one-on-one, they quickly showed interest and listened to what I had to say. Gradually, I became convinced that what I had to say was worth listening to, and that motivated me to talk about it more. I shared my knowledge and it strengthened my adherence to my new core beliefs and way of being. Instead of only *thinking* of the new philosophies, I *BECAME* the new philosophies.

I was going to learn how to be a speaker and I started watching TEDx lectures — a forum where the world's best speakers give their inspirational talks on innovation and new ideas. I knew that if I was going to be good at giving lectures, I'd have to practice and do it again and again and again. That's how to teach the subconscious mind new programs and behaviors, but I also now knew that I was able to prepare myself in an entirely different way. Meditation enabled me to prepare mentally. And so, my new routine was to imagine that I was giving the lecture, and each time it ended brilliantly. I visualized giving the talk, saying everything I wanted to say, and eventually receiving a standing ovation. The more I thought these thoughts, the more I looked forward to it happening. I gave my body a taste of what a good experience it would be; I didn't focus on what could go wrong. I focused only on all the positive aspects of my plan. It quickly dawned on me that this was the most demanding of the four challenges!

As described before, I'd given many presentations and I felt uncomfortable every time. Part of my job was to present in an entertaining and inspirational way, but I was always unhealthily nervous before my presentations. My body was stressed and, most of all, I wanted to flee screaming. Once I'd forced myself to do what my body was fighting against me doing—giving the presentation—then 99 percent of the time it went really well and I, subsequently, felt an amazing sense of victory. And my skills in presenting and inspiring were affirmed.

But it was something I always forgot when I went to make another presentation. It was weird—you'd have thought, that at some point, the subconscious would have learned not to be nervous. The problem was that I never consciously and purposefully tried to change the automatic reactions that were evoked just before a presentation. I always thought about what could go wrong. I sensed the insidious nervousness and my hands getting clammy, and that reaction caused me to get angry with myself. *Why the hell are you getting nervous now, Morten? It's the same every time! Pull yourself together, you wimp.*

And the more the inner voice was allowed to play bad coach, the more my body reacted with uncertainty. My heart began pounding hard and the voice said: *Stop bloody well pounding!*

But the more the voice terrorized, the more viciously my body reacted.

My willpower and fear of failure had to deal with the situation then: *You have to do it, Morten. People are waiting and you can't afford to disappoint them.*

My perfectionism, and my belief that I was only good if I competently delivered a satisfactory presentation, enabled me to collect myself enough to go out on stage and complete the mission—and almost always without anyone discovering my inner struggle.

I think many people can recognize themselves in what I describe here. Psychologists and scientists in the USA conducted a study to identify what Americans were most afraid of, and 40 percent of respondents had "dying" in third place, while "public speaking in front of an assembly" came in at number one! Wow! Think about that for a moment—people would rather die than speak in public. I suspect the situation would be a little different if you asked those people the same question while they were hanging in the abyss, but in their minds, public speaking was the worst thing that could befall them.

When people talk about being nervous before giving a presentation or performing in some way, I have often experienced people's response to be "without nerves and butterflies in your stomach, you can't perform optimally." When Danish folk singer Kim Larsen died, I watched an old interview with him on TV, where he mentioned always having the same routine before going on stage. He said, "A few hours before the concert, I get really nervous and feel really bad, and when I get on stage it all goes away and I really enjoy playing music. The next day, when I go back on stage, it all starts over again."

I recognized myself in his words when I had to make

a presentation at work; I'd just accepted that this is how it was because even professionals feel this way! So, if you didn't feel your stomach churning before a performance, you wouldn't be able to give your absolute best. So, you just had to accept that fear was the motivation that could drive you toward your goals!

Having to accept what is happening NOW is not the same as not influencing how the next NOW develops. First, it's about accepting things as they are now, without judging or denying them. And then it's up to *you* to learn from these things NOW and to decide what the next NOW should be. This is how you create your life.

For instance, one day you discover that you're practically a permanent resident of Hopelessness Street, but that you'd like to find Possibility Road. You're neither denying nor judging your current presence on Hopelessness Street; you're acknowledging it with your conscious awareness. Without judging that you're on Hopelessness Street, you can now celebrate and praise yourself for discovering that you no longer want to stay there. And you can calmly and gradually figure out how you're going to reach Possibility Road instead. There's no judgment or criticism for not having yet made it to Possibility Road. Only love for yourself, that you have realized it and want to do something about it—NOW. You find that you're no longer willing to be a victim in your own life, but the creator of your own life.

Equipped with my new knowledge of mindfulness and meditation, and how the psyche works, I was now able to use this mindfulness trick. Instead of fighting the situation I found myself in—getting so frustrated that my body would start emitting warning signals—I now accepted instead that they were there and that it was okay. I accepted the Now, as it was, without trying to fight it, for the more I tried to fight it, the more I nourished it. *"The wolf you feed is the wolf that wins."* And so, I developed a new strategy.

All pressure was going to be removed from my lecture, and I was going to make sure that the inner voice became my friend—not my enemy—on this mission. When the day of the lecture at LEGO came, I was obviously nervous, which was fine. I was about to give a lecture to forty people in English on something very personal, something I'd never spoken about in public before. This forum was, in a way, allowing me to exhibit the limiting thoughts that had haunted me for years. I was going to expose my weaknesses, reveal my visual impairment, and I didn't know how I—or the audience—would react, so, naturally, I was nervous. My colleagues only knew the side of me where I acted as though I had everything under control. I didn't, and that illusion was about to be broken in public! GULP!

All morning, I could feel the nervousness in my body, but like I'd done when I was about to jump from an altitude of nearly three miles, I was always able to spot the nervousness and put it into perspective. *What's the worst that can happen, Morten? Remember, they all like you and they're all wishing you well. You're being very brave and cool, and nothing can change that.*

People arrived, and sat expectantly and smiling, waiting for me to commence my lecture. I got everything ready, and then I began. My heart pounded and my voice shook a little as I said, "Welcome, and thanks for being here."

I was off—I continued like this: "Three things could happen today. One, I might forget everything I'd prepared to say today, and I'll stand up here, stammering my way through the lecture. Or two, I might break down sobbing, because everything I'm going to share with you today is super personal. Or three, everything will go really well, and you'll leave here inspired on how to move on from a difficult life situation and once again be able to see this amazing life we've been given. I hope, of course, that it's option number three we're going to experience today, but if it ends up being one of the other possibilities, then that' okay too. The very fact that I'm standing here talking to you at all is a victory for me."

And after I'd said that I felt a huge weight fall away from my shoulders. I could now just be myself without having to perform or try to be someone other than myself.

I could sense people squirming a little uneasily in their chairs when I talked about breaking down. But—ha ha—luckily, that didn't happen!

The lecture was a success. People were inspired and I got a lot of subsequent inquiries from people who were surprised at how I'd managed so well for so long with such poor eyesight and how inspired they were by how I handled it. Some people inquired about what books I'd read. My great fear of jumping out from the "blind closet" turned out to be a great relief.

I'd faced all my challenges—so now what?

A new core belief: Retinitis Pigmentosa isn't what limits me!

It's now clearly evident to me that my efforts to change my way of seeing my world, reality and myself have borne fruit. I can see a distinct difference in my everyday life in both how I perceive it and the people I meet in it. All the challenges I had in my life—my stress, my depression and my problems—were mostly self-created. And an even more important realization came to light:

It's not my ability to see with my eyes that determines

whether I'll lead a good life. The way I choose to handle it does. The way I take responsibility for it.

And this discovery freed — and frees — me. I'm no longer the visually impaired person facing a dark future. No, I'm the person who decides how he wants to be, and my life is exactly what I decide it to be. With or without an eye disorder. Blaming my visual impairment for not living my life the way I want it is a grotesque misunderstanding that I've held on to — for far too many years.

I've now stopped thinking that I'm limited. I take responsibility for my life and I control my destiny myself. I'm no longer a victim of my disappearing eyesight — I'm free and I know that the only limitations I have are created in my mind. I now know that my attitude toward my problems is what always determines how great they become. Problems are no longer problems; they're challenges I can deal with if I don't categorize them as good or bad. They're just there and if I view them with openness and curiosity, they become fascinating challenges that I can learn from.

It's a major paradigm shift, and it enables me to say yes to possibilities that I'd never have voluntarily agreed to. I inspire my two boys and a lot of other people, and I'm grateful for everything that my wife Mette does on her own, now that I can no longer drive a car. I dare to look my life situation in the eye. I can look openly at everything and perceive the world as a playground where anything can be done if I just dare to allow it.

What I choose to focus on and think about becomes my life. I meet people with a beginner's mind, and I've stopped interpreting what people say to me. I've stopped taking responsibility for the feelings, attitudes and actions of others. I can now keep an open mind and not interpret too much of the sensory input I get from my outside world. I try to judge neither that nor the people through the filters I created over time to keep my secret and my identities. It enables me to perceive the familiar in a new way. Old prejudices and attitudes can always be overturned.

What I focus on and think about becomes my reality! I may well lose my eyesight and go blind, but I am significantly more than my eyes and my eyesight—I am what I decide to be. So, with a changed perspective, I can now look back at the life I've lived and view it with a completely different pair of eyes. In reality, I've done something quite remarkable.

Where I once saw a limited man struggling through life, I now see a pretty awesome man who works with visual communication at LEGO and manages a busy life with only four degrees of vision! I now see everything that I've created and lived through from a new perspective. I think of all the campaigns I created—as someone who is legally blind! It's absurd that I was unable to see how amazing and unique that is. Imagine that I was ashamed of being ME instead of being proud. I recognize that now. I've gotten a new perspective. I've gotten a new inner voice. I've made my way to Possibility Road!

I can now look at my boys and be proud of how they're developing and how amazing they are, and I am so grateful and happy to have them. I can look at my wife Mette with brand new eyes. I've always loved her, and now I can see even more clearly just how unique she is. I'm now able to see the gift that my life is and how amazing it is. That overshadows all the sadness. The light is now far stronger than the dark. I'm slowly going blind, yes, but I've changed my view of losing my sight. It's no longer so tragic. It just IS. I accept it now without trying to fight the emotions and thoughts it evokes. And that act of surrendering to what is, dissolves the struggle.

I don't need my eyes to see how amazing my life is. It's a gift and I'm going to live it and be grateful for it every single day. The irony is that I had to lose my eyesight before I could see that.

I've been given a gift in the form of a visual disability that has enlightened me and taught me that my life is precious. Something many people may only realize when it's too late—if they realize it at all—but I've discovered it in my mid-forties. I become what I think!

A long and exciting life lies ahead of me that needs to be lived to the full and I look forward to every second of it. More than ever before. THANKS FOR TEACHING ME TO SEE, RETINITIS PIGMENTOSA.

Six Steps to Possibility Road

I've learned a lot on my journey from Hopelessness Street to Possibility Road, which others may only learn in a lifetime, and I'd like to share with you six important experiences I had along the way. It's a kind of summary—I use these six experiences as a guide in my life. And I hope, of course, that by reading my book you can take some of its messages with you into your life and your world.

Step #1
Become aware of who you are, where you are in your life, find your life goal and decide to realize it!

Only when I was able to recognize that I was stuck in life, and then defined my life goal, "Despite RP, I want to live a happy life and see possibilities rather than limitations," was I able to set a course for myself. Only then was I able to focus my efforts on something tangible. Writing my life goal down on paper was the first vital step in reaching Possibility Road.

Step #2

Stop fighting. Accept where you are NOW and then move on. NOW is the only thing that exists!

I noticed that I never really lived in the now—my thoughts and my focus were often somewhere in the past or the future. I realized that the only thing that actually exists is the NOW, and fighting it by not accepting it as it is, is futile and, in reality, a battle against life itself. Surrendering to the isness of now enabled me to accept that I was losing my eyesight, and thereby let go of thoughts about why I was the one who inherited this eye disorder. And let go of thoughts about what life would have been like if I hadn't developed the condition. By letting go of these thoughts, I went from being a victim to taking responsibility for my life. I could see the wonderful life right in front of me—and it was absolutely amazing and unique as it was.

Step #3

The subconscious mind controls our lives!

I discovered that our subconscious mind controls our lives. That we are very much a collection of learned and repeated programs that run automatically for 95 percent of our waking hours. And that most of the programs in our subconscious come from other people and were created during the first seven years of our lives. Knowing this, it no longer makes sense to blame ourselves for not living the life we wish for. Instead, it makes sense to acknowledge yourself for wanting to change the automatic programs with your conscious awareness, and that this can be done through repetition and meditation. The subconscious mind and the automatic programs can be changed, and that realization means there are no limits for what we can achieve in life. We just have to decide to change the programs that limit us and create new "possibility" programs.

Step #4
You are what you think. Decide to change your thoughts with new experiences!

I discovered that my thoughts and my focus revolved constantly around my limitations and problems. By continuously focusing on them, I gave them sustenance and life. By focusing on them, I couldn't create space to see all the good in my life. My thoughts were focused on everything that could go wrong; not on everything I could create and achieve. Teaching myself to focus on what I'd like to do in my life, instead of on what I didn't think I could do, was another vital step toward changing course from Hopelessness Street to Possibility Road. Teaching my body to take new chances evoked new emotions and feelings, which gave birth to new thoughts. I got off the "think-feel-think" circle.

"You can't get wet from the word 'water'!" – *Alan Watts*

"We can't solve problems by using the same kind of thinking we used when created them." – *Albert Einstein*

Step #5
How you experience your world is YOUR choice. You decide that with your attitude and perspective.

How we see the world, our lives and the people in it is our own choice. How we choose to look at an illness or other unhappy conditions of life is also our choice. I noticed that I was always quick to determine whether a situation was good or bad, whether a person was nice or not-so-nice, whether the weather was good or bad. Once I realized that these labels were, in fact, my own filters, I decided to use a positive filter.

All the problems, people and conditions in our lives are exactly what we decide them to be. We don't think we have that choice, but it's the greatest realization you can make. We ourselves choose, and I decided that the people I meet in my life are beautiful, lovely and gracious; that problems are opportunities to learn and that the conditions of my life are okay as they are, exactly as they are presented to me at all times.

In reality, I've discovered that we don't have to seek out Possibility Road, because you can't arrive where you already are. Nothing in the materialistic world has changed on my journey to MY Possibility Road. The only thing that has changed is my perspective on the world and the way I now think. Happiness and joy can't be found in the future. They're here right now. You just have to teach yourself to see them—NOW.

Step #6

We are the stories we tell ourselves and other people about ourselves. If you change the story, you change your life!

The stories we tell ourselves again and again about ourselves become our life stories. The more we repeat them, the more integrated they become in our subconscious mind—our personality. These stories are our own creations, based on our past and our desires for the future, and once I was able to put my past, present and future into perspective, I was able to create a new story. That's the story you've just read, and it's just a story. It's my perspective, and it could have been told in countless other ways. I decided that my story is about a man who is about to lose his eyesight, but who decided to change course from a life in the shade on murky Hopelessness Street to a life in the warm bright sunlight on Possibility Road.

Becoming One

Tuesday, December 19, 2017:
A late night in December. I'd just given my first lecture at the LEGO Group and I was sitting in front of the computer writing about the experience and my thoughts upon completing the fourth challenge. Having completed the four challenges was a crazy feeling—I was on a total high and was happy to have overcome myself on so many points. The Letter Men came to mind. I hadn't heard from them for a while. Not since Mr. P had encouraged me to turn my thoughts into reality—to translate my new philosophies into action in my life.

It had gone tremendously well. The last four months had been life-changing. I couldn't help but smile at all the new sensory input. Now, I understand absolutely that if changes are to happen in your life, you have to decide it's going to happen, once and for all, and then act on it! New knowledge had motivated new actions, which had, in turn, created new thoughts, which had then given new feelings, which had created new programs that had now become new core beliefs.

I reviewed the outline for my book and could now see my journey through the years in the chapter titles. I realized there and then that I'd done what most people said was impossible: to change their habits and patterns of reaction and to create a new, better "SELF." I thought about that statement—maybe it wasn't right to say, "a new, better 'SELF'" but rather "a new 'SELF' better aligned with my wishes and goals for my life."

I had genuinely changed course from Hopelessness Street to Possibility Road, and I wanted to hold even more lectures on this topic. I thought my experience might benefit others. Others with challenges in life or people who just needed a road map to find the way to change course from their Hopelessness Streets to their Possibility Roads.

I reflected over what had happened over the past few months and I felt a relieved joy deep inside me. Something had happened to me. I no longer had the old familiar feeling of deep-seated sadness, which I'd realized had lived in me for years. The critical voice was no longer critical and reproachful, but positive and motivating.

I'd learned to see possibilities rather than limitations, and my new way of being and thinking had changed something deep in me. I was no longer afraid of losing my eyesight. I was grateful for my life and the people around me whom I love and value even more than ever before. I was happy for life's little miracles that I'd never noticed or appreciated before. Little things, like when a stranger gives you a heart-warming smile; the wind blustering around my bald head; leaves dancing little spirals in the wind; clouds forming amazing paintings in the sky.

They are miracles. Everything is a miracle. Life is a miracle. I could — and can — see that clearly now.

Oh, the irony: I had to lose my sight before I could see how beautiful and amazing life is. Being sentenced to blindness taught me to see. It was almost as if the universe had realized that this man from Denmark, who was so engrossed in the thoughts of his little universe, his thought-created problems, his disability, needed precisely a disability or a shock to his monotonous one-track life to see how amazing it all really is. I was deeply grateful and actually quite happy. Christmas was coming and I was glad.

It was while focused on these thoughts that my computer screen flashed, and a little dialog box appeared on the screen.

Hello Morten. It's time to meet. Meet us in the Koldinghus Tower tomorrow at midnight. There is no need to bring the manuscript. Just yourself and remember to wear warm clothes!

I'd long stopped being surprised by these messages appearing on my screen, phone or elsewhere. I'd grown accustomed to them and, once again, couldn't help but smile at the huge realization I'd made through my research as well as through my challenges — that determined repetition can rewrite our habits and beliefs.

I thought about whether Mr. N had returned and caught myself actually missing him. Something about him reminded me of myself. Somehow, all three Letter Men felt like they were a part of me. I shut down the thought, deciding it was bedtime. Tomorrow was going to be a long day with work and my meeting with the Letter Men. I needed sleep.

The next night, a few minutes before midnight, I was traipsing my way up the long staircase in the nearly 250-foot-high tower above the Banqueting Hall of the more than 750-year-old Koldinghus Castle. It was a crystal-clear crispy frost December night and I was excited about my meeting with the Letter Men. Had Mr. N returned and why didn't they want to see my manuscript? I was no longer nervous at heading into these meetings. I was calm and confident that I could cope with whatever situation I ended up in. I was no longer so dependent on knowing what was going to happen when new challenges reared their heads. I'd learned to realize that any situation I was exposed to was best resolved in the NOW. Spending energy worrying about them or imagining all sorts of scenarios that kept my focus away from the present wasn't worth it.

Finally being able to live like that was a major relief, and so, armed with that feeling and core belief I went up the last step and stepped out into the open air on the top of Koldinghus. At first, I couldn't see anything in the dark icy night, but decided it was okay. I didn't want to break the darkness with my powerful flashlight, so I waited for my eyes to slowly adjust a little to the conditions. Though, I sensed I was alone. It was completely still as I slowly made my way out to the middle of the tower. I took a deep breath and felt the biting cold in my nostrils. I stood for a few minutes looking up at the stars, and the longer I looked, the more stars appeared—one after the other. The more my eyesight got used to the darkness, the more stars appeared. But I was well aware that I could only see a tiny fraction of the stars that were visible to the naked eye.

For a moment, the grief at my loss of this vision gripped me, but I caught myself in my pity and immediately thought that this limited eyesight was still a miracle. I remembered myself as a boy, looking up at the night sky for hours and scanning for the Big Dipper. The childhood memory filled me with delight. I was again intrigued by how sensory input like this could evoke old memories that had long since been forgotten by the conscious mind. Experiences saved via the senses and stored as emotions, which I now recalled simply with the thought of this well-known constellation.

I knew now that all these old memories were part of my subconscious mind, and I smiled at having broken the code of how to understand a better way to manage unconscious thoughts and feelings that I'd let myself be controlled by for years. Again, I noticed the cold passing through my nostrils and down into my lungs, and I thought about how something as simple, yet simultaneously as miraculous, as breathing was one way for me to better control which thoughts I allowed to delve into and be carried away by. How long I wanted to remain deep in thought before drawing my awareness back to the present was my choice. Having that control was intoxicating, and I noticed at once how my body radiated inner life and the bubbling joy I felt when I encountered this life. I controlled which thoughts I wanted to immerse myself in, and which ones I wanted to let pass, like clouds in the starry frosty night sky.

"You need to watch your back, dear Morten," said a voice before me.

I started—I hadn't heard anyone pass me, and they must have done because the stairs were behind me, and the voice that had broken the silence had come from in front of me.

I looked around. I couldn't see anyone in the dark, but I didn't need my eyes to know who had spoken. It was Mr. P.

"Are you alone?" I asked calmly in the dark, already knowing the answer.

"No, we're all here, Morten, but you knew that already, didn't you?" replied Mr. P.

I nodded.

"Yes, you're all here together, because we can't really let each other go, can we?" I asked.

I heard movements from both sides and turned my head to the left and looked to the right but couldn't see anything.

"Yes, you're all here. I understand that now, and finally, I accept it, too."

I heard footsteps approaching from all sides, and my initial reaction was to defend myself, but I stopped the impulse by being present. I knew this was an illusion, and I knew that, as with all illusions, I decided how the illusion was to manifest.

"You've returned, Mr. N," I said in the blind darkness, sure it was Mr. N slowly moving toward me from the left.

"Well, that's not quite true, is it? Because you never really left, did you?"

A deadly silence descended, as if all the sounds in the world had disappeared. As though we were in a vacuum.

"It took me a while to realize, but it's all clear to me now, and it's what we're going to talk about here tonight, isn't it?"

I could hear my own voice, and it seemed to have changed. There was a new determination and resolve that I'd never noticed before. As if a new voice was speaking or perhaps new ears hearing. A new inner ability to listen and understand.

I looked to my left, where the figure was now less than

six feet away from me.

"You were only gone because I found the will and focus to keep you away—isn't that right, Mr. N?" I asked the figure slowly approaching. "That day, out on the road when you attacked me, I did something unexpected. I decided not to fight you anymore, Mr. N. I stopped fighting and it broke your hold over me."

The figure was now very close to me, but I didn't feel either fear or discomfort. It felt like a family member approaching me. I felt safe.

"Once I decided to look for possibilities and only focus on positive thoughts for an entire month, you were gone, and that was because there was no room for you anymore. Because we both know well what you are, Mr. N."

The figure, now also standing very close to me, lay a hand on my shoulder.

"I have underestimated you, Morten, and I would like to acknowledge that to you here tonight, in front of my two colleagues." It was Mr. N's voice, and it sounded more peaceful than it ever had before. "I did not believe you could change us, but you did."

"WE did it, Mr. N," I replied. "I know what binds us together—actually I can't understand how it didn't occur to me ages ago."

I was able to glimpse everyone's faces now. I looked directly into Mr. N's eyes and it was a completely different person who looked back at me. His eyes shone with life as if there was balance in his eyes. A calm that I hadn't seen before.

I looked to the right, and there next to me was Mr. F. He had tears in his eyes and looked like he wanted to say something, but I beat him to it.

"And you, Mr. F, I know what you would say. You'd say that for years you've felt worried and held back, but that something happened recently. Something you can't explain. But I can explain it because I felt the same way."

Mr. F took another step forward and lay his hand on my shoulder.

"I know that's what you're thinking because I know what you're all thinking. Before, I couldn't see things in depth, but now I see everything. I know who you are.

"When I first met you, Mr. F, I felt only contempt for you. I thought you were weak and indecisive, and I was angry with you because you made me feel weak and fearful. Every time I looked at you or were close to you, you made me feel weak and worthless, and that's what you were about to tell me when I beat you to it—that you no longer feel that way. Am I right?"

Mr. F's eyes were misty as he tried to pull himself together to speak, and when he finally managed to start talking, it was with a completely different voice than the one I knew. He spoke with certainty and with an authority previously unheard. He was obviously touched, but his voice was resolute.

"Yes, Morten, I feel that something has happened to me, though I'm not quite sure what."

I lay my hand on Mr. F's shoulder.

"Mr. F, we have known each other our entire lives, but we only really got to know each other over the last year. I know it sounds paradoxical, but that's how it is. You know that too, don't you?"

Mr. F nodded quietly.

"You've always been scared and felt worthless, but that's changed now, hasn't it?"

He nodded again.

"Let me tell you what happened," I continued. "When I performed my second challenge—the parachute jump from an altitude of about three miles, I realized something. I discovered that I've been fighting against you all my life and I decided to stop fighting you. I decided to accept you exactly as you are, and the second I did so, you felt different. Isn't that right, Mr. F?"

Mr. F nodded but remained silent. I looked him in the eye and continued.

"I realized that I'd despised you my whole life, and my decision to love you changed you."

Mr. P, who had remained completely silent while I'd been talking to Mr. N and Mr. F, now took a step forward toward us. I looked straight ahead, and our eyes met each other.

"You've come a long way, Morten," said Mr. P. "Much

quicker than I'd dared hope, but you have achieved what I knew you would, eventually. I've always known that one day we would stand here."

I was standing very close to the other two and Mr. P was now also within reach. He lay his hand on my shoulder, and now the four of us stood there, at the top of Koldinghus—as one. I put my hand on Mr. P's shoulder and we stood there for a while without saying a word.

We remained there without saying anything, and I remembered it being the most serene and complete moment.

"Yes, I've come a long way, Mr. P, or should I call you what you truly are?" I asked. "When you called me during the summer and introduced yourself and told me about your plan, it didn't make any sense to me. But you promised me that if I did as you said, everything would make sense eventually and you said I'd change. I have to admit I didn't wholeheartedly believe in you, but I was desperate enough to try. Sometimes you have to be in a hopeless situation, right at the bottom of a dark pit before you are ready to make changes. We have to be in a deep crisis or have survived something dramatic before we're able to step out of our rehearsed identity."

I looked at Mr. P and continued: "When you called me that night in August, I was well and truly stuck in my life. I was suffering from stress and depression, and everything looked bleak to me." I turned my gaze to Mr. F.

"An inner voice ran on repeat. It kept whispering: *You're going to be blind, and there's nothing that can change that.* That voice was yours, wasn't it, Mr. F? You represent that part of my mind in which FEAR lives. It was you. And when you called, Mr. P, it was another part of my mind that spoke to me, that part that can see possibilities rather than limitations. You are my POSITIVE voice, and when you called me, it was, in fact, the part of my mind that could see the light at the end of the tunnel, and what is amazing about life, that spoke to me. You are my POSITIVE inner voice."

Mr. P smiled and looked over at Mr. N.

I kept going: "And you, Mr. N. You, of course, represent the inner voice that always sees the NEGATIVE in life. The voice that kept me from seeing all the good, despite it always being right in front of me. You made sure I couldn't see the good in either myself or those around me. I made you disappear for over a month, but that's not how it works. We are one. We belong together, but we have always fought each other. I couldn't see that at first. I was shocked that you could access my computer, my phone and even my thoughts, because back then I was unaware of your existence in my mind.

"When I thought negative or fearful thoughts, I REMAINED in those thoughts in my mind. They absorbed me; carried me off on wild journeys. I couldn't see you for what you are. You're a part of me too, but I am not the thoughts that each of you represents. I am the consciousness that lies deeper. The consciousness that can observe you and lovingly take care of you. Without you, FEAR, NEGATIVITY and POSITIVITY, I wouldn't be able to see life in its entirety.

"But I've let you control me unconsciously for years. We created an imbalance, and no one believed there was room for the other. I'm here tonight to tell you that I'm taking control now. From now on—and in the future—there'll be room for all of us, because without the whole, there'll never be balance. Only by accepting that life contains NEGATIVITY, FEAR and POSITIVITY will I become whole. There is no light without darkness, no joy without sorrow, and we are now ready to face our future. It doesn't matter that my eyesight is disappearing, because as long as there is light in my soul, there will always be joy and strength to withstand the darkness."

I closed my eyes and turned my face toward the night sky. And so, I stood for what felt like an eternity. The silence was deafening, and here, in this moment, I genuinely realized that when something dramatic happens in our lives—loss of eyesight, loss of identity or loss of what we fearfully cling to—then something within us dies. We feel a great loss and lose what we think we are. And when we lose what we think we are—what we've identified ourselves with—we're left in a void. Trying to deny what *is*—the sadness, the pain and the void—is to give it life. I saw it all so clearly now. I can do precisely what I want. I decide my course in life, and I decide what ideals I want to live up to—right now. It is me who has decided who and what I am and who I want to be.

The world I live in is exactly the way I've chosen to perceive it, because I made it what it is. Would I like to change and go down another path in life? View losing my eyesight through other eyes? View myself as the creator of my own life? Yes! I would like to face my future with courage despite my eye disorder and be able to see possibilities rather than limitations because I've decided to. I opened my eyes and found myself all alone, but forever at one with myself.

~ THE END ~

Reading List

Braden, Gregg
- *The Divine Matrix*
- *The Isaiah Effect*

Coelho, Paulo
- *The Alchemist*

Dispenza, Joe
- *Breaking the Habit of Being Yourself*
- *You Are the Placebo: Making Your Mind Matter*
- *Evolve Your Brain*

Frankl, Viktor E.
- *Man's Search for Meaning*

Harari, Yuval Noah
- *Sapiens: A Brief History of Humankind*

Hawkins, David R.
- *Letting Go*

Hill, Napoleon
- *Think and Grow Rich*

Holmes, Ernest
- *Creative Mind and Success*

Isaacson, Walter
- *Einstein: His Life and Universe*

Jung, Carl Gustav
- *Memories, Dreams, Reflections*

Lakhiani, Vishen
- *The Code of the Extraordinary Mind*

Lao-Tzu (Stephen Addiss, trans.)

• *Tau te ching*

Lipton, Bruce

• *The Biology of Belief: Unleashing the Power of Consciousness, Matter and Miracles*
• *The Honeymoon Effect: The Science of Creating Heaven on Earth*

Maxwell, John C. (and Jim Dornan)

• *How to Influence People: Make a Difference in Your World*

McTaggart, Lynn

• *The Field*

Moorjani, Anita

• *Dying to Be Me: My Journey from Cancer to Near Death, To True Healing*

Nightingale, Earl

• *The Strangest Secret in the World (audio from YouTube)*

Sadhguru, Jaggi Vasudev

• *Inner Engineering: A Yogi's Guide to Joy*

Schucman, Helen

• *A Course in Miracles*

Singer, Michael A.

• *The Surrender Experiment*

Thich Nhat Hanh

• *Peace Is Every Step: The Path of Mindfulness in*

Everyday Life

Tolle, Eckhart

- *The Power of Now: A Guide to Spiritual Enlightenment*
- *Practcing the Power of Now: Teachings, Mediations and Exercises from the Power of Now.*
- *Stillness Speaks: Whisper of the Now*
- *A New Earth: Awakening Your Life's Purpose*
- *Gateways to Now (Inner Life)*

Walsch, Neale Donald

- *Conversations with God: An uncommon dialogue Book 1*

Watts, Alan

- *The Meaning. of Happiness: The Quest for Freedom of the Spirit in Modern Psychology and the Wisdom of the East*

Yogananda, Paramahansa

- *Autobiography of a Yogi*

Young, Shinzen

- *The Science of Enlightenment, How Meditation Works*

Zinn, Jon Kabat

- *Full Catastrophe Living: How to Cope with Stress, Pain and Illness using Mindfulness Meditation*
- *Wherever You Go There You Are: Mindfulness Meditation in Everyday Life.*

Made in the USA
Middletown, DE
20 July 2021